Living in Christ

The Paschal Mystery

Christ's Mission of Salvation

Second Edition

Brian Singer-Towns

Saint Mary's Press®

The Subcommittee on the Catechism, United States Conference of Catholic Bishops, has found that this catechetical high school text, copyright 2016, is in conformity with the *Catechism of the Catholic Church* and that it fulfills the requirements of Core Course III of the *Doctrinal Elements of a Curriculum Framework for the Development of Catechetical Materials for Young People of High School Age.*

Nihil Obstat: Rev. Fr. Timothy J. Hall, STL
               Censor Librorum
               September 30, 2014

Imprimatur: †Most Rev. John M. Quinn, DD
             Bishop of Winona
             September 30, 2014

The nihil obstat and imprimatur are official declarations that a book or pamphlet is free of doctrinal or moral error. No implication is contained therein that those who have granted the nihil obstat or imprimatur agree with the contents, opinions, or statements expressed, nor do they assume any legal responsibility associated with publication.

The content in this resource was acquired, developed, and reviewed by the content engagement team at Saint Mary's Press. Content design and manufacturing were coordinated by the passionate team of creatives at Saint Mary's Press.

Printed in the United States of America

1163 (PO5689)

ISBN 978-1-59982-433-8

Contents

Unit 3 ◆ God's Plan for Salvation Is Fulfilled

Unit 4 ◆ The Paschal Mystery and Your Life

Unit 5 ◆ Prayer and the Paschal Mystery

Introduction

When I was a young man, I spent several years searching for something I didn't know I had lost. From birth I grew up in a devout Catholic family, as a teen I was an altar server and lector in my parish, and as a college student I continued to attend Mass every Sunday. But after a while, I felt like I was just going through the motions. If you were to see the brave face I presented to the world, you would have thought I was just fine. But inside I was a confused and lonely person.

What I didn't know then was that deep inside myself, in my soul, I was missing a crucial connection with God. I tried to fill that void in many ways. I tried making new friends, joining new groups, and reading about different religions. But it wasn't until I joined a Bible study group that was reading the Gospel of Mark that I found what my soul was missing: a close and intimate relationship with the Trinity—the Father, Son, and Holy Spirit.

I share this story because there is a danger in writing a student book about Jesus Christ. The danger is that it can make faith in Jesus seem like just another intellectual exercise, just another subject to master on your way to adulthood. Yet as I discovered those many years ago, yes, faith involves the intellect, but there is more to it. God wants to be in an intimate relationship of love with each of us. He has worked throughout history to reveal that desire and make it possible for us to bridge the "gap" that separates us from his love.

The Paschal Mystery is the name we give to the process of God's plan of salvation, which is principally accomplished through the life, death, Resurrection, and Ascension of Jesus Christ. This book explores that plan, from its beginnings in the Garden of Eden to its glorious conclusion at the Parousia. We will see how God has been at work throughout all of history to restore what was lost—our full and intimate communion with the Holy Trinity. Perhaps most important, we will look at how God calls each of us to be an active participant in his plan.

When I gave myself over in faith to God's loving invitation those many years ago, my whole life was renewed. I discovered a deeper and more profound relationship with God. And because of that, I entered into deeper and more loving relationships with other people. My faith in Christ saves me from sin and will save me from death. It saves me from confusion, loneliness, and despair. Every day it gives my life meaning, joy, and hope even when times are hard and when bad things happen. As a member of the Body of Christ, the Church, I have met and been loved by many amazing and wonderful people, people who inspire me to deeper commitment in my journey of faith.

That is what I pray for you. I hope that as you study this book, you take seriously what it teaches about Jesus Christ and the Paschal Mystery. There is an important intellectual dimension to belief. We must believe in the right things, the truths revealed by God. But I also hope this will be more than an intellectual exercise for you. I pray that you will let the love of Christ that is expressed in the Paschal Mystery touch your heart and motivate your every action. I pray that you will see your study of the Paschal Mystery as an invitation from God to draw closer to him and to let this Mystery become the spiritual center of your life. Let God fill the hunger in your soul.

Blessings,
Brian Singer-Towns

God's Plan for Salvation: The Big Picture

In this unit, we will learn about the creation of the world and how God's creation reveals his plan for humanity. In the beginning, God created the heavens and the earth and all that is in them. Everything that God created was good, and it developed according to God's plan, which is for us to live in communion with him and with one another.

But we will see that when the first human beings sinned, they broke that communion. What did God do then? He didn't just leave us to struggle with sin on our own. Instead he promised right then and there to save all of humanity from sin and death.

After the Original Sin and the Fall, God put a plan in motion to send his Son to redeem humanity and restore what we lost through sin—communion with God and eternal life. God's plan of salvation culminated in the Passion, death, Resurrection, and Ascension of Jesus, the events we call the Paschal Mystery.

Throughout the course of salvation history, the pattern of events in which God revealed his presence and saving actions, God made covenants with his people, to show them that he would always be faithful and that he would never forsake them. Even though God's people continued to sin and turn away from him, God did not abandon them. God chose to remain faithful to his covenants, and he sent prophets to continually call God's people back to himself.

The enduring understandings and essential questions represent core concepts and questions that are explored throughout this unit. By studying the content of each chapter, you will gain a more complete understanding of the following:

Enduring Understandings
1. God created the entire world as essentially good.
2. Sacred Scripture uses figurative and symbolic language to convey religious truth.
3. Original Sin entered the world when Adam and Eve chose to reject a God-centered life in favor of a self-centered life.
4. After the Fall, God continued to find a way to communicate his love for humanity and his desire to restore humanity's communion with him.

Essential Questions
1. How do we know that the world is essentially good, despite the presence of sin?
2. How does Scripture use literary forms to convey religious truth?
3. If God created the entire world essentially good, why do people, beginning with Adam and Eve, choose to sin?
4. What characterized God's relationship with humanity after the Fall?

The Goodness of Creation

Introduction

God has a plan, and *you* are a part of it. Modern science has come a long way in explaining creation, growth, and even the end of stars and galaxies. We have some intriguing theories, such as the big bang theory, about how the universe came into existence. Through the gift of our intellect, we can continue to learn about the workings of the universe; through faith we know that the universe was made by God, so we know that what has been created was made out of the uncreated.

We begin this chapter by looking at the Scripture accounts of Creation. Although these accounts might not be scientifically true, we can accept them as religious truth because of what they reveal about God and his plan for creation. Creation, both visible and invisible, is the work of the Trinity.

You will read that God created the universe out of love. God's creation is good, and he loves all of it, every particle, every grain of sand, every blade of grass, and every form of life that swims, crawls, walks, or flies. And in his plan, human beings—the summit of God's creation—have a special place. God has made us "little less than a god, / crowned [us] with glory and honor" (Psalm 8:6). God has a plan and *you* are a part of it.

Article 1: The Primeval History

As we explore God's plan, it makes sense to start with his intention in creating the world in the first place. Was God bored? Was he lonely? Was he looking for some free labor? No, no, and no! The creation stories of other ancient cultures claimed these as reasons for why the gods created the earth and human beings. But the two Creation accounts in Sacred Scripture, found in the first two chapters of the Book of Genesis, give very different reasons, which makes them special in teaching us about Creation. These chapters contain the familiar accounts of the six days of Creation, the creation of Adam and Eve, and Adam and Eve's Fall from grace.

primeval history
The time before the invention of writing and recording of historical data.

Although the two accounts of Creation originated at different times, both reveal important truths about God. God is revealed as the one, true God, who sustains the whole universe. He created the world out of love, because he is Love. He created the world to be good, because he is Goodness. He revealed the serpent's words as lies, because he is Truth. Even after Adam and Eve's sin, God's love for humanity remains steadfast and faithful, because he is Faithfulness.

The two Creation accounts are part of a section of Genesis (chapters 1–11) called "The Primeval History" in some Bibles. *Primeval* sounds like *prehistoric,* and it means kind of the same thing. Describing the accounts of Creation in Genesis as **primeval history** means that these are symbolic accounts about things that happened long before we have any kind of historical records—written or archaeological. These texts probably came from several different ancient Jewish sources. By the inspiration of the Holy Spirit, these stories were told, refined, and edited together over the course of several centuries before they became the final text we have today. Through the primeval history, God reveals some very important truths that we will take a closer look at in this chapter.

© Robert Simon / istockphoto.com

Sacred Scripture
The sacred writings of the Old and New Testaments, which contain the truth of God's Revelation and were composed by human authors inspired by the Holy Spirit.

literary forms (genres)
Different kinds of writing determined by their literary technique, content, tone, and purpose.

Literary Forms in the Bible

Before examining the meaning of the Creation accounts in **Sacred Scripture**, it is helpful to understand **literary form** and how it relates to Scripture. Literary form is also called literary genre. A newspaper, for example, has many literary forms: news stories, editorials and opinion pieces, comics, advice columns, sports scores, and many others. They all can teach us something true, but we don't interpret a comic strip the same way we interpret a front-page news story.

We must always remember that God is the primary author of Sacred Scripture. But this does not mean that God took away the creativity of the human authors, who were inspired by the Holy Spirit. So Sacred Scripture also has many literary forms, including figurative language, hymns, parables, short stories, law codes, hero stories, prophetic oracles, Gospels, letters, proverbs, religious histories, and even love poetry. God works through all these different literary forms to reveal his truth. To interpret the Bible's truth correctly, we must take into account what the human authors intended to communicate through the different literary forms as well as what God wanted to reveal through their words.

Religious Truth and Scientific Truth

The primeval history in Sacred Scripture teaches religious truth, not science. We know this because these chapters are written in **figurative language**. Figurative language uses symbolic images, stories, and names to point to a deeper truth. It can teach us important religious truths, but it is usually not meant to be scientifically or historically accurate. So, for example, the seven days of creation in chapter 1 of Genesis teach us that God created

the world with order and purpose. But we should not interpret this story to mean that God literally created the universe in six 24-hour days. We should also not interpret figurative language as pure fantasy; the first chapters of Genesis affirm real events that took place at the beginning of human history.

Another example of figurative language is the account in Genesis 2:21 in which God made the first woman from one of the ribs of the first man. This verse is not trying to teach that God literally made the first woman from a piece of the first man. (In an effort to "prove" this, some people even say that men have one less rib than women, but, of course, this is not true.) Instead, through this text, God reveals that men and women are intimately connected; we are equal, each gender complementing the other. Man and woman are called to be "one flesh" in the Sacrament of Matrimony.

Religious truth and scientific truth ultimately never contradict each other. God has given us both our faith and our reason, and he would not cause his gifts to us to

figurative language
A literary form that uses symbolic images, stories, and names to point to a deeper truth.

Primary Sources

Protecting Creation

In the homily for his inauguration Mass on the Solemnity of Saint Joseph, Pope Francis took his theme from Saint Joseph's role as protector of the Holy Family. The Pope urged all human beings to be protectors—of the environment and of those who are poor, and those who are in need. The Pope said:

> "In [Joseph], dear friends, . . . we also see the core of the Christian vocation, which is Christ! Let us protect Christ in our lives, so that we can protect others, so that we can protect creation! . . . [This] means respecting each of God's creatures and respecting the environment in which we live. It means protecting people, showing loving concern for each and every person. . . . In the end, everything has been entrusted to our protection, and all of us are responsible for it. Be protectors of God's gifts!"
>
> ("Homily of Pope Francis, Mass, Imposition of the Pallium and Bestowal of the Fisherman's Ring for the Beginning of the Petrine Ministry of the Bishop of Rome," March 19, 2013)

be in conflict. If religion and science seem to contradict each other, it means that we have misunderstood one or the other. Trying to interpret the figurative language in the Bible as scientific truth is a misunderstanding that causes an unnecessary conflict between our faith and our reason.

How would you explain the difference between religious truth and scientific truth to a friend?

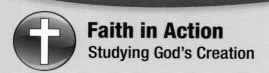

Faith in Action
Studying God's Creation

© MarcelClemens / Shutterstock.com

Deep in the southern Arizona desert, an astronomer searches the skies as he studies God's beautiful creation. That astronomer is a Jesuit priest, and he is using one of the two telescopes set in this observatory. The larger telescope is run by the University of Arizona. The smaller telescope, run by the Vatican, is known as the VATT (Vatican Advanced Technology Telescope). The only other telescope in the world run by the Vatican is in the Vatican Observatory in Rome.

The goal of the Vatican Observatory is to promote education and research opportunities for scientists interested in astronomical research. Why would the Church be interested in maintaining an observatory? Because we can learn so much about God and the goodness of creation from studying the world around us. In fact, the Church sponsors a special group, the Pontifical Academy of Sciences, consisting of scientists from all over the world. They meet periodically to study important topics in science and to share their findings with one another.

Pope Benedict XVI considered the work of the Pontifical Academy of Sciences to be of great importance. He said: "I am convinced of the urgent need for continued dialogue and cooperation between the worlds of science and of faith in the building of a culture of respect for man, for human dignity and freedom, for the future of our human family and for the long-term sustainable development of our planet" ("Address of His Holiness Pope Benedict XVI to Members of the Pontifical Academy of Sciences on the Occasion of the Plenary Assembly," November 8, 2012).

Article 2: Creation Reflects the Glory of God

Throughout all history human beings have repeatedly experienced a particular kind of awe-inspiring moment, perhaps while gazing at the stars, watching the waves on the ocean, or seeing a brilliant sunset. At such moments one might exclaim aloud or silently, "Praise God!" This is a recognition that creation itself gives glory to the Creator. God created the world to reveal his glory. Every creature is meant to share in God's truth, goodness, and beauty.

> Praise the Lord from the heavens;
> > praise him in the heights.
> Praise him, all you his angels;
> > give praise, all you his hosts.
> Praise him, sun and moon;
> > praise him, all shining stars.
>
> . . . .
>
> Young men and women too,
> > old and young alike.
> Let them all praise the Lord's name,
> > for his name alone is exalted,
> > His majesty above earth and heaven.
> > (Psalm 148:1–3,12–13)

This image of God creating the sun and the moon is from the famous mural painted by Michelangelo in the Sistine Chapel of the Vatican.

Trinity

From the Latin *trinus*, meaning "threefold," referring to the central mystery of the Christian faith that God exists as a communion of three distinct and interrelated Divine Persons: Father, Son, and Holy Spirit. The doctrine of the Trinity is a mystery that is inaccessible to human reason alone and is known through Divine Revelation only.

Creation: The Work of the Three-in-One

Sacred Scripture joyfully proclaims that creation is evidence of the power of God. Of course, there are those who say the opposite and claim that creation simply happened, that there is no divine Creator. But faith and reason lead us to the sure knowledge that there is one God who created the universe and continues to sustain it through his love. He exists outside of space and time. Even more accurately, space and time are the creation of God. God and God alone freely created the universe without help from anyone or anything.

Sometimes Christians mistakenly believe that Creation is the work of only God the Father. Instead Sacred Scripture tells us that Creation is the work of all three Divine Persons of the **Trinity**: Father, Son, and **Holy Spirit**. The role of Jesus Christ, the Word of God and the second Person of the Trinity, is explicitly mentioned at the beginning of the Gospel of John:

> In the beginning was the Word,
> and the Word was with God,
> and the Word was God.
> He was in the beginning with God.
> All things came to be through him,
> and without him, nothing came to be.
> (1:1–3)

© Zvonimir Atletic / Shutterstock.com

The involvement of the Holy Spirit, the third Person of the Trinity, is a bit more hidden. The opening of Genesis describes "a mighty wind sweeping over the waters" (1:2). *Wind* can also be translated as "the spirit of God," because in Hebrew the word *ruah* means "breath," "wind," and "spirit." In other words, the sentence could be read as "the spirit of God sweeping over the waters." You might also take a look at Psalm 33:6 and notice that it too says that the Lord created the heavens by his Word (Jesus Christ) and his breath (Holy Spirit). Sacred Tradition makes it clear that

Bible passages like these teach us that Creation is the work of all three Divine Persons of the Holy Trinity.

Creation Visible and Invisible

In the modern world, people put a lot of emphasis on science. This means we tend to believe solely in things we can observe through our five senses. But Sacred Scripture and **Sacred Tradition** teach that part of God's creation includes things unseen too. We profess our belief in this every time we pray the Nicene Creed, which begins, "I believe in one God, the Father almighty, maker of heaven and earth, of all things visible and invisible." The invisible creation, which we usually call the spiritual, is every bit as real as the visible reality, which we call the earthly realm.

So what creatures exist in the spiritual, or heavenly, realm? **Angels**. Angels are witnessed to in both Scripture and Tradition. They are spiritual beings who are

Holy Spirit
The Third Person of the Blessed Trinity, the personal love between the Father and the Son, who inspires, guides, and sanctifies the life of believers.

Did You Know?

Angels in Scripture

The Bible mentions three angels by name and two by type. The three named angels are:

- **Raphael** Raphael appeared in the Book of Tobit. He was a companion and protector of Tobiah.
- **Gabriel** Gabriel appeared to Daniel and explained the meaning of Daniel's visions (see Daniel 8:16, 9:21). He appeared to Zechariah and Mary in the Gospel of Luke (see 1:19,26).
- **Michael** In the Book of Daniel, Michael is revealed as the protector of Israel (see 10:21, 12:1). He is mentioned in the Book of Jude (see verse 9) and is the archangel who led the fight against Satan in the Book of Revelation (see 12:7).

The two types of angels are:

- **Cherubim** These angels are close to God, directly serving him. Images of them adorned the Ark of the Covenant (see Exodus, chapter 25) and Solomon's Temple (see 1 Kings, chapter 6). They appeared in the prophet Ezekiel's visions (see chapter 10).
- **Seraphim** These angels are mentioned in Isaiah, chapter 6. They serve God and proclaim his glory.

Sacred Tradition
"Tradition" comes from the Latin *tradere*, meaning "to hand on." Sacred Tradition refers to the living process of passing on the Gospel message. It began with the oral communication of the Gospel by the Apostles, was written down in Sacred Scripture, and is interpreted by the Magisterium under the guidance of the Holy Spirit. Both Sacred Tradition and Sacred Scripture have their common source in the revelation of Jesus Christ and must be equally honored.

angel
Based on a word meaning "messenger," a personal and immortal creature with intelligence and free will who constantly glorifies God and serves as a messenger of God to humans to carry out God's saving plan.

the servants and messengers of God. They are present throughout all of salvation history and appear to human beings at key moments. For example, an angel stopped Abraham from sacrificing Isaac (see Genesis 22:11–12). An angel announced to Joseph and Mary the birth of Jesus (see Matthew 1:20 and Luke 1:26–27). Angels announced the Resurrection of Christ (see Matthew 28:2–7). The angels glorify God without ceasing, and in Heaven we will join our voices with theirs in praising and glorifying God (see Revelation 5:11).

When have you experienced awe that reminded you of God's presence in creation?

Article 3: Human Beings: The Summit of Creation

As we explore God's plan for creation, we face a critical question: Do human beings have a special role, a special place in God's plan? Some people would answer this question by saying we are just the same as all the other animals; we are just a more highly evolved form of life with greater intelligence. So human life has no meaning other than what we give it. These people are wrong, however well-intentioned they might be. God has revealed that humanity indeed has a unique role, a very special place, in his plan.

Once again we turn to the Creation account in Genesis. "God created mankind in his image; / in the image of God he created them; / male and female he created them" (1:27). No other living being is created in God's image. We are the only creature God created with a body and an immortal **soul**. Our soul, created by God, is our spiritual principle. It is what makes us most like God. The union of our body and soul is so complete that we cannot distinguish or separate one from another until our death. At our death our soul will live on until it is reunited once again with our resurrected body.

"Male and Female He Created Them"

You may have noticed the line "male and female he created them" in the quotation from Genesis. Because this verse follows the literary form of Hebrew poetry, each line is a different way of saying the same thing. The biblical author is telling us that both sexes are made in the image of God. God created men and women to be of equal dignity, yet with distinct characteristics. Both maleness and femaleness reflect God's infinite perfection.

God created men and women for each other. "The Lord God said: 'It is not good for the man to be alone. I will make a helper suited to him'" (Genesis 2:18). The Genesis account makes it clear that we are not meant to be solitary creatures. God created us to be in communion with each other, a partnership in which we bring together our unique gifts as men and women. The loving relationship between a man and a woman is the first form of communion between persons, reflecting the perfect communion of the Trinity. In the union of a man and a woman in marriage, God even shares with us his creative power to bring new life into the world!

soul
Our spiritual principle, it is immortal, and it is what makes us most like God. Our soul is created by God at the moment of our conception. It is the seat of human consciousness and freedom.

© Imagezoo/Images.com/Corbis

Humanity's Role

It follows by reason that if human beings are unique among God's creatures, then we have a unique role in his plan. Humanity's special role in God's plan has two dimensions: (1) to be in communion with God and to respond to his love by loving him in return, and (2) to serve him, particularly as stewards of his creation. Let's take a closer look at each of these dimensions.

Notice the symmetry in this image of Adam and Eve. What does this communicate about their relationship?

Love for God

Of all God's creatures, we are the only ones who can freely choose to return his love, to choose to share in his own life. God has given us free will and self-knowledge. Because of this we have a dignity that surpasses all other creatures. We are not just something, we are someone!

The greatest testimony to human dignity and our importance in God's plan is the Incarnation. From the beginning humanity has been destined to "reproduce the image of God's Son made man, 'the image of the invisible God' (Colossians 1:15)" (*Catechism of the Catholic Church [CCC]*, 381). When the fullness of human dignity was lost through Original Sin, God put in motion a plan to restore what we had lost. When the time was right, the Son of God assumed our human nature, restoring the fullness of human dignity. Jesus Christ, true God and true man, became the firstborn of God's sons and daughters. Through Baptism we are his brothers and sisters, sons and daughters of God.

Live It!
Be Whom God Created You to Be

Perhaps the hardest challenge in life is to be whom God created you to be. We're not talking about whether you should be an athlete, a doctor, a priest, or a teacher, but about believing that you and every person you meet are made in the image and likeness of God. This means treating yourself and every person the same way you would treat Jesus.

Wouldn't it be a perfect world if we did this? Everyone would be patient, kind, unselfish, and slow to anger (see 1 Corinthians, chapter 13). Guess what? The seed of this perfect world is already here. We call it the Kingdom of God. The Father sent his Son, Jesus, who announced the Kingdom of God and made it present through his life, suffering, death, and Resurrection. The Holy Spirit empowers us to live it. So what do you need to do to truly be the person God created you to be? How will you show that every person is made in the image of God? Take time to answer these questions. Follow up by making your answers a part of how you live.

Our Responsibility for Creation

The Creation account in Genesis summarizes the second dimension of humanity's unique role in God's plan: "God blessed them, and God said to them: 'Be fertile and multiply; fill the earth and subdue it. Have dominion over the fish of the sea, the birds of the air, and all the living things that crawl on the earth'" (1:28). This passage teaches us that God has given human beings all the other creatures for our benefit. He has put the earth and everything that lives on it in our care.

God willed into being the great diversity of creatures that exists. Each living thing has its own goodness and its own unique place in creation. Further, there is an order and interdependence among all creatures. Scientists have discovered how complex these relationships are in the plant and animal world. The removal of just one species can threaten a whole ecosystem. And God has given us the responsibility for nurturing his creation. We must respect each creature's goodness and place in the order of creation. We are called to care for the earth until the time Christ returns and brings about "a new heaven and a new earth" (Revelation 21:1).

These people are rescuing animals from an oil spill. How would you rate humanity's care of the earth in recent years?

© SEAN GARDNER / Reuters / Landov

Do human beings have a special place in God's plan? How do you know?

original holiness
The original state of human beings in their relationship with God, sharing in the divine life in full communion with him.

original justice
The original state of Adam and Eve before the Fall, a state of complete harmony with themselves, with each other, and with all of creation.

Article 4: The Garden of Eden: The Perfect Life

How would you describe the perfect life? Can you even imagine what such a life would be like? Would you be on a tropical island, with perfect weather every day, with delicious food nearby just waiting to be picked and eaten? Well, one man and one woman did have a perfect life, at least at first. Adam and Eve started out not only in a perfect place, the Garden of Eden, but also in perfect relationship with God and with each other.

Original Holiness and Original Justice

Adam and Eve appear in Genesis 2:4–3:24. Because this account was written in figurative or symbolic language, the elements must be interpreted symbolically.

As you read about Adam and Eve, it is important to focus on the quality of their relationships. First, notice the relationship between Adam and God. God breathed his life directly into Adam, a very intimate act. God walked in the garden, talking to Adam as a friend. He was concerned for Adam's happiness and worked to make the perfect partner for him. All of this is a symbolic way of saying that God intended the first human beings to

Pray It!

Prayers for Creation Stewardship

In God's plan, he gave the care of all creation to human beings. In the Church's Liturgy, we ask for God's help in caring for the earth. This is the opening prayer for the Mass for the Sanctification of Human Labor. Pray to ask God to guide you in making good choices to care for creation.

O God, who willed to subject
the forces of nature to human labor,
mercifully grant
that, undertaking in a Christian spirit what we are to do,
we may merit to join our brothers and sisters
in practicing sincere charity
and in advancing the fulfillment of your divine work of creation.
(Roman Missal)

share in his life, to be in direct communion with him. We call this state **original holiness**.

In this Scripture account, the human author of Genesis describes God anthropomorphically, meaning God is depicted in a human way. This technique relies on the use of analogy—that is, describing God as being like a human being and with human characteristics. We must, of course, understand that this analogy, like any description of God, is imperfect. "Our human words always fall short of the mystery of God" (CCC, 42). However, by describing him with human characteristics the biblical author emphasizes God's closeness to Adam and Eve.

Next, notice the relationship between Adam and Eve and their relationship with the rest of creation. Adam and Eve were of one mind and one body, a relationship symbolized by Eve's being made from a part of Adam. They felt no shame in each other's presence, even though they were naked. This symbolizes their complete honesty and respect for each other. At the beginning their work of caring for the garden and producing food was not a burden. This symbolizes their harmony with the rest of creation. This state of complete harmony between Adam and Eve and the rest of creation is called **original justice**.

The state of original holiness and original justice is God's will, his plan for all humanity. God wants us to be happy. That happiness comes from our friendship and full communion with God, with other people, and with creation. Even though this plan was interrupted, God's will is not blocked. Those with faith in God— the Father, Son, and Holy Spirit—will experience a taste of original holiness

The artist who created this painting is trying to convey the Garden of Eden before the Fall. How would you describe what is being portrayed here?

Museum of Fine Arts, Boston, Massachusetts, USA / Gift of Maxim Karolik for the M. and M. Karolik Collection of American Paintings, 1815–1865 / Bridgeman Images

and original justice in this life and will know it completely in Heaven.

> **How does faith in God help you to glimpse original holiness and original justice in this life?**

Chapter Review

1. Explain what is meant by *primeval history.* Where do you find an example in the Bible?

2. Give two examples of the use of figurative or symbolic language in the first two chapters of Genesis.

3. What is the relationship between Creation and the Trinity?

4. What are angels and what do they do?

5. Give a theological definition of the word *soul.*

6. Give two reasons why God created humans as male and female.

7. What is original holiness?

8. What is original justice?

The Fall from Grace

Introduction

God has a plan for us, but as you will read in this chapter, our first parents, Adam and Eve, decided not to cooperate with the plan. They disobeyed God's direct command, and this sin resulted in an event called the Fall. The Fall refers to Adam and Eve's fall from their state of original holiness and original justice. The result is that every person (except Jesus and Mary) born since Adam and Eve is born with Original Sin. Original Sin deprives us of our original holiness and original justice and is a wound in our relationship with God. It weakens our ability to resist temptation, making it easier for us to commit sin.

This chapter introduces a key character in the account of the Fall: the serpent, the deceiver. Sacred Scripture and Sacred Tradition identify the serpent as Satan, a fallen angel who is opposed to God. Satan and the other fallen angels rejected God completely. Now Satan tempts others to do the same. But God's power is infinite, and his saving plan will prevail over the power of Satan and evil.

Original Sin
From the Latin *origo*, meaning "beginning" or "birth." The term has two meanings: (1) the sin of the first human beings, who disobeyed God's command by choosing to follow their own will and thus lost their original holiness and became subject to death, (2) the fallen state of human nature that affects every person born into the world, except Jesus and Mary.

Fall, the
Also called the Fall from Grace, the biblical Revelation about the origins of sin and evil in the world, expressed figuratively in the account of Adam and Eve in Genesis.

Article 5: Adam and Eve's Disobedience

In his Letter to the Romans, Saint Paul said: "What I do, I do not understand. For I do not do what I want, but I do what I hate" (7:15). He was describing an experience that all people since Adam and Eve have had, with the exception of Jesus Christ and his Mother, Mary. You have probably had this experience. We sin even when we know it is wrong. We make choices that hurt others, and even ourselves, for very selfish reasons. People who have serious addictions struggle with this experience every day, but all of us are capable of doing what we know is wrong. Why would God make us like this? Well, he didn't—not exactly. The attractiveness of sin and the many ways we delude ourselves into thinking sin is okay are, to a large degree, results of the sin of our first parents.

The Fall

We now come to a truly tragic moment in human history. We must take a closer look at the second part of the symbolic account of Adam and Eve: Genesis 3:1–24. You are probably familiar with this passage, but read it again. Earlier in Genesis we learn that God gave Adam and Eve only one command: "You are free to eat from any of the trees of the garden except the tree of knowledge of good and evil. From that tree you shall not eat; when you eat from it you shall die" (2:16–17). Then the serpent came along and told Eve the exact opposite. Eve ate the forbidden fruit and offered it to Adam, who did the same.

Immediately Adam and Eve realized they were naked, which is a symbolic way of saying they felt guilt and shame. These are two feelings God did not intend for humans to know. Adam and Eve were ashamed to be seen by each other (the reason they covered themselves with fig leaves) and ashamed to be seen by God (the reason they hid from him). When God confronted them about their disobedience, they played the blame game. Adam blamed Eve for his sin, and Eve blamed the serpent. In their shame, they could not be honest with God and accept responsibility for their actions.

All of this—the shame at their nakedness, their hiding from God, their blaming others for their choices—is a symbolic way of saying that Adam and Eve lost their original holiness and original justice. They were no longer in loving communion with God, nor were they in harmony with each other. They had to leave the Garden of Eden; they could no longer live in Paradise.

Why are Adam and Eve trying to conceal themselves in this image? What does this teach us about sin?

Adam and Eve's disobedience in the Garden of Eden, known as **Original Sin**, affected all humanity. No other human beings would ever be conceived with their holiness and justice intact. This is why we now find it harder to obey God's Commandments and easier to do what is sinful. **The Fall** of Adam and Eve is the origin and the consequence of Original Sin.

© Willie Rodger, reproduced by permission of the artist / Bridgeman Images, "Adam and Eve in Deep Water, Willie Rodger RSA RGI DUniv, oil, 2000"

Live It!
Think about the Consequences

Most people do not intend to do evil things. We are often tempted when something sinful looks or feels good to us. In the Lord's Prayer, we ask God to "lead us not into temptation," to keep us out of tempting situations and to help us not give in to the temptations that do cross our path.

Avoiding temptation completely is impossible. Even Jesus had to face temptation. "The Spirit drove [Jesus] out into the desert, and he remained . . . tempted by Satan" (Mark 1:12–13). With God's help we can face our temptations and see them for what they are: evil disguised as good. The next time you are tempted, think about what would happen if you decide to give in. What would happen the next day? the next month? How would it affect you? your friends? your family? What are the false promises? the real consequences? Considering the effects of your choices in this way can help you to resist temptation and choose what is good.

What Was the Sin?

You might wonder exactly why Adam and Eve's action was a sin. Yes, they disobeyed God's command, but why would God not want them to eat from the tree of knowledge of good and evil? Wouldn't having that knowledge be a good thing? To understand this sin, we must consider the culture of the time and the use of figurative language. For the sacred writer of Genesis, the full knowledge of good and evil belongs to God alone, who is the source of everything. So the tree symbolizes what human beings can never be: God himself. Eating the fruit from that tree is a symbolic way to say, "We don't need God; we can be gods ourselves." The tragic irony is that God had already given Adam and Eve the greatest gift possible: They were made in God's image (see 1:27), and they had the grace of full communion with God. Seduced by the serpent's lie, "you will be like gods" (3:5), they lost the grace of original holiness and original justice.

Accepting our own goodness is key if we are to recognize and respect the goodness in one another and in creation. Doing so helps us to live in right relationship with God and with one another.

© The Metropolitan Museum of Art / Art Resource, NY

Their sin was their misuse of human freedom and their lack of trust in God. They did not accept the gift of their humanity and instead tried to replace God with themselves. In some way, these two things—not accepting our own goodness and not trusting in God—are at the root of every sin.

Adam and Eve's sin showed a lack of trust in God. Have you observed similar kinds of sin in your own life?

Article 6: Original Sin: A Consequence of the Fall

If someone asked you to list five doctrines that are essential for understanding Christianity, what would you say? Would Original Sin make your list? Of course, all the truths of our faith are important. They all fit together and support one another to help us see more clearly God's will and plan for us. The doctrine of the Trinity is the most essential truth, but without Original Sin there would have been no need for the Son of God to become flesh and live among us. We would still be living in Paradise. So we need to understand Original Sin in order to understand other doctrines of our faith. But we should always remember that sin does not defeat God. As Saint Paul said, "Where sin increased, grace overflowed all the more" (Romans 5:20).

Original Sin Affects Our Human Nature

Original Sin is the name for the fact that "Adam and Eve transmitted to their descendants human nature wounded by their own first sin and hence deprived of original holiness and justice" (CCC, 417). Sacred Scripture and Sacred Tradition do not explain exactly how this happens. We accept it as a mystery that we cannot fully understand. What we know is that Adam and Eve were created in a state of original holiness not for themselves alone but for all human nature. Therefore, when they sinned, their sin affected not just themselves but also their human nature, which was passed on to all their descendants.

Perhaps the following analogy will help you to understand. If for some reason a genetic abnormality develops in a person's DNA—such as nearsightedness—it may get passed on to that person's children. The children didn't do anything to deserve this physical defect, but they still receive it. In a similar way, a defect was created in Adam and Eve's human nature that now gets passed on to all people (with the exception of Jesus and his Mother,

concupiscence
The tendency of all human beings toward sin, as a result of Original Sin.

etiology
A story that explains something's cause or origin.

Mary). We didn't do anything that led us to be in this state. We were born into the state of Original Sin before we ever had a chance to commit a personal sin ourselves.

The Results of Original Sin

Because of Original Sin, human nature is weakened. The loss of original holiness and original justice makes things that should be natural to us more challenging. Relationships with others that should come naturally are marked by tension and misunderstanding. Moral decisions that should be easy and straightforward become more difficult and confused. We are more inclined to sin. This inclination is called **concupiscence**. All of these struggles lead to more pain and suffering in our lives.

Did You Know?

Biblical Etiologies

© Stefano Bianchetti / Corbis

After the Fall, God listed several consequences for Adam and Eve and the serpent. This list is one example of a literary type called an **etiology**. An etiology is a story that explains something's cause or origin. Genesis 3:14–19 gives the answers to a number of questions ancient people had:

- Why are snakes shunned by other animals?
- Why don't snakes have legs?
- Why is childbirth so painful?
- Why is it so hard for men and women to get along?
- Why is earning a living so much work?
- Why do we have to die?

Today we have scientific explanations for many of these questions. But in symbolic language, this etiology explains the spiritual result of the Fall. Life is now hard and often painful, and we die. Fortunately, God has a plan to restore us to full communion. His plan was set into motion even as Adam and Eve experienced the consequences of their disobedience.

But we have suffered an even more serious loss because of Original Sin. Our relationship with God is now clouded and hidden. We no longer naturally walk in the garden with God as with a close friend. Even though God desires to be just as close to us as he was to Adam and Eve, we struggle to find him. And the most serious loss of all is that we now experience death. What God warned Adam about has come true: "From that tree you shall not eat; when you eat from it you shall die" (Genesis 2:17).

But it is also important to recognize that Original Sin does not cause us to lose our goodness or make us completely spiritually corrupt. Some of the Protestant reformers taught that Original Sin completely perverted human nature and destroyed our freedom to choose between right and wrong, and some Protestants today still hold that belief. In response, the Catholic Church has more clearly articulated her teaching on God's Revelation. Namely, Original Sin does not completely pervert human goodness, but it does weaken our natural powers for relating to God and for choosing to do good.

Death is a consequence of Original Sin, but death is not our final end. Jesus Christ has conquered death and opened the gates of Heaven.

© Judi Ashlock / istockphoto.com

Primary Sources

The Voice of Conscience

With the gift of God's grace—the free and undeserved help that he gives us to respond to his call—we are able to know and do what is good despite our fallen state. We may not always immediately prefer what is good, but if we allow our conscience to speak to us, we will more easily choose what is good and avoid evil. Pastoral Constitution on the Church in the Modern World (Gaudium et Spes, 1965) reminds us of this:

In the depths of his conscience, man detects a law which he does not impose upon himself, but which holds him to obedience. Always summoning him to love good and avoid evil, the voice of conscience . . . speaks to his heart: do this, shun that. For man has in his heart a law written by God; to obey it is the very dignity of man. (16)

The Spiritual Battle

The doctrine of Original Sin lies behind another important concept in Scripture and Tradition. The concept is this: since the Fall of Adam and Eve, the human race has been involved in a spiritual battle between good and evil. On one side of this battle is Satan, the evil one, who continues to tempt human beings to reject God and God's

Faith in Action
The Community of Sant'Egidio

© Monkey Business Images / Shutterstock.com

The Community of Sant'Egidio (named after a parish church of Saint Giles) was founded in Rome shortly after Vatican Council II. The founding members were high school students who simply wanted to live the Gospel in a more intentional way. With the early Christian communities as their model, the students began to visit poor people in Rome and started a school for children.

Today living the Gospel concretely is still the goal of the community, which now has sixty thousand members all over the world and includes laypeople of all ages. Members live by these essential elements:

- prayer, both privately and in common
- communicating the Gospel (evangelization)
- solidarity with the poor
- ecumenism (friendship, prayer, and the search for unity among Christians)
- dialogue (as a path to peace and cooperation among religions, and as a means of resolving conflicts)

The Community of Sant'Egidio USA has communities in several cities, including Boston, New York City, and Minneapolis–Saint Paul. The worldwide Community of Sant'Egidio has been officially recognized by the Vatican as a public lay association.

The Community of Sant'Egidio has been recognized for its work for peace and reconciliation among warring nations, particularly in Algeria, the Balkans, and the Democratic Republic of the Congo. The group has also been nominated for the Nobel Peace Prize. All of this has come from a meeting of high school students! The Community of Sant'Egidio has grown from a small mustard seed into a mighty tree, supporting life in every way (see Luke 13:19).

laws. On the other side of the battle is God—the Father, Son, and Holy Spirit—who has promised to help us win this battle against evil. In fact, Jesus Christ's life, Passion, death, and Resurrection have already won the battle. We just have to decide whose side we are going to be on.

What do you imagine your relationship with God would be like without Original Sin?

Satan
The fallen angel or spirit of evil who is the enemy of God and a continuing instigator of temptation and sin in the world.

Article 7: Satan and the Fallen Angels

Who is the deceiving serpent we first meet in the account of the Fall? Tradition identifies the serpent as **Satan**. Satan is a popular character in television, movies, and music. Sometimes he is pictured in demonic form with goat horns. This image is taken from Matthew 25:31–46, Jesus' explanation of his Second Coming, when he will separate the sheep, who will go to Heaven, from the goats, who will go to Hell. Sometimes Satan is presented as a smooth-talking, well-dressed, but always deceptive businessman. These images tell us something true about Satan. He is a liar, and he is dangerous to our spiritual well-being. The danger in the media portrayal of Satan is that it might lead us to believe that he is not real. He and his false promises are very, very real.

This painting depicts Michael the Archangel in battle against Satan and his demons. Why does the artist depict the demonic forces as bestial?

The Origin of the Fallen Angels

The Bible gives us only a hint of the nature of Satan and his demons. The Second Letter of Peter has this passing reference: "God did not spare the angels when they sinned, but condemned them to the chains of Tartarus and handed them over to be kept for judgment" (2:4; see also Jude, verse 6). This mention supports what God has revealed through Sacred Tradition. The devil and his demons are fallen angels.

© Bildarchiv Preussischer Kulturbesitz / Art Resource, NY

These angels, through their own free choice, totally and completely rejected God and his Reign. As a result they could no longer be in the presence of God and were cast from Heaven (see Luke 10:18).

The greatest of these fallen angels is Satan, also called the devil or Lucifer. Satan's identity develops over time in Sacred Scripture. Some people are surprised to discover that in Satan's earliest appearances in the Bible, he was a member of God's heavenly court. The Old Testament mentions him only three times: Job, chapters 1 and 2; 1 Chronicles 21:1; and Zechariah 3:1–2. The Books of Job and Zechariah portray Satan as an angel whose role is to direct God's attention to human sinfulness.

By New Testament times, Satan emerged as God's fierce opponent. Unlike the Old Testament, the New Testament includes many references to Satan, who is also called the devil and Beelzebub. Satan was bold enough to tempt Jesus himself at the beginning of Jesus' ministry (see Luke 4:1–11). Jesus called him "a murderer from the beginning" and "the father of lies" (John 8:44). In the New Testament, Satan is now understood to represent the powers of evil in the world. He is described as the leader of a kingdom of darkness (see Mark 3:23–26) and "the prince of demons" (Luke 11:15). The devil was even partially responsible for the death of Jesus, entering Judas and leading him to betray Jesus (see John 13:27). Early Christians were warned to be on the alert for Satan, who was "prowling around like a roaring lion" (1 Peter 5:8) looking to devour the unwary. The New Testament also identifies Satan as the spiritual power behind the empires that persecuted the Israelites and the early Christians. This depiction is particularly evident in the Book of Revelation, which also characterizes Satan as a dragon (see chapters 12, 13, and 20).

Jesus recognized Satan for who he is: a deceiver who wants to turn us away from God's love. Through his life, death, and Resurrection, Jesus helps us to follow God and to resist the devil's temptations.

© Jeff Preston/Licensed from GoodSalt.com

All of these different images of Satan in the Bible offer another example of why we must consider all of Sacred Scripture and Tradition when we interpret a specific Bible passage.

Satan's Power Is Limited

As a spiritual force, Satan is powerful, but he is not all-powerful. He has already lost his war with God. Christ won his victory over Satan through his death on the Cross. Now all that remains is for Satan to be thrown into Hell forever at the Final Judgment (see Revelation 20:21).

It might be confusing to talk about a battle that has already been won on one hand, and on the other hand a battle that is still occurring. The battle that is ongoing is not a battle to determine whether good or evil will ultimately be victorious, because God has already defeated Satan. Rather, Satan continues fighting to persuade us to rebel against God.

As we await the **Parousia**, the devil continues to have the power to tempt us to sin. But he cannot force us to do

Parousia
The Second Coming of Christ as judge of all the living and the dead, at the end of time, when the Kingdom of God will be fulfilled.

Pray It!

Deliver Us from Evil

When thinking of evil, some people envision a red creature with horns and a pitchfork. But evil comes in more real and concrete forms. We sometimes convince ourselves that evil is "out there," perpetrated by other people, but the truth is that we often participate in evil. It is easy to point a finger at the evil carried out by others, but it is extremely painful to admit the evil committed by our own hands.

Let us prayerfully acknowledge where we have fallen short and ask God to deliver us from these evils.

Lord Jesus, you taught us that repentant souls will be forgiven. Help me to turn from the selfish acts that lead me away from communion with you and with others: gossip . . . cheating . . . addiction . . . greed . . . racism . . . drug abuse . . . bullying . . . pornography . . . hatred . . . abortion . . . lies . . . poverty . . . violence . . . sexual promiscuity . . . selfishness. Help me to recognize evil for what it is and to choose to act out of love instead. In your name I pray, Amen.

temptation
An invitation or enticement to commit an unwise or immoral act that often includes a promise of reward to make the immoral act seem more appealing.

anything against our will. We have received grace from the Holy Spirit to resist the devil's **temptations**. The pain and suffering in the world caused by human sin may start with Satan's temptations, but the choices we freely make as human beings actually cause the pain and suffering. So be on the watch for Satan's temptations, but do not fear him. The power of Christ will protect you.

What temptations do you recognize in your own life? How can Christ help you to resist them?

Chapter Review

1. How is the loss of Adam and Eve's original holiness and original justice symbolically expressed in Genesis, chapter 3?

2. Explain the deeper meaning of Adam and Eve's sin of disobedience.

3. How does Original Sin affect human nature?

4. Describe the spiritual battle that is occurring because of Original Sin.

5. What is the origin of Satan and his demons?

6. What are some of the different ways Satan is described in Scripture?

The Path to Restoration

Introduction

After Adam and Eve's Fall from grace, God sought
to restore to humanity what was lost in the Fall. In
this chapter, we continue to see God's plan revealed
through Scripture and Tradition. This plan began with
his promise to our first parents. We will then see the
covenants God made with Noah, Abraham, Moses,
and David. Through the covenants, God established
his intent to call a Chosen People to be his light for
all the nations. He gave them the Law to teach them
how to live in right relationship with him and with one
another. We will see the continued impact of Original
Sin as the Chosen People failed to uphold their end of
the covenant time and time again, suffering many ter-
rible consequences because of their lack of faith.

You might think that God would just give up
on the Chosen People. But God's love, patience, and
understanding have no limits. God called judges
and kings to lead his people. His prophets tirelessly
warned, directed, and comforted the Chosen People.
Their message contained hints of what was to come
in God's wonderful plan for our salvation. God would
send a Messiah, a chosen one, who would fully restore
humanity's original holiness and justice. He would
lead with justice, proclaim peace, and as the Suffering
Servant take upon himself all our sins. And the Chosen
People began to wait in hope.

literal sense
A form of biblical interpretation that considers the explicit meaning of the text. It lays the foundation for all other senses of Sacred Scripture.

spiritual sense
A form of biblical interpretation that goes beyond the literal sense to consider what the realities and events of Sacred Scripture signify and mean for salvation.

Article 8: God's Promise to Adam and Eve

After the Fall things seemed pretty bleak for the human race. We have already looked at the consequences of Adam and Eve's sin, found in Genesis 3:14–19. Adam and Eve, who are symbolic of all humanity, lost God's gifts of original holiness and original justice. Their relationships with God and with each other were more difficult and challenging. But hidden in the third chapter of Genesis is a great spiritual truth: even amidst the greatest of tragedies, God does not abandon us. For those who have faith, God will bring good even from sin and suffering.

The *Protoevangelium*

In Genesis, chapter 3, God delivered the consequences of Adam and Eve's disobedience. He said to the serpent:

> I will put enmity between you and the woman,
> and between your offspring and hers;
> They will strike at your head,
> while you strike at their heel.
>
> (Genesis 3:15)

This verse is called the *Protoevangelium*, which is a Latin word meaning "first gospel." The **literal sense** of this verse is that it is an etiology; it explains why snakes and people do not get along very well. But after the experience of Christ's life, death, and Resurrection, the Church Fathers saw a deeper, **spiritual sense** in this verse. They interpreted it as God's first promise to send a Savior to free humanity from the effects of the Fall. The following chart will help you to understand their interpretation:

Literal Sign	Spiritual Meaning
the serpent	Satan
the woman	Mary
the woman's offspring	Jesus Christ

Literal Sign	Spiritual Meaning
enmity between the serpent and the woman, between the serpent and her offspring	the spiritual battle between Satan and God for the future of humanity
"They will strike at your head, / while you strike at their heel" (Genesis 3:15).	Jesus Christ will win the battle with Satan. A strike at the heel is a position of weakness, but a strike at the head is a death blow.

So even as Adam and Eve were leaving the Garden of Eden, God was already making a promise, a covenant, that he would save humanity from the damage caused by Satan's deception. In this interpretation, Mary is the new Eve and Christ is the new Adam. They restored the original holiness and justice that were lost by Adam and Eve. As the Mother of God, Mary was the first to benefit from Christ's victory over sin. She was conceived without the stain of Original Sin and with special grace from God remained free from sin throughout her entire life.

According to Saint Leo the Great, humanity was not simply restored to our former state by Christ's victory, however. Saint Leo, who served as Pope from 440 to 461, expressed the wonder and joy of the great mystery of God's plan of salvation in one of his sermons:

> For today not only are we confirmed as possessors of paradise, but have also in Christ penetrated the heights of heaven, and have gained still greater things through Christ's unspeakable grace than we had lost through the devil's malice. For us, whom our virulent enemy had driven out from the bliss of our first abode, the Son of God has made members of Himself and placed at the right hand of the Father. ("Sermon 73")

God Remains Faithful

The accounts that follow the Fall in the primeval history serve two purposes. First, they show the growth and worsening of sin. Second, they show that no matter how bad humanity fell, God remained faithful in finding a way to preserve his plan of salvation.

Cain and Abel (Genesis 4:1–16)

The story of Cain and Abel, Adam and Eve's first two sons, is a story of jealousy and fratricide. Cain, a shepherd, and Abel, a farmer, offered the appropriate sacrifice to God. God liked Abel's sacrifice better (because he offered the best of what he raised), and Cain was jealous. He killed Abel. The first sin after the Fall was brother killing brother.

© ZU_09 / istockphoto.com

Adam and Eve weep over their dead son, Abel. Notice the two altars in the background. The smoke from Abel's sacrifice raises straight up, a symbol that his sacrifice was pleasing to God.

Again, in this account, the inspired biblical writer described God by way of an imperfect analogy that presents God in human terms, as acting in a human manner. First, God warned Cain not to let sin be his master. Second, after the murder, God marked Cain to prevent anyone from killing him in revenge. God's promise to save the descendants of Adam and Eve was already being fulfilled.

Noah and the Flood (Genesis 6:5–9:17)

The Book of Genesis gives two versions of the generations from Adam to Noah. Humankind had greatly increased in number. And humankind had also greatly increased in sin. God saw how "every desire that [humanity's] heart conceived was always nothing but evil" (6:5). God decided to start over again. Fortunately, there was one just man on earth: Noah. Through Noah and his family, God was able to continue his promise to save the descendants of Adam and Eve. But God went one step further this time. He made an explicit covenant or promise with Noah, and through Noah with all humankind and all creation: "Never again shall all creatures be destroyed by the waters of a flood" (9:11). God marked this promise with a rainbow. He committed to saving humanity by some different means than by destroying all sinners. God's plan continued to be revealed.

The Tower of Babel (Genesis 11:1–9)

Following the Flood, the Israelites resolved to build a city for themselves, with a tower "with its top in the sky" (Genesis 11:4). The account of the tower of Babel tells about a people who tried to make themselves like gods. To keep his promise not to destroy all the sinful people with a natural disaster, God instead made them speak different languages so they could not understand one another (another etiology). Once again God took action to keep his plan of salvation in motion.

All of these accounts from the primeval history reveal that humanity was simply not learning how to be faithful to God. Each time, something more was needed. As the Old Testament progresses, we see that God takes an increasingly direct approach in his saving plan by initiating and affirming specific, special covenants with his Chosen People.

How do you encounter God's presence and his promise of salvation even when you sin?

Article 9: The Old Testament Covenants

A covenant is a solemn agreement between two parties. Among the nations surrounding ancient Israel, covenants were usually made between two kings, outlining the responsibilities the kings had toward each other. Often the stronger king promised to protect the weaker king, and the weaker king promised to pay tribute or taxes to the more powerful king. But we do not have any records of these kingdoms' having covenants with their gods or goddesses. In their mythologies, their deities would never humble themselves to enter into a binding agreement with human beings.

This makes Israel unique. Their covenants were not with other kingdoms but with God. God initiated these covenants and stayed faithful to them. Through them he communicated the love he has for humanity and his

Paschal Mystery
The work of salvation accomplished by Jesus Christ mainly through his Passion, death, Resurrection, and Ascension.

polytheism
The belief in many gods.

desire to restore our communion with him. These covenants point us to the **Paschal Mystery**, the redemption of all humanity through Christ's Passion, death, Resurrection, and Ascension. We will look at four of these covenants—those with Noah, Abraham, Moses, and David.

The Covenant with Noah

In this chapter, you have already read about the covenant God made with Noah and, through Noah, with the whole human race. An important thing to consider about this early covenant is its universal nature. Chapter 10 of Genesis describes how, directly after God made this covenant, Noah's descendants multiplied to become all the nations of the world: "These are the clans of Noah's sons, according to their origins and by their nations. From these the nations of the earth branched out after the flood" (verse 32). This was a way of saying that God's covenant with Noah now extended to all the nations of

Did You Know?

An Enduring Relationship

© stevenallan/istockphoto.com

A close relationship exists between Christians and Jews because we share the same spiritual heritage, given to us by the patriarchs, Moses, and the prophets. Vatican Council II stated, "The apostle Paul maintains that the Jews remain very dear to God, for the sake of the patriarchs, since God does not take back the gifts he bestowed or the choice he made" (t], 4).

In our own time, Pope Francis invited the chief rabbi of Rome to the papal inauguration Mass. In the invitation, Pope Francis wrote, "Placing my trust in the protection of the Most High, I eagerly hope to be able to contribute to the progress that relations between Jews and Catholics have experienced . . .
in a spirit of renewed collaboration, and in service of a world that might be more and more in harmony with the Creator's will."

the earth and will remain in force as long as the world lasts.

However, because of sin these nations were always in danger of **polytheism**, which is the false belief in many gods. They were also always in danger of worshipping their nation and their king instead of God, which is another form of idolatry. Yet the covenant with Noah assures us that God was still at work among these nations. The Bible lifts up several non-Jewish leaders as examples of God's working through other peoples. These Gentiles, or non-Jews, were instrumental in God's plan of salvation. The following chart lists the most prominent ones:

Name	Importance
Melchizedek	The king of Salem and a "priest of God Most High" (Genesis 14:18). With Abraham he offered bread and wine in thanksgiving after a successful battle.
Rahab	A Canaanite woman who risked her life to help protect Joshua's spies in the city of Jericho (see Joshua 2:1–21).
King Cyrus	The Persian emperor who conquered Babylon and ended the Jewish Exile (see Ezra 1:1–4). He allowed the Judean slaves to return home and even helped to fund the reconstruction of Jerusalem (see 3:7).
Ruth	A Moabite woman who married an Israelite man. She is remembered for her trust in God and her commitment to her Jewish mother-in-law.

The covenant with Noah, which applied universally to all peoples, found its fulfillment in the New Covenant that Jesus Christ extends to all the people of the world.

The rainbow was God's sign to Noah of his love for humanity and his promise to save us.

© PHOTOCREO Michal Bednarek / Shutterstock.com

circumcision
The act, required by Jewish Law, of removing the foreskin of the penis. Since the time of Abraham, it has been a sign of God's covenant relationship with the Jewish people.

patriarch
The father or leader of a tribe, clan, or tradition. Abraham, Isaac, and Jacob were the patriarchs of the Israelite people.

The Abrahamic Covenant

The story of Abraham begins in chapter 12 of Genesis. Starting with Abraham, God began a new phase of his plan to restore humanity's holiness and justice: he called a Chosen People to be in a unique relationship with him. These people had a special role in his plan. God established this special relationship and its purpose in the covenant he made with Abraham. There are several places where God announced his covenant to Abraham: 12:1–3, 13:14–17, 15:1–19, and 17:1–27. But the later announcements are, for the most part, further elaborations on the covenant first made in chapter 12:

> I will make of you a great nation, and I will bless you; I will make your name great, so that you will be a blessing. I will bless those who bless you and curse those who curse you. All the families of the earth will find blessing in you. (Verses 2–3)

In his covenant with Abraham, God promised Abraham three things: (1) to make of him a great nation by promising Abraham many descendants, (2) to provide

Pray It!

Courage to Be Faithful to God

When God appears to someone in a movie, the moment is often presented as joyous, accompanied by a white light and angels singing. But in the Bible, God's appearances usually fill those who experience them with fear at encountering the mystery of God. When God established his covenant with Abraham, "a great, dark dread descended upon him [Abraham]" (Genesis 15:12). Before Moses received the Ten Commandments, Mount Sinai was "enveloped in smoke" and "trembled violently" (Exodus 19:18). We might interpret this as God's way of saying, "This isn't going to be easy." It is true: our life with God requires courage. Let us pray:

God, give me the courage . . .
  . . . to be present to you despite my fears,
  . . . to keep my promises to you even when there are obstacles,
  . . . to know you are here with me even in the turmoil of my life,
  . . . to live the New Law taught by and embodied in Jesus Christ.
Amen.

Abraham and his descendants with a land of their own, and (3) to make Abraham and his descendants a blessing for all the nations.

The third promise was the most important one in God's saving plan. The first two promises were the preconditions necessary in order for the third promise to be fulfilled. God's plan was for Abraham's descendants, who would later be called Hebrews, Israelites, and finally Jews, to be an example to all other people of how to live in right relationship with the one, true God. God asked Abraham and his descendants to commit to these things: (1) to walk with God—that is, to recognize the one, true God (see Genesis 17:1), (2) to be blameless—that is to live a life without sin (see 17:1), and (3) to practice **circumcision** as a physical mark of the covenant (see 17:9–14).

Abraham and his descendants—Isaac and Jacob (whom God renamed Israel)—are called the **patriarchs**, and they are revered as saints in the Church's liturgical tradition. The remaining chapters of Genesis tell of how they escaped many dangerous situations. Their stories show that God is faithful in keeping his covenant despite human sin and weakness. Original Sin continued to have its effect. The Israelites worshipped false gods and goddesses and were guilty of a variety of sins. But God remained faithful, and his will could not be overcome by human sin and weakness. God's covenant with Abraham prepared the way for the coming of the Messiah, Jesus Christ, in whom the ctovenant is fulfilled. Through Jesus Christ, a descendant of Abraham, God's blessing is brought to all the nations.

Abraham is a gracious host to his mysterious visitors. Notice how he kneels before them in the foreground and serves them at a table in the background.

© DeA Picture Library / Art Resource, NY

The Mosaic Covenant

One of the most awe-inspiring events in the Old Testament is the **theophany** at Mount Sinai, which is described in Exodus 19:16–25. The Israelites had escaped from Egypt because of God's miraculous intervention and had been journeying for three months. They had come to the Sinai desert and camped at the base of a large mountain. On the third day after their arrival at the mountain, the air was filled with lightning and thunder, the ground shook, and smoke and fire appeared on the mountaintop. These dramatic signs of God's presence are meant to call attention to the critical importance of what comes next.

God summoned Moses to the mountaintop and renewed with him the covenant God made with Abraham. And God gave Moses a set of laws that the Israelites were required to follow as their part of the covenant. This Law is summarized in the Ten Commandments (see Exodus 20:1–17), but the full Law is spelled out in the rest of Exodus and Leviticus. It is summarized again in Deuteronomy. This Law is also called the Mosaic Law or the Old Law. It is called the Old Law because it has been fulfilled in Jesus Christ, who is the New Law.

From this point on, the covenant and the Law were so closely linked that they were understood to be two sides of the same coin. Keeping the Law was the most important sign of faithfulness to the covenant. Breaking the Law was the same as being unfaithful to the covenant. The Jewish people eventually call the first five books of their Scriptures—the same five books that begin the Old Testament—the **Torah**, which is the Hebrew word for "law" or "teach-

Moses receives the Ten Commandments from God to teach the Israelites how to live in right relationship with God and one another. Obeying the Commandments was an important part of the Israelites' covenant with God.

ing." Through these laws God taught his Chosen People how to be in right relationship with him and with one another. The Old Law was a step in God's plan for restoring our original holiness and justice. It became the rule by which the prophets measured the faithfulness of the kings and the people.

The Davidic Covenant

God made one more promise in the Old Testament that can also be called a covenant. This promise was delivered to King David by the prophet Nathan. David wished to build a permanent dwelling for the **Ark of the Covenant**, the sacred box in which the tablets with the Ten Commandments were kept. God instructed Nathan to tell David not to build this Temple (see 2 Samuel 7:4–13). Instead David's heir would build it. God then promised David that "your house and your kingdom are firm forever before me; your throne shall be firmly established forever" (2 Samuel 7:16).

In this context, a "house" means a bloodline or direct line of descendants. Even though a descendant of David was always ruler of Israel or Judah (the southern kingdom), the kingdom itself was destroyed in 598 BC. After this there were no more Davidic kings. The Gospels help us to understand how this promise was fulfilled. Jesus Christ was a direct descendant of David (see Matthew 1:6, Luke 3:31). Christ established the Kingdom of God, which will endure forever and over which he reigns for eternity. Through him the covenant with David is fulfilled.

Covenants: Part of God's Plan

Through all of these covenants—with Noah, Abraham, Moses, and David—God was establishing and affirming his Chosen People, a people who are our ancestors in faith. We find this explicitly described in the Book of Deuteronomy, which portrays Moses' final speech to the Israelites: "For you are a people holy to the Lord, your God; the Lord, your God, has chosen you from all the

theophany
God's manifestation of himself in a visible form to enrich human understanding of him. An example is God's appearance to Moses in the form of a burning bush.

Torah
A Hebrew word meaning "law," referring to the first five books of the Old Testament.

Ark of the Covenant
A sacred chest that housed the tablets of the Ten Commandments, placed within the sanctuary where God would come and dwell.

peoples on the face of the earth to be a people specially his own. It was not because you are more numerous than all the peoples that the Lord set his heart on you. . . . It was because the Lord loved you and because of his fidelity to the oath he had sworn to your ancestors" (7:6–7).

All the Old Testament covenants are part of God's plan. They assure us of God's loving commitment to humanity. They teach us how to live in right relationship with God and with one another. They point us toward the restoration of our original holiness and justice. But these covenants by themselves are not enough to bring God's plan of salvation to fulfillment. So they also point the way to something more. That something more is the Messiah, Jesus Christ, whose life, death, Passion,

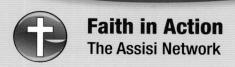

Faith in Action
The Assisi Network

The persecution of Jews is a sad fact of human history. The human family from which our Savior was born has often been identified as a scapegoat for problems in wider society.

During World War II, Germany implemented a program of genocide, now called the Holocaust, with the aim of purging Germany of Jews, gypsies, the disabled, Catholics, homosexuals, and others deemed undesirable.

When the persecution of Jews spread to Italy, Bishop Giuseppe Nicolini of Assisi responded quickly. He ordered Fr. Aldo Brunacci to hide Jewish people in the numerous churches, monasteries, and convents of Assisi. Some were even disguised as monks and nuns! Others who passed through Assisi were given false papers so that they might survive in other countries. Laypeople risked their own lives to make these false documents look as authentic as possible. This circle of rescue was known as the Assisi network.

During the war the people of Assisi did their best to help fulfill the religious needs of the Jews in hiding. After the war the entire town celebrated Yom Kippur (the Day of Atonement, a day of fasting and the most solemn day in the Jewish calendar), and a community of nuns prepared the meal to celebrate the end of the fast.

In 1977, Bishop Nicolini and Father Brunacci were honored as Righteous Among the Nations, a title given by the State of Israel to those who risked their lives to save Jews during the Holocaust. Luigi Brizi and his son Trento, who printed the false papers, were named Righteous Among the Nations in 1997.

Resurrection, and Ascension—the Paschal Mystery—
bring these ancient covenants to their final and complete
fulfillment. By sending his own Son, God has revealed
himself fully to the world.

> **How do the covenants with Noah, Abraham,
> Moses, and David point the way to Jesus Christ, the
> Messiah?**

confederation
An alliance of
tribes or nations
with no central
authority.

Article 10: Covenant Keeping: Successes and Failures

The historical books and the writings of the prophets
reveal the Israelites' struggles to keep the covenant they
had made with God. You might have covered this history
in greater detail in a previous course. Now let's examine
three important elements in the Israelites' history: the
time of the judges, the time of the monarchy, and the role
of the prophets.

The Judges of Israel

After the Israelites, led by Joshua, settled in the land of
Canaan, they had no central government—no king, no
high priest, no president. They existed as a **confederation**
of tribal groups. When they faced any threat, such as an
outside invader, God raised up a hero who rallied one or
more tribes in defense of their land. These leaders were
called judges, but they were not judges as we know them
today. Though they may have settled disputes, judges
were primarily military leaders. The Book of Judges contains the accounts of twelve of these charismatic leaders,
telling about six of them in more detail.

There is a cycle in Judges related to the covenant. It
would seem that after taking possession of the Promised Land, the Israelites forgot the Law and the covenant
again and again. "[T]he Israelites . . . abandoned
the Lord, the God of their ancestors, the one who had
brought them out of the land of Egypt. They followed
other gods, the gods of the peoples around them, and

monarchy
A government or a state headed by a single person, such as a king or queen. As a biblical term, it refers to the period of time when the Israelites existed as an independent nation.

bowed down to them, and provoked the Lord" (Judges 2:11–12). God allowed them to fall into the hands of their enemies. When they realized their sin and repented and called out to God for deliverance, God raised up a judge to lead the victory against their enemies. Then for a while, the Israelites kept the covenant before falling into the cycle of disobedience again.

The Book of Judges shows another step in God's plan of salvation. God wanted his Chosen People to be completely committed to him, which they could demonstrate by keeping the Law and the covenant. As long as they did this, they would not need an intermediary, such as a king, to lead them. But they proved incapable of doing this. As the period of the Judges continued, even the judges themselves became less exemplary in their behavior. Gideon introduced idolatry (see Judges 8:24–27), Jephthah sacrificed his own daughter (see 11:29–40), and Samson was driven by his own selfish concerns (see chapters 13–16). The period ended with a bloody civil war (see chapter 20). Despite these setbacks God was faithful to the covenant and did not abandon this seemingly hopeless people.

© Providence Collection/Licensed from GoodSalt.com

Deborah, the only female judge of Israel, is depicted with her palm tree, where the Israelites came to her for guidance (see Judges 4:5).

The Monarchy

The history of the kings of Israel is told in First and Second Samuel and First and Second Kings and is then repeated in First and Second Chronicles. The **monarchy** began with the Israelites' approaching Samuel, the last judge of Israel, and asking him to appoint a king. Samuel was reluctant to do this because he believed the people were rejecting God as their king. Despite this, God directed him to anoint the first king of Israel, Saul (see

1 Samuel, chapter 8). The first three kings of Israel were all heroically committed to God and promoted the Law and the covenant. All three were also tragically flawed: Saul with lack of trust, David with lust, and Solomon with greed. Despite their sin and weakness, God worked through them to unite the twelve tribes into a strong, united kingdom and eventually to build a Temple in Jerusalem, the center of authentic Israelite worship.

After Solomon's death, however, the united monarchy was split into two kingdoms: Israel and Judah. The Books of First and Second Kings chronicle the successes and failures of the kings of both kingdoms. The very first king of the northern kingdom (Israel), Jeroboam, got off to a bad start by setting up idolatrous places of worship. He and the kings who followed him "did what was evil in the Lord's sight" (1 Kings 15:26). The kings of the southern kingdom (Judah) did not do much better. "Judah did evil in the Lord's sight and they angered him even more than their ancestors had done" (1 Kings 14:22). But there were good kings of Judah, like Asa, Hezekiah, and Josiah, who brought religious reform and destroyed the places of idolatry and called the people to be faithful again to the covenant.

Samuel unexpectedly anoints David, the youngest of eight brothers, as the future king of Israel. Why do you think God's choices are often not what people expect?

As another step in God's plan of salvation, the monarchy firmly established the Israelites as God's Chosen People. The practices of religious ritual and worship were established at the Jerusalem Temple. And the great kings, such as David and Solomon, foreshadowed the kingship of Jesus Christ. As earthly kingdoms, Israel and Judah did not last. But the noble intention of these Israelite nations—to be kingdoms committed to the Law and the covenant—finds its fulfillment

© Art Resource, NY

in the Kingdom of Heaven and the eternal Reign of Jesus Christ.

The Prophets

The Israelite prophets played a key role in relation to the covenant. In a very real sense, they were the overseers of the covenant and the Law. As God's spokespeople they called the kings and the people to be faithful to the covenant and warned of the consequences of failing to do so. "Thus says the Lord, the God of Israel: Cursed be anyone who does not observe the words of this covenant, which I commanded your ancestors the day I brought them up out of the land of Egypt" (Jeremiah 11:3–4). But the prophets also assured the people that God would not abandon his covenant commitment:

> Though the mountains fall away
> and the hills be shaken,
> My love shall never fall away from you
> nor my covenant of peace be shaken,
> says the Lord, who has mercy on you.
> (Isaiah 54:10)

Live It!
What Would the Prophets Tell Us?

The prophets of the Old Testament often cried out against the hypocrisy of the Israelites. They pointed out the great gap between the demands of the covenant and how the Israelites actually lived. For example, Amos tells the people that their worship means nothing to God because they do not live a good and just life. Their prayers have become empty and hollow. Only when they "let justice surge like waters, / and righteousness like an unfailing stream" (Amos 5:24) will their worship have any meaning again. Today the words of the prophets remind us to be faithful to the teachings of Christ by being peacemakers, caring for the poor, and loving those whom we do not like. Our worship at Mass is most authentic when we are faithful to Christ's teachings. "Faith . . . if it does not have works, is dead" (James 2:17).

Does your faith have works? Look for opportunities each day to put your faith into action by doing good works, especially for those most in need.

The books of the prophets contain the writings of four major prophets—Isaiah, Jeremiah, Ezekiel, and Daniel—and the writings of twelve minor prophets. But there were many more prophets than these who are part of salvation history. These faithful men endured ridicule and torture and even risked death to speak God's Word. They did this out of love for God's People. They knew that the Israelites' faithfulness to the covenant was essential for God's plan of salvation. They already were beginning to see that God was planning something big, something new, to complete his plan to redeem all humanity and restore our right relationship with God and with one another. The prophets foreshadowed Christ's own role as prophet, for Jesus Christ will not just proclaim the Word—he is the Word of God Made Flesh.

> **"A child is born to us, a son is given us." (Isaiah 9:5)**

Why do you think the people repeatedly forgot the lessons they had learned about being faithful to their covenant with God?

Primary Sources

On Christian Hope

Pope Benedict XVI's second encyclical specifically addresses Christian hope. In this beautiful letter, he outlines the importance of the virtue of hope in the life of the believer. The Pope's letter begins as follows:

> According to the Christian faith, "redemption"—salvation—is not simply a given. Redemption is offered to us in the sense that we have been given hope, trustworthy hope, by virtue of which we can face our present: the present, even if it is arduous, can be lived and accepted if it leads towards a goal, if we can be sure of this goal, and if this goal is great enough to justify the effort of the journey. (Spe Salvi, 1)

You can easily find Pope Benedict's encyclical online. It is enlightening and inspiring reading.

Article 11: The Growing Messianic Hope

Hope. It is an important virtue and a gift of faith. Hope creates in us a desire and an expectation for our salvation and the Kingdom of God. The prophets were God's instruments of hope to his Chosen People. He revealed to the prophets a vision of a **New Covenant** and a new

Location	Description	Connection to Christ
Isaiah 9:1–6	Isaiah prophesied that the "people who walked in darkness have seen a great light." A child will be born to lead them and among his names will be "God-Hero" and "Prince of Peace." His Kingdom will be just and peaceful forever.	Jesus Christ is the Prince of Peace and the Son of God who forever rules the Kingdom of Heaven.
Isaiah 11:1–9	Isaiah prophesied about a coming ruler from the "stump of Jesse." He shall "judge the poor with justice" and "with the breath of his lips he shall slay the wicked." Even natural enemies will play together peacefully in his Kingdom.	Jesus Christ is a descendant of Jesse (David's father).
Isaiah 52:13–53:12	This is one of the Suffering Servant passages in Isaiah. Isaiah prophesied of a servant of the Lord who is "struck for the sins of his people." "The LORD laid upon him the guilt of us all" and "by his wounds we were healed."	This prophecy is an accurate description of Christ's Passion. He suffered and died for our salvation.
Jeremiah 31:31–34	Jeremiah prophesied about a new covenant God will make with Israel and Judah: "I will place my law within them, and write it upon their hearts."	The New Covenant is established in Jesus Christ. Through the power of the Holy Spirit, Christ lives in every believer's heart.
Ezekiel 34:11–31	Ezekiel prophesied that God will act like a good shepherd, rescuing his people, giving them safe pasture, and healing their injuries. He will "make a covenant of peace with them" and "deliver them from the power of those who enslaved them."	In the Gospel of John, Christ declares that he is the Good Shepherd.
Ezekiel 37:1–14	Ezekiel had a vision of a valley of dry bones being resurrected and coming alive again. "You shall know that I am the LORD, when I open your graves and make you come up out of them."	With the coming of the New Covenant, all the faithful who have died will rise again, having been saved through the Passion, death, and Resurrection of Jesus Christ.
Zechariah 9:9–10	Zechariah prophesied about a king and a "just savior." He shall "proclaim peace to the nations" and "his dominion will be from sea to sea."	Jesus Christ is the promised King and just Savior.

heavenly Kingdom. This vision would be brought about through the work of a messiah, which literally means "anointed one."

The chart outlines some of the more important prophecies of hope proclaimed by the prophets and explains how each prophecy is connected to Christ.

By proclaiming these visions of a messiah, the prophets gave the Chosen People hope for a future in which humanity's relationship with God would be fully restored. In the centuries preceding the birth of Christ, many faithful Jews waited in expectant hope for the promised Messiah who would deliver them from their earthly and spiritual bondage. Their wait was over when Jesus Christ, the only begotten Son of the Father, was conceived by the power of the Holy Spirit and born of the Virgin Mary.

What is hope? How does the virtue of hope make it easier to endure suffering and uncertainty?

New Covenant
The covenant or law established by God in Jesus Christ to fulfill and perfect the Old Covenant or Mosaic Law. It is a perfection here on earth of the Divine Law. The law of the New Covenant is called a law of love, grace, and freedom. The New Covenant will never end or diminish, and nothing new will be revealed until Christ comes again in glory.

Chapter Review

1. Give an interpretation of the *Protoevangelium* using both the literal and spiritual senses of the passage.

2. How do the accounts of Cain and Abel and Noah and the Flood explain both the effects of Original Sin and God's promise of salvation?

3. How is God's covenant with Noah different from his covenant with Abraham?

4. What does God promise in his covenant with Abraham?

5. Explain the connection between the Mosaic Covenant and the Mosaic Law.

6. How is God's promise to David fulfilled?

7. Describe two Old Testament prophecies of hope and how they are fulfilled in Jesus Christ.

Jesus Christ's Mission Is Revealed

When a friend or relative you haven't seen in a long time plans to visit, do you sit back and just assume everything will go smoothly? You probably do exactly the opposite—as soon as you mark the date, you tell your other friends about the upcoming visit and get busy preparing.

God did something similar before sending his Son into the world to carry out his work of salvation. God had promised to send a Savior to his people. He wanted them to look forward to the Savior's coming and to be ready to receive him. In this unit, we will see how God, through his prophets, prepared the Chosen People for Jesus, the Savior. God also prepared two very special people for a unique role in the Savior's birth: Mary and Joseph.

We know that the Son of God was incarnated, or became man, to save us from sin. In this unit, we will explore other important effects of the Incarnation, including that Jesus showed us the depth of God's love, modeled how to be holy, made us partakers of the divine nature, and destroyed the power of the devil. As a model of holiness, Jesus taught us how to live by his teachings and his example. He lived in poverty and accepted all people. He obeyed his Father to show us how to humbly obey God in all things. He showed compassion to all, healing people both physically and spiritually. Jesus' life made it clear: the Kingdom of God is at hand. But what is the Kingdom of God? In this unit, we will discover what the Kingdom of God means and how it was made present in Jesus.

The enduring understandings and essential questions represent core concepts and questions that are explored throughout this unit. By studying the content of each chapter, you will gain a more complete understanding of the following:

Enduring Understandings

1. The promise of a Messiah is fulfilled in the person of Jesus Christ.
2. The Word of God became flesh for our salvation.
3. Jesus' life and teachings are signs that the Kingdom of God is present to all who believe in him.

Essential Questions

1. How does Jesus' birth fulfill the promise made by God to the Israelites?
2. Why did the Word of God become flesh and dwell among us?
3. How is Jesus' life part of God's plan of salvation?

Chapter
4

The Word Became Flesh

Introduction

In the previous chapter, we studied how God took patient steps to call and prepare his Chosen People. But despite God's gifts of the Covenant and the prophets, his Chosen People could not maintain their faithfulness. In unit 2, we will study how God's plan to offer redemption to all humanity is brought to fulfillment. The angel's announcement to Mary that she would bear the Son of God was the beginning of what Saint Paul called "the fullness of time" (Galatians 4:4). Through the power of the Holy Spirit, Mary conceived a son and named him Jesus, meaning "God saves." Mary became the Mother of God and was supported by Joseph, her husband and Jesus' human foster father.

This great mystery, that the Eternal Son of God assumed a human nature in order to save us, had been foreshadowed through God's relationship with his Chosen People. In recognition of this, the sacred writers of the New Testament showed how many of the Old Testament prophecies applied to Jesus. They made clear that in obedience to his Father, Christ redeemed us from the tyranny of sin and death. He showed us the depths of God's love, enabling us to share in his divine nature. We will see that the names and titles the Gospels use for him—Jesus, Christ, Son of God, and Lord—teach us about his redemptive role. This is the heart of the Paschal Mystery that we are invited into, and it is a cause for great rejoicing!

Article 12: God Prepares the Way: The Roles of Mary and Joseph

God intends that families reflect the love and communion between the Divine Persons of the Holy Trinity: the Father, Jesus Christ the Son, and the Holy Spirit. We have a model for this in Mary, Joseph, and Jesus, the Holy Family. Though we do not know many details of Mary and Joseph's life together, the Gospels give us glimpses of their love and devotion and their faith and trust in God. It was through their family that God set in motion

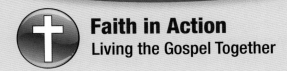

Faith in Action
Living the Gospel Together

© Bill Wittman / www.wpwittman.com

The Christian Family Movement emerged from two separate groups of married couples who, unknown to each other, were meeting simultaneously—one at the University of Notre Dame, the other in Chicago. They were seeking ways to both serve the Church and enrich family life. When the lead couples of both groups met at a Cana Convention for family renewal in 1948, they realized that joining together would benefit Christian families. This meeting of two couples was the nucleus of the Christian Family Movement.

Today members of the Christian Family Movement (parents and adult family members) meet together in local groups to help one another focus on Christian values, rooted in love at home and service to others. They do this through a simple method: observe, judge, and act. *Observe* what is going on around you, *judge* whether this situation is good and helpful, and *act* to improve the situation. This method can be applied from the smallest unit of society, the family, to larger issues in the community and in the world. The Christian Family Movement uses this method to put faith into action.

Members of the movement find that it has helped them to grow in faith, to improve their own family life, to make friends, and to reach out to their communities in loving service. Children benefit because their families meet other families who share the same values. Together they discover ways to live the Gospel and to share their gifts and talents with others.

fiat
Latin for "let it be done," the words Mary spoke to the angel Gabriel at the Annunciation.

Annunciation
The biblical event in which the Archangel Gabriel visits the Virgin Mary to announce that she is to be the Mother of the Savior.

Theotokos
A Greek title for Mary meaning "God bearer."

the events that would bring his plan for our salvation to completion. This is one of the many reasons the Church holds the family unit to be of central importance for our faith.

Mary's Faith and Trust

Over two thousand years ago, the angel Gabriel visited a poor, young, Jewish girl. He told her, "[Y]ou will conceive in your womb and bear a son, and you shall name him Jesus" (Luke 1:31). Faced with what must have been a confusing and overwhelming announcement, Mary showed her complete trust and faith in God with her simple but profound answer: "I am the handmaid of the Lord. May it be done to me according to your word" (verse 38). Because of God's grace, Mary's faith was possible. In her unhesitating "yes," her *fiat*, to God's invitation at the **Annunciation**, Mary committed to her role in God's plan of salvation and became *Theotokos*, meaning "God-bearer." By giving her consent to the Incarnation,

Pray It!

In This Valley of Tears

N ear the entrance of Saint Peter's Basilica in Vatican City sits an extraordinary statue by Michelangelo called *La Pieta*. It depicts Mary, the Mother of God, in her anguish as she embraces Jesus after he was taken down from the cross. Mary knows the depths of whatever suffering you are enduring. In times of difficulty or suffering, pray to Mary with the following prayer, known as the *Salve Regina*, or Hail, Holy Queen.

Hail, holy Queen, Mother of mercy:
Hail, our life, our sweetness and our hope.
To you do we cry, poor banished children of Eve.
To you do we send up our sighs,
mourning and weeping in this valley of tears.
Turn then, most gracious advocate
your eyes of mercy towards us;
and after this our exile,
show unto us the blessed fruit of your womb, Jesus.
O clement, O loving, O sweet Virgin Mary.

Mary was already collaborating with all that her Divine Son would bring about.

God the Father chose Mary from all the descendants of Eve to bear his Eternal Son. From the moment of her conception, Mary was free of Original Sin and she remained blameless and without personal sin for the whole of her life. This is a doctrine called the **Immaculate Conception**. Mary's cousin, Elizabeth, recognized this truth in her greeting to Mary: "Most blessed are you among women, and blessed is the fruit of your womb" (Luke 1:42). Thus God equipped Mary to be able to give herself completely to his plan of salvation.

According to the Father's plan, Jesus Christ was born of a virgin as a sign of his divine identity. When Mary asked how she could give birth, because she was a virgin, Gabriel replied: "The holy Spirit will come upon you, and the power of the Most High will overshadow you. Therefore the child to be born will be called holy, the Son of God" (Luke 1:35). Jesus' birth is a result of divine initiative with the Virgin Mary as his mother and God the Father his only father. Joseph was not his physical father but was his earthly foster father. The virgin birth also symbolizes that Jesus is the New Adam (who also did not have an earthly father) who will usher in the new Heaven and earth that is our ultimate destiny. Mary remained a virgin her entire life, a sign of her total commitment, body and soul, to God.

> **Immaculate Conception**
> The dogma that the Virgin Mary, from the moment of her conception, by a singular grace of God, was free of Original Sin and remained free from personal sin throughout her entire life.

© Vibrant Image Studio / Shutterstock

Joseph's Faith and Trust

It is not only Mary who displayed great faith and trust in God's plan. While the Gospel of Luke emphasizes Mary's role, the Gospel of Matthew emphasizes Joseph's role. From the very beginning, we learn that Joseph was a

What emotions do you see on Mary's face in this beautiful icon? Why might she have experienced these emotions?

compassionate man. Upon learning that Mary was pregnant, Matthew's Gospel tells us, "Joseph her husband, since he was a righteous man, yet unwilling to expose her to shame, decided to divorce her quietly" (1:19). As a betrothed woman, Mary would have been subject to harsh penalties, even death by stoning, had Joseph chosen to accuse her of adultery.

This is where God stepped in. An angel (perhaps Gabriel) appeared to Joseph in a dream and told him the same thing the angel told Mary in the Gospel of Luke—that Mary's child was conceived through the Holy Spirit and that he was to be named Jesus. The angel told Joseph to take the pregnant Mary into his home, which Joseph did without question (see Matthew 1:20–25). Later the angel appeared to Joseph in another dream and warned him to flee with Mary and the infant Jesus to Egypt (see 2:13–14). They fled to avoid the infant massacre ordered by King Herod. After Herod died the angel told Joseph it was safe to return with his family to Israel (see 2:19–21). The Gospel recounts that after both dreams Joseph rose and took the child and his mother, emphasizing his unhesitating obedience and trust in God's call. He didn't even wait until the night was over!

Joseph was a model husband and father. He put his complete trust in God, accepting both Mary's virgin pregnancy and the need to uproot his family at a moment's notice. He loved Mary wholeheartedly and did whatever he could to protect her. He cared for Jesus as his own son. He was a carpenter, most likely a stonemason, and supported his family through hard work. Because there is no mention of Joseph after the account of the lost

In this image of the events of Jesus' birth, why do you think Joseph is reaching out toward the Magi?

Laura James, (Contemporary Artist) / Private Collection / Bridgeman Images

child Jesus being found in the Temple, it is assumed that
Joseph died before Jesus' public ministry. We honor Saint
Joseph as the patron saint of the universal Church, of
happy death, of workers, and of fathers. He is also the
patron saint of many countries. His feast days are March
19 and May 1.

Jesus' Brothers and Sisters

Some people ask, "How is it possible that Mary remained
a virgin her whole life when the Gospels speak about
Jesus' brothers and sisters?" (see Mark 3:31–35 and 6:3,
for example). This is possible because of the close kinship
relationships in biblical times. Extended families lived
next to one another and were together every day. So a
child's aunts and uncles were considered to be another set
of parents, and cousins were commonly called brothers
and sisters. So Jesus' brothers and sisters in the Gospels
were likely members of his extended family, not Mary's
other children. There is also a tradition that says Joseph
was a widower and had children from his first marriage.
If that were the case, Jesus could also have had stepbroth-
ers and stepsisters.

> **Whom do you know in your own life who models
> faith and trust in God's plan? How do they do this?**

Article 13: The Gospels and Christological Prophecies

By reading the Gospels and the letters in the New Testament, we begin to recognize the important truth that the
Eternal Son of God assumed human nature in order to
save us. The Gospels tell us how Jesus was born of the
Virgin Mary, through the power of the Holy Spirit, and
grew up in a loving family. The Gospels go on to describe
Jesus' public ministry, death, Resurrection, and Ascension. But the Evangelists and the other sacred writers of
the New Testament provide us with more than historical
accounts of Jesus' life and ministry. They also show how

foreshadow
To represent or prefigure a person before his or her life or an event before it occurs.

Christological
Having to do with the branch of theology called Christology. Christology is the study of the divinity of Jesus Christ, the Son of God and the Second Divine Person of the Trinity, and his earthly ministry and eternal mission.

many Old Testament prophecies apply to Jesus, helping us to believe that he is the Messiah and Savior who was promised.

Toward the end of the Gospel of Luke, two confused disciples were traveling home to their village after Jesus' Crucifixion (see 24:13–32). The Risen Christ appeared and walked with them, but they did not recognize him. They told Jesus all that has happened, "and he said to them, 'Oh, how foolish you are! How slow of heart to believe all that the prophets spoke! Was it not necessary that the Messiah should suffer these things and enter into his glory?' Then beginning with Moses and all the prophets, he interpreted to them what referred to him in all the scriptures" (24:25–27).

Following Jesus' example the first Christians realized how much of Jesus' life and mission was **foreshadowed** in the Old Testament Scriptures. In chapter 3, "The Path to Restoration," we looked at some of these **Christological** prophecies. God was revealing how his plan would be fulfilled through his relationship with his Chosen People. The sacred writers of the New Testament frequently made reference to these Old Testament connections in order to help others believe. Those with the gift of faith recognize the truth of these prophetic passages, confirming our faith in Christ. The following chart provides many examples of Christological prophecies and how they were fulfilled by God's Word Made Flesh, Jesus Christ. Only selected parts of the passages are quoted in the chart; you may wish to look up and read the complete reference.

Old Testament Prophecy	New Testament Fulfillment
The Savior will be born of a virgin.	

Isaiah 7:14: "Therefore the Lord himself will give you a sign; the young woman, pregnant and about to bear a son, shall name him Emmanuel."	Matthew 1:22–23: "All this took place to fulfill what the Lord had said through the prophet:
	    'Behold, the virgin shall be with child
	        and bear a son,
	        and they shall name him Emmanuel,'
	which means 'God is with us.'"

The Savior will be born in Bethlehem.	
Micah 5:1–4: "But you, Bethlehem-Ephrathah / least among the clans of Judah, / From you shall come forth for me / one who is to be ruler in Israel . . ."	Luke 2:4–7: "And Joseph too went up from Galilee from the town of Nazareth to Judea, to the city of David that is called Bethlehem. . . . While they were there, the time came for her to have her child, and she gave birth to her firstborn son."
The Savior will be full of zeal for God's house, the Temple.	
Psalm 69:10: "Because zeal for your house has consumed me, / I am scorned by those who scorn you."	John 2:17: "His disciples recalled the words of scripture, 'Zeal for your house will consume me.'"
The Savior will be filled with the Spirit of God.	

Isaiah 61:1–2: "The spirit of the Lord God is upon me . . ."	Luke 4:16–21: "He [Jesus] unrolled the scroll and found the passage where it was written:
	    'The Spirit of the Lord is upon me.'
	  . . . .
	He said to them, 'Today this scripture passage is fulfilled in your hearing.'"

The Savior will come into his glory, arriving on an ass (donkey).	

Zechariah 9:9: "Behold, your king is coming to you; / a just savior is he, / Humble, and riding on a donkey, / on a colt, the foal of a donkey."	Matthew 21:4–5: "This happened so that what had been spoken through the prophet might be fulfilled. . . .
	    'Behold, your king comes to you,
	        meek and riding on an ass,
	        and on a colt, the foal of a beast
	          of burden.'"

The Savior will be betrayed for thirty pieces of silver.	
Zechariah 11:12–13: "And they counted out my wages, thirty pieces of silver."	Matthew 27:3–10: "Judas, his betrayer, seeing that Jesus had been condemned, deeply regretted what he had done. He returned the thirty pieces of silver. . . ."

Old Testament Prophecy	New Testament Fulfillment
The Savior will suffer and die.	

Psalm 22:
My God, my God, why have you abandoned me?
. . . .
All who see me mock me;
. . . .
As dry as a potsherd is my throat;
. . . .
     they divide my garments among
     them;
     for my clothing they cast lots.
(Read the whole Psalm for many more connections to Jesus' Crucifixion.)
	Mark 15:34: "Jesus cried out in a loud voice, *'Eloi, Eloi, lema sabachthani?'* which is translated, 'My God, my God, why have you forsaken me?'"
	Mark 15:29: "Those passing by reviled him."
	John 19:28: "Jesus said, 'I thirst.'"
	John 19:23–24: "So they said to one another, 'Let's not tear it, but cast lots for it.'"
	(Read the complete accounts of Jesus' Crucifixion to see other connections.)

The Savior will be the Son of God and will overcome death.	

Psalm 2:7–8:
"I will proclaim the decree of the
    LORD,
  he said to me, 'You are my son;
  today I have begotten you.'"
Psalm 16:10:
"For you will not abandon my soul to
    Sheol,
  nor let your devout one see the pit."
	Acts 13:32–35: "It is written in the second psalm, 'You are my son; this day I have begotten you.' . . . That is why he also says in another psalm, 'You will not suffer your holy one to see corruption.'"

analogy of faith
The coherence of individual doctrines with the whole of Revelation. In other words, as each doctrine is connected with Revelation, each doctrine is also connected with all other doctrines.

How might studying the Old Testament deepen your faith?

Article 14: Why the Word Became Flesh

All the great mysteries of our faith fit together and support one another, kind of like a three-dimensional jigsaw puzzle. This is called the **analogy of faith**. A good example of this is how the Incarnation and the Paschal Mystery are deeply connected to each other. The Paschal Mystery could not have happened without the Incarnation, and without the Paschal Mystery there is no need for the Incarnation.

The Incarnation: A Quick Review

The mystery of the union of Jesus' divine and human natures in one Divine Person is called the **Incarnation**. Like the Trinity, the Incarnation is a mystery we will never be able fully to understand. But we do know that at the time appointed by God, Jesus Christ, the Word of God, became incarnate; that is, without losing his divine nature, he became fully man. This is expressed in the Nicene Creed when we say, "For us men and for our salvation he came down from heaven, and by the Holy Spirit was incarnate of the Virgin Mary, and became man."

Incarnation
From the Latin, meaning "to become flesh," referring to the mystery of Jesus Christ, the Divine Son of God, becoming man. In the Incarnation, Jesus Christ became truly man while remaining truly God.

The Reasons for the Incarnation

Jesus Christ is true God and true man, in the unity of his Divine Person. Because of this, he is the one and only

Did You Know?

The Church of the Nativity

© Saint Mary's Press / Brian Singer-Towns

On Good Friday each year, a worldwide collection is taken up to maintain the Christian holy places in the Holy Land. One of these is the Church of the Nativity in Bethlehem, which marks the traditional place of Christ's birth—a cave venerated since apostolic times.

Early in the fourth century, Emperor Constantine commissioned a church to be built over this cave. A hole was cut into the floor above the cave so that visitors could look down into it. In the sixth century, Emperor Justinian commissioned the large church that remains today. In 1852, shared custody of the Church of the Nativity was granted to the Roman Catholic, Armenian, and Greek Orthodox Churches.

In 2012, the United Nations Educational, Scientific, and Cultural Organization (UNESCO) designated the site of the Church of the Nativity and its pilgrimage route a World Heritage Site, the first to be designated in Palestine. In January 2013, the Vatican offered a large donation for the repair of the church, the cost of which is estimated at ten to fifteen million dollars. Long-needed repairs are now being made.

expiation
The act of atoning for sin or wrongdoing.

mediator between God and humanity. Here are some of the spiritual results of the Incarnation, and the reasons why it was needed.

To Reconcile Us with God through the Forgiveness of Sins

After the Fall human beings were separated from full communion with God because of our sins. But through the Incarnation, Christ took upon himself all human sin so that we might be reconciled with God. As Saint Paul explains, "For just as through the disobedience of one person the many were made sinners, so through the obedience of one the many will be made righteous" (Romans 5:19). Or put another way by the author of the First Letter of John, "In this is love: not that we have loved God, but that he loved us and sent his Son as **expiation** for our sins" (4:10).

To Help Us Know the Depth of God's Love

After the Fall and the resulting shame that accompanies sin (for example, Adam and Eve hiding from God), humanity did not experience or understand the true nature of God's unconditional love for us. Thus the first Christians were astounded at the realization that God loved us so much he would take on human nature and even suffer a torturous death to redeem us. This is referred to again and again in the New Testament writings. "For God so loved the world that he gave his only Son, so that everyone who believes in him might not perish but might have eternal life" (John 3:16). "But God proves his love for us in that while we were still sinners Christ died for us" (Romans 5:8).

To Be Our Model of Holiness

As God, Jesus Christ is perfect holiness. As a man, he shows us how to be holy in our everyday lives. We are given frequent commands in the Gospel to imitate Christ's holiness. At the Transfiguration, God the Father commands: "This is my beloved Son. Listen to him" (Mark 9:7). In the Gospel of John, at the Last Supper,

Jesus tells his disciples (and us), "This is my commandment: love one another as I love you" (15:12).

To Make Us Partakers of the Divine Nature

Christ wants us to share in his divinity. This amazing truth means God wants us to share in his divine life and to become the image of God we were created to be. Saint Athanasius (297–373), a Church Father who lived in the fourth century, explained it like this:

Brooklyn Museum of Art, New York, USA / Bridgeman Images

> He [the Son of God] became man so that we might be made God; and he manifested himself in the flesh, so that we might grasp the idea of the unseen Father; and he endured the insolence of men, so that we might receive the inheritance of immortality. *(Treatise on the Incarnation of the Word)*

Moses and Elijah appear with Jesus in the Transfiguration. Moses represents Jesus' being the fulfillment of the Law of God, and Elijah represents Jesus' fulfillment of the mission of the prophets.

To Destroy the Power of the Devil

In chapter 2, "The Fall from Grace," you read about the spiritual war between the devil and the forces of evil on one side and God and the forces of good on the other. On our own, humanity could not hope to defeat Satan. But Jesus resisted the temptations of Satan in the desert, anticipating his complete victory over evil with his

Primary Sources

We Are Christ's Body

The following reflection, commonly attributed to Saint Teresa of Ávila (1515–1582), reminds us that we can be Christ for others whenever we model his holiness and reach out to others with love and compassion:

Christ has no body now but yours;
No hands, no feet on earth but yours;
Yours are the eyes through which He looks compassion on this world;
Yours are the feet with which He is to go about doing good.
Yours are the hands with which He is to bless us now.

Passion, death, and Resurrection. "Indeed, the Son of God was revealed to destroy the works of the devil" (1 John 3:8). We share in Jesus' victory over Satan. Because we are strengthened by our faith and the gifts of the Spirit, Satan has lost his power over us.

Do any of these reasons for the Incarnation surprise you? Why?

Article 15: The Titles Say It All

We commonly give titles to people to recognize their role and their importance in society. Titles like Father, Doctor, Captain, Professor, President, or Bishop immediately tells us important information about a person. The same is true for Jesus. In the New Testament, Jesus is given a variety of titles that indicate his central role in salvation history. How many from this list do you recognize?

Title	Location
Alpha and Omega	Revelation 22:13
Bread of Life	John 6:48
Bright Morning Star	Revelation 22:16
God Our Savior	Titus 3:4
Good Shepherd	John 10:11
High Priest	Hebrews 3:1
King of Kings	Revelation 19:16
Lamb of God	John 1:29
Light of the World	John 8:12
Lord of Lords	Revelation 19:16
Paschal Lamb	1 Corinthians 5:7
the Resurrection and the Life	John 11:25
the Way, the Truth, and the Life	John 14:6
the Word	John 1:1

We conclude this chapter by reflecting on the meaning of the name of Jesus and then on three of his most important titles: Christ, Son of God, and Lord. Think about these titles for Jesus as you use them in your prayer, reverently remembering the tremendous love of God each of them represents.

Jesus

In the beginning of the Gospel of Luke, the angel Gabriel told Mary, "You will conceive in your womb and bear a son, and you shall name him Jesus" (1:31). *Jesus* means "God saves" in Hebrew (Joshua is another form of Jesus' name). Jesus' very name reflects his divine identity and his mission as Savior of the world. It is through the

© Hazlan Abdul Hakim / istockphoto.com

Paschal Mystery that we are saved from our sins, which is why the Father "bestowed on him the name / that is above every name, / that at the name of Jesus / every knee should bend, / of those in heaven and on earth and under the earth" (Philippians 2:9–10).

Christ

Christ is a formal title for Jesus that is used more than four hundred times in the New Testament. *Christ* is the Greek translation of the Hebrew word *messiah,* which means "anointed." To be anointed in the religious sense is to have oil placed on you in preparation for a special mission. In the Old Testament, kings, priests, and prophets were anointed in God's name. Jesus is Christ because the Father anointed him with the Holy Spirit and established him as priest, prophet, and king.

After their kingdom collapsed, many Jews believed God would send a new anointed one, the Messiah (or Christ), who would fulfill all God's promises for salvation. Peter was the first to proclaim about Jesus, "You are the Messiah" (Mark 8:29), announcing that Jesus was the savior the Jews had been hoping for. So when you say "Jesus Christ," you are really saying "Jesus, the Anointed One sent by God to be the Savior of the world."

Son of God

Another important title of Jesus is Son of God. In the Old Testament, the title Son of God is sometimes used for angels, for the people of Israel, and for Israel's kings. The title signifies their special relationship with God. But when it is applied to Jesus in the New Testament, it takes on additional meaning. We are all children of God, but Jesus has a unique relationship with the Father. At both Jesus' Baptism and his Transfiguration, the Father's voice announces, "This is my beloved Son" (Matthew 3:17, 17:5). Jesus is the only begotten Son of the Father, and he is the Second Person of the Trinity, fully God himself. It

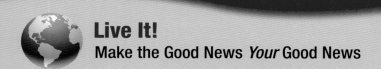

Live It!
Make the Good News *Your* Good News

It is important to have a deep knowledge of Sacred Scripture. It is also important to apply all that Scripture teaches to your life. Here are ten ways you can make the Word of God an integral part of your life:

1. Join or start a Bible study group.
2. Set aside a time each week to read the next Sunday's readings.
3. Keep a journal devoted to your reflections on the Sunday readings.
4. Read the Gospel of Mark from beginning to end. It will take only an hour or two!
5. Find a Catholic Bible commentary online to learn more about the background and history of the four Gospels.
6. Each month choose just one of Jesus' teachings and focus on incorporating it into your life.
7. Find a Bible passage you find personally meaningful and post it in your locker to inspire you.
8. Read about how saints chose to live the Good News.
9. Find a good daily reflection book that has short Bible readings for each day of the year.
10. Pray with the Sunday Gospel readings or other Bible passages (*lectio divina*).

is because Jesus is both true God and true man, that he is the one and only mediator who can restore the damaged relationship between God and humanity.

Lord

Jesus is frequently referred to as **Lord** in the New Testament. Lord was a title of respect in Jesus' time, and often people who were approaching Jesus respectfully called him Lord. But the word had another unique meaning. *Lord* is the Greek word the Jews used for God instead of calling him *Yahweh,* the Hebrew name often used for God in the Old Testament. *Yahweh* was considered too sacred to be pronounced out loud in public. When Thomas called Jesus "My Lord and my God!" (John 20:28), he was calling Jesus by a title the Jews used for God. Today whenever we call Jesus Lord, we too recognize his divinity and acknowledge that he alone is worthy of our worship and our complete obedience.

> **Which title for Jesus helps you to feel most connected with him?**

Lord
The word used in the Old Testament to refer to God and in the New Testament for both God the Father and Jesus Christ, to reflect awareness of Jesus' divine identity as the Son of God.

Chapter Review

1. Why was it important that Mary conceived and gave birth as a virgin?

2. How did Joseph show his trust in God and his love for Mary and Jesus?

3. Give three examples of the Christological prophecies.

4. Why is Jesus the perfect and only mediator between God and humanity?

5. Give three reasons for the Incarnation.

6. What is the meaning of the name Jesus?

7. What does the title Christ reveal about Jesus?

Chapter 5

The Redemptive Nature of Christ's Earthly Life

Introduction

The Father's saving plan is revealed through his Son, Jesus Christ, and fully understood with the guidance of the Holy Spirit. All of Jesus' life teaches us about God's saving plan: his poverty, his humility, his prayer, whom he lived with, whom he called to be his disciples, his teaching and preaching, his healings, his exorcisms . . . everything.

Christ's Passion, death, Resurrection, and Ascension most clearly reveal his and his Father's glory (see John 13:31). These events, which we identify with the Paschal Mystery, the fulfillment of God's plan of salvation, are the focus of unit 3. Here in chapter 5, we will focus on how the mystery of redemption was already at work in the words and actions of Jesus that preceded his Passion. We will start by considering Christ's earthly life through the lens of the Luminous Mysteries of the Rosary. The Luminous Mysteries were proposed by Pope Saint John Paul II in 2002 as an opportunity for us to meditate on the events in Jesus' public ministry in which he was truly revealed as the "light of the world" (John 9:5). Then we consider the mystery of our redemption in Christ by examining his teachings on poverty, his example of obedience, his moral preaching, and his healing miracles.

Article 16: The Luminous Mysteries

As Pope, in 2002 Saint John Paul II issued the apostolic letter "Rosarium Virginis Mariae" ("The Rosary of the Virgin Mary"). In the letter, the Pope recommended a change in the way the Rosary is prayed. In addition to the three traditional sets of mysteries that are meditated on when praying the Rosary—the Joyful Mysteries, the Sorrowful Mysteries, and the Glorious Mysteries—the Pope recommended another set of mysteries, which he called the Luminous Mysteries, or the Mysteries of Light. The following chart introduces these five mysteries with their scriptural origins. Each of the five mysteries commemorates a significant moment in Jesus' public ministry. In these events, he is "the light of the world" (John 9:5) shining for all to see!

Mystery	Scripture Passage	Description
The Baptism in the Jordan	Matthew 3:13–17, Mark 1:9–11, Luke 3:21–22, John 1:31–34	The voice of the Father declared Jesus the beloved Son.
The Wedding at Cana	John 2:1–12	Christ changed water into wine, his first public miracle.
The Proclamation of the Kingdom	Mark 1:15 is a good summary.	Jesus called his listeners to conversion (see Mark 1:15) and forave the sins of all who drew near to him.
The Transfiguration	Matthew 17:1–8, Mark 9:2–8, Luke 9:28–36	The glory of the Godhead shone forth from the face of Christ.
The Institution of the Eucharist	Matthew 26:26–30, Mark 14:22–26, Luke 22:14–23, 1 Corinthians 11:23–25	Jesus offered his Body and Blood as food under the signs of bread and wine.

In his letter, Saint John Paul II wrote, "Each of these mysteries is *a revelation of the Kingdom now present in the very person of Jesus*" (21). Think of the Kingdom of God as that "place" (although it is not a place in the geographic sense) where the fullness of God's grace is present and human beings are restored to full communion with God and with one another. The full realization of the **Kingdom of God** is the end result of God's saving plan. What Saint John Paul II is saying is that Jesus does not just talk about God's saving plan; he makes it real. When Jesus speaks and acts, the Kingdom of God is present to those who listen to him and believe in him. So let us consider what the five Mysteries of Light reveal about the Kingdom of God and the Paschal Mystery.

The Baptism in the Jordan

The account of Jesus' Baptism is told in all four Gospels, which in itself is a sign of its importance. Jesus was baptized by his cousin John. John prepared the way for Jesus, and his ministry was seen as a fulfillment of a prophecy by Isaiah (see Mark 1:2–3). John prepared the way by urging people to reform their lives and turn away from sin. As a sign of their cleansing and renewal, John baptized people in the waters of the Jordan River.

The Baptism of Jesus is the first luminous mystery. Jesus is without sin, so why did he choose to be baptized?

Even though Jesus was free from all sin, he came to John to be baptized at the beginning of his public ministry. In doing this, he showed his willingness to completely identify with the human condition. By identifying himself with human sin, Jesus Christ became the perfect offering to save us from our sin. Saint Paul put it this way: "For our sake he [the Father] made him [the Son] to be sin who did not know sin, so that we might become the righteousness of God in him" (2 Corinthians 5:21).

Jesus' Baptism is an example of his perfect obedience to his heavenly Father (see the section "Christ's Obedience" later in this chapter). His Baptism also reveals the mystery of the Holy Trinity. The three Divine Persons of the Trinity work together in the plan of salvation. The Holy Spirit descended upon the Son in the form of a dove and the Father pronounced, "You are my beloved Son; with you I am well pleased" (Mark 1:11). The first luminous

Brooklyn Museum of Art, New York, USA / Bridgeman Images

mystery shows that Jesus is the Second Person of the Trinity and he has come to save us from our sins.

The Wedding at Cana

The second luminous mystery is recorded in the Gospel of John only. A few days after Jesus' Baptism, Jesus attended a wedding feast with his new disciples. When the wedding party ran out of wine (an embarrassing situation for the hosts), Jesus' mother asked him to help. You probably know Jesus' response; he turned the water, in six large ceremonial jars, into excellent wine. The Gospel of John tells us that "Jesus did this as the beginning of his signs in Cana in Galilee and so revealed his glory, and his disciples began to believe in him" (2:11).

John's Gospel contains only seven miracles. Each of these is a sign that reveals Jesus as the Son of God. This first sign shows his power over creation. We see that his mother already believed in him, because she asked him to do something miraculous. But now his disciples began to believe too. The second luminous mystery recalls the beginning of Christ's public ministry.

The Proclamation of the Kingdom

The third luminous mystery is not just one event or one teaching. Through many miracles and many teachings, Jesus proclaimed that the Kingdom of God is at hand. His very first words in the Gospel of Mark were these: "This is the time of fulfillment. The kingdom of God is at hand. Repent, and believe in the gospel" (1:15). The prophets had prophesied about the coming of the Kingdom of God (see Isaiah 2:2–4 and Micah 4:1–4) when original justice and original holiness would be restored and people would live in peace with God and one another. They prophesied that a messiah would usher in this kingdom by bringing good news to the poor and freedom to captives (see Isaiah 61:1–2).

Jesus fulfilled these ancient prophecies. His words were good news for the poor and challenging news for the wealthy (see the section "The Poverty of Jesus" later

Kingdom of God
The culmination or goal of God's plan of salvation, the Kingdom of God is announced by the Gospel and present in Jesus Christ. The Kingdom is the reign or rule of God over the hearts of people and, as a consequence of that, the development of a new social order based on unconditional love. The fullness of God's Kingdom will not be realized until the end of time. Also called the Reign of God or the Kingdom of Heaven.

synoptic Gospels
From the Greek for "seeing the whole together," the name given to the Gospels of Matthew, Mark, and Luke, because they are similar in style and content.

Passion
The sufferings of Jesus during the final days of his life: his agony in the garden at Gethsemane, his trial, and his Crucifixion.

Passover
The night the Lord passed over the houses of the Israelites marked by the blood of the lamb, and spared the firstborn sons from death. It also is the feast that celebrates the deliverance of the Chosen People from bondage in Egypt and the Exodus from Egypt to the Promised Land.

in this chapter). He lived a life of unconditional love and forgiveness, even forgiving his torturers and killers. He called everyone to forsake hate, revenge, violence, and greed. He helped the blind to see and the lame to walk. He brought freedom to those held captive by demons, disease, sin, and even death. Wherever he went, the Kingdom of God was present for those who put their faith in him. The third luminous mystery reveals that the Kingdom of God is present in Jesus Christ and that his life brings salvation to our world.

The Transfiguration

The fourth luminous mystery is described in all three **synoptic Gospels**. The event took place soon after Peter proclaimed that Jesus is the Messiah, the Son of God (see Matthew 16:16). Jesus responded to this act of faith by predicting his own **Passion**, death, and Resurrection (see verse 21). Jesus wanted to be clear that as Messiah he would not be a warrior leader but a Suffering Servant. This was hard for the disciples to hear (see verse 22).

Just a few days later, Jesus took Peter, James, and John to the top of a mountain by themselves. There Jesus was transfigured and the three disciples saw him in his glory; Christ's face and clothes shone like the sun, and both Moses and Elijah appeared with him (see Matthew 17:1–3). God the Father's voice came from the clouds saying, "This is my beloved Son, with whom I am well pleased; listen to him" (verse 5).

To faithful Jews, Moses represented the Law, and Elijah represented the message of all the prophets. Their appearance with Jesus was a sign that Jesus was the fulfillment of the Law and the prophets. The Transfiguration reassured Peter, James, and John that Jesus was indeed the Messiah, and it strengthened their faith before the ordeal of Jesus' Passion and death. The fourth luminous mystery reveals that Jesus was the one they had been waiting for, but they would not fully understand the plan of salvation until the principal events of the Paschal

Mystery—Christ's Passion, death, Resurrection, and Ascension—had come to their conclusion.

The Institution of the Eucharist

The fifth luminous mystery is testified to in the synoptic Gospels and in Paul's First Letter to the Corinthians. It is also strongly alluded to in the Gospel of John. These accounts all testify that soon before his death, at a **Passover** meal, Jesus turned ordinary bread and wine into his sacred Body and Blood and shared these with the Twelve Apostles. Then he commanded them to "do this in memory of me" (Luke 22:19). This was the first celebration of **the Eucharist**, which today we also call the Mass. By instituting the Eucharist, Jesus gave the Church a great gift—the gift of himself—present to us in his Body and Blood.

This luminous mystery, the Institution of the Eucharist, reveals that Jesus Christ is the Lamb of God, whose life was given that we might be freed from sin and death. Just as the original **Paschal Lamb** was offered to free the people of Israel from their slavery in Egypt, Jesus' life was offered up for us through his Passion, death, Resurrection, and Ascension. This is the core of the Paschal Mystery, which we enter into every time we participate in the Eucharist. This is why "the Eucharist is the heart and

Eucharist, the
Also called the Mass or Lord's Supper, and based on a word for "thanksgiving," it is the central Christian liturgical celebration, established by Jesus at the Last Supper. In the Eucharist, the sacrificial death and Resurrection of Jesus are both remembered and renewed. The term sometimes refers specifically to the consecrated bread and wine that have become the Body and Blood of Christ.

Paschal Lamb
In the Old Testament, the sacrificial lamb shared at the seder meal of the Passover on the night the Israelites escaped from Egypt; in the New Testament, the Paschal Lamb is Jesus, the Incarnate Son of God who dies on a cross to take away "the sin of the world" (John 1:29).

© Zvonimir Atletic / Shutterstock.com

Notice how the color of Jesus' clothing stands out in this image of the Last Supper. What symbolic meaning might his red garment have?

redeem, Redeemer, redemption
From the Latin *redemptio*, meaning "a buying back"; to redeem something is to pay the price for its freedom. In the Old Testament, it refers to Yahweh's deliverance of Israel and, in the New Testament, to Christ's deliverance of all Christians from the forces of sin. Christ our Redeemer paid the price to free us from the slavery of sin and bring about our redemption.

summit of the Church's life, for in it Christ associates his Church and all her members with his sacrifice of praise and thanksgiving offered once for all on the cross to his Father; by this sacrifice he pours out the graces of salvation on his Body which is the Church" (Catechism of the Catholic Church [CCC], 1407).

> **Which of the Luminous Mysteries most clearly reveals Jesus as "light" to you? Why?**

Article 17: Jesus' Humble Beginnings

In the musical *Jesus Christ Superstar*, Judas rhetorically asks Jesus why he chose to reveal himself the way he did. Why be born and live in an unimportant place? Why be born in a poor and unimportant family? Wouldn't Jesus' message be accepted more easily if he were born into an important family? Wouldn't it be heard more easily if he went to Rome and preached and lived in the center of the world's politics and economics?

These are important questions because everything in Jesus' life does indeed teach us about God's plan for our **redemption**. Let us start with Jesus' humble beginnings. There is a reason he was born into poverty and lived in relative poverty—it has something to teach us and will lead us more deeply into the Paschal Mystery.

The Poverty of Jesus

In the United States, we are used to a socioeconomic system divided into three classes: those who are wealthy, those who are poor, and those in between, grouped into what we call the middle class. In Jesus' time, there were basically two economic classes: the elites (the wealthy) and the non-elites (the poor). The elites were a very small minority of the population, but they owned most of the land, lived in luxury and plenty, and held all the political and economic power. They lived almost exclusively in cities and rented out their land to tenant farmers, who paid high rents and taxes.

The non-elites were the vast majority of the people. They were lucky to make just enough to survive. If they owned a small plot of land, they were constantly in danger of hunger or starvation if their crops failed. Many worked as day laborers for the wealthy landowners who grew cash crops, not subsistence crops. Some non-elites were "self-employed," but they had to pay high fees (to fish, for example) or rents (to use someone's fishing boat, for example). They all had to pay high taxes to support both the elite Jewish leaders and the elite of the Roman Empire. Many non-elites sold themselves into slavery to work for the elites because slaves were at least usually assured food and a place to sleep.

This was Jesus' world. The Gospel of Luke emphasizes Jesus' poverty, living as a non-elite. First, it shows Mary and Joseph under the power of the elites of the Roman Empire. At the order of the emperor, Caesar Augustus, they had to make the difficult trip from Nazareth to Bethlehem even though it was late in Mary's pregnancy (see 2:1–5). The only reason for this trip was for a census, to determine the amount of taxes the Romans would collect. The birth of Jesus in Bethlehem emphasized Mary and Joseph's low status again: "She wrapped him [Jesus] in swaddling clothes and laid him in a manger, because there was no room for them in the inn" (verse 7).

Olives were a cash crop grown by wealthy landowners in Jesus' time.

You might think that in his life Jesus would have shown us how to get ahead by working hard to become an elite. Instead he did just the opposite; he embraced the poverty he was born into. He resisted Satan's temptation to become an elite and replied to Satan, "One does not live by bread alone" (Luke 4:4). When a scribe wished to follow him, Jesus warned the scribe about the poverty that would be

© Saint Mary's Press / Brian Singer-Towns

Son of Man
A messianic title from the Book of Daniel, used to describe a figure who receives authority over other nations from God; the only messianic title in the Gospels used by Jesus to describe himself.

poverty of heart
The recognition of our deep need for God and the commitment to put God above everything else in life, particularly above the accumulation of material wealth.

involved in following Jesus: "Foxes have dens and birds of the sky have nests, but the **Son of Man** has nowhere to rest his head" (Matthew 8:20). In the parable of the Final Judgment, Jesus identified with the poor, saying, "Whatever you did for one of these least brothers of mine, you did for me" (25:40).

Material Poverty and Poverty of Heart

Jesus embraced material poverty for one simple reason: he was teaching that we do not achieve salvation through material wealth, contrary to popular belief at the time. Many Jews believed that material wealth was a sign that you were blessed by God and living a righteous life. Jesus taught just the opposite: "Blessed are you who are poor, / for the kingdom of God is yours. . . . But woe to you who are rich, / for you have received your consolation" (Luke 6:20,24).

Not only did Jesus teach that God had not abandoned the poor, but he also taught that the elites, the wealthy, have a special obligation to help the poor. There are several Gospel stories about this:

- Parable of the Rich Young Man (see Matthew 19:16–24)
- Parable of the Final Judgment (see Matthew 25:31–46)
- Parable of Whom to Invite to Eat with You (see Luke 14:12–14)
- Parable of the Great Feast (see Luke 14:15–24)
- Parable of the Rich Man and Lazarus (see Luke 16:19–31)

Jesus' life and teaching revealed that **poverty of heart** (sometimes called spiritual poverty) is necessary for us to be truly in communion with God. People with poverty of heart recognize their need for God. This is why Jesus says, "Blessed are the poor in spirit" (Matthew 5:3). Without God we are truly empty and alone; no amount of material wealth can fill that void. In fact, material wealth often gets in the way of our recognizing our need for God. For this reason, Jesus warns us that material wealth can be dangerous to our salvation: "How hard it is for those who have wealth to enter the kingdom of God!" (Mark 10:23). He calls us to be unattached to material wealth. Material wealth is not bad in and of itself, but it is very easy to let it take the place of God in our lives.

Here are some other examples from the four Gospels of Jesus' teaching about the importance of poverty of heart:

- "Store up treasures in heaven." "No one can serve two masters." (Matthew 6:19–21,24)
- Parable of the Treasure Buried in the Field, Parable of the Pearl of Great Price (Matthew 13:44–46)
- the widow's contribution (Mark 12:41–44)
- Parable of the Rich Fool (Luke 12:16–21)
- the importance of dependence on God (Luke 12:22–32)
- "Where your treasure is, there also will your heart be." (Luke 12:33–34)

Did You Know?

The Evangelical Counsels: Good Advice

© mylifeiscamp/Shutterstock.com

The evangelical counsels are the counsels of poverty, chastity, and obedience. They are called counsels because they are *advised* as an excellent way to follow Christ. The evangelical counsels are the essence of a vowed commitment in religious life. Priests, brothers and sisters, and monks and nuns all vow, in some form, to live these evangelical counsels.

The word *evangelical* comes from *evangelion*, the same Greek word from which we get the word *gospel*. These counsels come directly from the Gospel. They are the values Christ lived and proclaimed. For that reason, they are not limited to vowed religious life. Every Christian is called, according to each one's particular state of life, to live these Gospel values: poverty (simplicity and sharing), chastity (respect for ourselves and others), and obedience (listening to God and lawful authority in family, Church, and civil life).

© James B. Janknegt

Consider the two homes in this image. Do people seem happier in the large, more extravagant home, or in the smaller home?

Our culture places a great deal of importance on having money. We often measure our worth by how much we have. We get stressed when we think we don't have enough— which for many people is most of the time. We sometimes compromise our values and even our physical and emotional well-being in order to get more. The poverty of Jesus challenges us to put our trust in God, not in money. When we do this, we are one step closer to the Kingdom of God.

What does it mean to trust in God and not in material comfort or security? Do you find this easy or difficult?

Article 18: Christ's Obedience

Obedience is a topic that can irritate many people. We sometimes rebel or complain when we are told what to do by people in positions of authority. Part of our resistance to the idea of obedience is likely rooted in our historical struggle against unjust situations. For example, the United States was born when our ancestors rejected the English monarchy and disobeyed unfair laws. So why is obedience such an important value to our faith?

The answer lies in whom we are obedient to. We owe our obedience to God, our Creator, who calls us back to full, loving communion with him. To redeem Adam's disobedience and to be an example for us, the Son of God lived a life of perfect obedience to his Father.

Redeeming Adam's Disobedience

Our first parents disobeyed God and, through their disobedience, brought sin and death into the world. To rescue us the Son of God assumed a human nature, becoming our perfect mediator. Through Christ's perfect obedience to his Father's will, he restored human nature to its original holiness. We read in the Letter to the Romans, "For just as through the disobedience of one person the many were made sinners, so through the obedience of one the many will be made righteous" (Romans 5:19). This is why we call Jesus the New Adam.

Brooklyn Museum of Art, New York, USA / Bridgeman Images

The Letter to the Philippians contains a hymn that may have been used by the first Christians. Saint Paul, inspired by the Holy Spirit, uses this hymn to praise Jesus' obedience to his Father in taking on a human nature.

This painting portrays Jesus' suffering in the garden at Gethsemane. What are the angels showing Jesus that causes him such agony? When does obedience require you to make a personal sacrifice?

> Have among yourselves the same attitude that is also yours in Christ Jesus,
>
> Who, though he was in the form of God,
> did not regard equality with God
> something to be grasped.
> Rather, he emptied himself,
> taking the form of a slave,
> coming in human likeness;
> and found human in appearance,
> he humbled himself,
> becoming obedient to death,
> even death on a cross.
>
> (2:5–8)

Jesus' Example of Obedience

Paul introduces the Philippians' hymn with these directions: "Have among yourselves the same attitude that is also yours in Christ Jesus" (2:5). Jesus' obedience to his Father's will is the model for us of how to live a life of obedience to God. First, Jesus was obedient in his human relationships, respecting the order his Father created. We read how as a child he respected his earthly parents: "He went down with them and came to Nazareth, and

conscience
The "inner voice," guided by human reason and Divine Law, that enables us to judge the moral quality of a specific action that has been made, is being made, or will be made. This judgment enables us to distinguish good from evil, in order to accomplish good and avoid evil. To make good judgments, one needs to have a well-formed conscience.

was obedient to them" (Luke 2:51). Tradition teaches us that in the hidden years of Jesus' life, which are not recorded in the Gospels, he remained obedient to Mary and Joseph.

Second, Jesus was obedient to his heavenly Father. In the garden at Gethsemane, we see his obedience even when it would lead to torture and death. Knowing that his Passion and death were coming, Jesus prayed that he might escape this ordeal. But he concluded his prayer with a commitment to obediently follow his Father's will: "If it is not possible that this cup pass without my drinking it, your will be done!" (Matthew 26:42). We should not assume that obedience always came easily to Jesus or that he never struggled with it.

We are called to follow Jesus' example to be obedient to the Father's will, not because God wants to control us as a puppeteer controls puppets but because God is a perfectly loving parent who wants what is best for us. When we are obedient to God, we grow in holiness, which is to say we grow to be in closer communion with him. The First Letter of Peter gives excellent advice on this subject:

> Like obedient children, do not act in compliance with the desires of your former ignorance but, as he who called you is holy, be holy yourselves in every aspect of your conduct, for it is written, "Be holy because I [am] holy." (1:14–16)

How do you follow Jesus' example by obeying the Father's will?

Article 19: Christ's Moral Teaching

Christ's moral teaching is perhaps the section of the Gospels that Christians struggle with most. In his moral teaching, Jesus goes beyond the letter of the Old Law to challenge us to live the spirit of the Law—the deeper moral truths it is intended to teach us—thus revealing its ultimate meaning. In his life and teaching, Jesus perfectly fulfills the Old Law and ushers in the New Law. Even more, through the Paschal Mystery, he redeems us from all our sins against the Law. Living the New Law is a return to original holiness and original justice. It can be lived only with the sanctifying grace given by the Holy Spirit through Baptism.

The New Law is part of the Paschal Mystery; through the New Law, Christ redeems us by purifying our **conscience**. When we live according to the New Law, our moral choices are based not only on what is good or bad for us, or on legalistic morality, but also on what truly brings us into full communion with God and with one another. Jesus sums up the New Law in two great commandments: "The first is this: 'Hear, O Israel! The Lord our God is Lord alone! You shall love the Lord your God with all your heart, with all your soul, with all your mind, and with all your strength.' The second is this: 'You shall love your neighbor as yourself'" (Mark 12:29–31). Let's take a closer look at Jesus' expression of the New Law in the Sermon on the Mount.

© The Artchives / Alamy

Primary Sources

Christ Our Teacher

Saint Clement of Alexandria (AD 150–211) traveled from Greece to Italy to Palestine and finally to Egypt to find Christian teachers to instruct him in the faith. Here is an excerpt on his thought about Christ as our Teacher:

> The Word by whom all things were made, has appeared as our Teacher; and he, who bestowed life upon us in the beginning, when, as our Creator, he formed us, now that he has appeared as our Teacher, has taught us to live well so that, afterwards, as God, he might furnish us abundantly with eternal life. *(Exhortation to the Greeks)*

The Sermon on the Mount

The Sermon on the Mount is found in Matthew, chapters 5–7. Some have called the Sermon on the Mount a kind of "mini-Gospel" because it is a summary of the key teachings of Jesus. The following outline of the entire Sermon on the Mount will help orient you to this important passage:

- 5:3–12   the Beatitudes
- 5:13–16   salt of the earth, light of the world
- 5:17–20   teaching about the Law
- 5:21–37   teachings about anger, adultery, divorce, and oaths
- 5:38–48   teachings about retaliation and love of enemies
- 6:1–18   teachings about almsgiving, prayer, and fasting
- 6:19–34   teachings about poverty of heart
- 7:1–12   teachings about judging others, relying on God, the Golden Rule
- 7:13–23   teachings on discipleship
- 7:24–29   the result of acting on Jesus' teachings

Our focus will be three of the "You have heard it said" statements in the part of the sermon found in Matthew, chapter 5. These statements are good examples of how Jesus purifies our conscience by teaching us the true meaning of God's Law. If you haven't read the Sermon on the Mount recently, it would be good to do so before reading the rest of this section.

"You have heard that it was said to your ancestors, 'You shall not kill; and whoever kills will be liable to judgment.' But I say to you, whoever is angry with his brother will be liable to judgment" (Matthew 5:21–22). The Old Law commands us not to kill. This may seem obvious, but recall the story of Cain and Abel and that the first sin after the Fall was murder. The Old Law is meant to teach us that thoughts and attitudes—anger, hatred, lack of forgiveness, revenge—that lead to violence are wrong in themselves. They have no place in the King-dom of God. They will not lead to love and communion with other people and with God.

Does this mean that you are sinning every time you have an angry thought? No, those thoughts are part of life, especially as we are on the journey to perfect holi-ness. It is sinful to hang on to feelings of anger and hurt, letting them grow inside us until they become thoughts of revenge. At that point, we are only one step away from actually hurting another person. The New Law calls us to let go of our anger and replace it with forgiveness and compassion, even for those who hurt us.

"You have heard that it was said, 'You shall not com-mit adultery.' But I say to you, everyone who looks at a woman with lust has already committed adultery with her in his heart" (Matthew 5:27–28).

The Old Law commands us not to have sex outside of marriage. Again Jesus says this is just a minimum requirement. The Old Law is meant to teach us that the thoughts and attitudes that lead to sexual promiscuity are wrong in themselves. Christ's New Law commands us to live a life of **chastity** and not to think or act in ways that might lead us to sexual sin.

This is a difficult commandment to live out in our culture. Sexuality and sexual suggestion are often used as marketing techniques, and we are constantly bom-barded with sexual messages. This makes it difficult to go through a day without having a sexual thought! Again this doesn't mean that having a brief sexual thought is sinful. It is sinful is to hang onto those thoughts, letting them grow into sexual fantasies and then convincing ourselves that acting on those thoughts and fantasies is okay. The New Law asks us to let go of sexual fantasies and to avoid sexual temptations and live a chaste life. "You have heard that it was said, 'You shall love your neighbor and hate your enemy.' But I say to you, love your enemies, and pray for those who persecute you" (5:43–44).

chastity
The virtue by which people are able to successfully and healthfully integrate their sexuality into their total person; recognized as one of the fruits of the Holy Spirit. Also one of the vows of religious life.

Jesus quoted Leviticus 19:18, which says that you should love your neighbor as yourself (it does not say anything about hating enemies). In Jesus' time, people were fiercely loyal to their own family and social groups, distrusting everyone who was outside those groups. By his example Jesus showed a different way of living. He gathered people together who weren't blood relatives or even from the same social groups. He brought together fishermen, tax collectors, and zealots; these people usually distrusted one another, but Jesus taught them how to love one another.

This doesn't seem to be much different today. People often fear and distrust people who come from somewhere else. Sometimes cultural differences lead to hatred and attacks on people and their way of life. Jesus tells us these attitudes are wrong and sinful. His New Law asks us to love everyone, even those who aren't like us and those who attack us. Through prayer, and with the help of God, we will find ways to overcome misunderstanding, distrust, and even hatred.

Live It!
Loving Beyond Boundaries

Jesus gathered people from many different walks of life who probably, in most circumstances, hated one another. Similarly, in many schools today, certain social groups dislike and avoid one another because of their race, religion, economic status, or even something as trivial as involvement in particular extracurricular activities. Jesus saw beyond the external ways people define one another. He saw the common humanity of the fisherman and the tax collector, the Jew and the Gentile, the prostitute and the Pharisee, the Zealot and the Roman soldier. And he loved them all.

Christ also asks us to look beyond the things that divide us. Though it is easy to love people we like, God requires more from us. Christians are called to love and respect athletes, band members, cheerleaders, slackers, artists, and straight-A students—everyone—whether we like them or not. How do you take up that call?

Jesus' moral teaching shows us what our relationship with God and others must be in order to participate in the Kingdom of God. Through Baptism we receive the grace that is necessary to live according to the New Law. Through the other Sacraments, we receive additional graces that strengthen us as we journey to perfection in our lives as true children of God, members of the Body of Christ, and citizens of the Kingdom of Heaven.

> **Why is it important to live by the spirit, and not just the letter, of God's Law as well as other rules?**

Article 20: Christ's Healings

Being sick is no fun. Illness makes our daily routine challenging, if not impossible. It can isolate us from other people. People with lifelong disabilities must face these challenges every day. And serious illness and disease force us to face death itself, which can be frightening for many people.

In his public ministry, Jesus performed many miraculous healings. He cured those who were blind, deaf, and lame. He brought health and wholeness to lepers so they could rejoin the community. He cast out evil spirits from those who were possessed. Jesus had great compassion for those who were suffering and outcast. But he didn't try to heal everyone, even though there was great need. Have you ever wondered why Jesus did not make healing his full-time ministry? The answer is that Jesus' mission was bigger than just being a miracle worker.

Jesus' healings are a sign that the Father's plan of salvation is being fulfilled. Every healing is a sign that Christ is restoring the wholeness of body, mind, and spirit he intended people to have. The healings are also signs that Jesus is the Messiah who is making the Kingdom of God present to all those who believe in him. Jesus himself pointed to this. When asked, "Are you the one who is to come, or should we look for another?" he replied, "Go and tell John what you hear and see:

the blind regain their sight, the lame walk, lepers are cleansed, the deaf hear, the dead are raised, and the poor have the good news proclaimed to them" (Matthew 11:3,4–5). Finally, Jesus' healings are a promise that in the Kingdom of Heaven we will all be made whole, physically and spiritually, and there will be no more suffering or sickness or disease for all God's holy ones.

Sickness and Health in Biblical Cultures

The culture Jesus lived in did not make the distinction that we make between the natural world and the spiritual world. Illness and disability were most often associated with impurity and sin. When someone is sick today, we look for a natural cause. When someone was ill at the time of Jesus, people looked for a supernatural or spiritual cause. In the Book of Job, Job's friends were convinced that his sufferings were sent by God as punishment for sins. In the Gospel of John, Jesus was asked, "Rabbi, who sinned, this man or his parents, that he was born blind?" (9:2). Jesus denied that suffering is a direct punishment for sin (see 9:3, Luke 13:1–5). But he did seem to acknowledge that there is a relationship between sin and illness. For example, before he healed the paralytic, he asked the scribes, "Which is easier to say— 'Your sins are forgiven,' or 'Rise and walk'?" (Matthew 9:5).

During Jesus' time people also believed that illness and disease were the direct result of demonic possession. Some of the Gospel accounts make this connection. Luke tells about a woman who was crippled by a spirit for eighteen years (see 13:11). In Matthew's Gospel, Jesus cast out a demon from a boy who had seizures, curing him

Imagine the joy that comes from being healed of a serious mental or physical illness. Why is such healing a sign of the presence of the Kingdom of God?

Laura James, (Contemporary Artist) / Private Collection / Bridgeman Images (see 17:14–18). For these reasons, we probably should not see Jesus' physical healings and his **exorcisms** as two different things. They were all miracles in which Jesus restored people to both physical and spiritual wholeness at the same time.

The Church Continues Christ's Healing Ministry

In our culture today, we also see a connection between our spiritual health and our physical health. People are more prone to physical illness when they are feeling stressed, depressed, and yes, when they are engaged in sinful activities, such as sexual promiscuity and illegal drug use. In addition, studies show that people of faith and prayer, people who are part of a loving family and community, often recover more quickly than those who are not.

exorcism
The act of freeing someone from demonic possession. Exorcisms are also part of the Church's worship and prayer life, calling on the name of Christ to protect us from the power of Satan.

Pray It!

Comfort for the Sick

Being sick can be awful. Aside from just making us feel bad, illness can cut us off from our friends, cause us to fall behind in our school work, and make us anxious and upset about everything we have to do after we get better. It can be depressing! It is obvious that our physical health has an impact on our mental and spiritual health. The next time a loved one is sick, offer a prayer to God like this one from the Sacrament of Anointing of the Sick:

> Father in heaven,
> through this holy anointing
> grant (name) comfort in his / her suffering.
> When he / she is afraid, give him / her courage,
> when afflicted, give him / her patience,
> when dejected, afford him / her hope,
> and when alone, assure him / her of the support of your holy people.
> We ask this through Christ our Lord.
> Amen.

(Pastoral Care of the Sick, 125)

chaplains
Specially prepared
priests to whom
the spiritual care
of a special group
of people, such as
hospital patients,
military personnel,
or migrants, is
entrusted.

The Church supports the work of doctors, nurses, and other medical professionals to continue the healing ministry of Christ. In fact, many of the hospitals around the world were founded by Catholic religious orders. In the United States, there are over six hundred Catholic hospitals with over 500,000 staff who treat nearly six million patients a year. At most Catholic hospitals, **chaplains** work with other medical professionals to care for the whole person, both body and soul. And, most important, the Sacrament of Anointing of the Sick makes Christ's healing grace available through the power of the Holy Spirit.

How can you help to bring Christ's healing presence to those who are sick or dying?

Faith in Action
Serving the Sick and the Poor

© Karen Kasmauski / Corbis

In 1869, a young woman in New York City, on her way to work as a laundress, found a little girl crying on the sidewalk. This young woman was Mary Walsh, an immigrant from Ireland. The little girl explained that her mother was very sick. Mary went upstairs to the little girl's apartment, and found the mother, very ill, with a dead infant by her side. For the next four days, Mary sacrificed her own job and her own pay to help this family. This was the beginning of a new community, the Dominican Sisters of the Sick Poor. The compassionate young woman became known as Mother Mary Walsh.

In 1922, four Dominican Sisters of the Sick Poor arrived in Denver, ready to help those who were poor, elderly, or chronically ill. They visited the people in their homes, giving nursing care and other help as needed. Their work lives on in the Dominican Sisters Home Health Agency of Denver. Under the leadership of the Dominican Sisters, the lay nursing staff of this agency provides free home nursing care to people in need. The motto of this agency is "Charity in Action."

The Dominican Sisters Home Health Agency depends on donations for its survival, and, in addition to support from local Catholic parishes, is also supported by donations from local businesses and grants from charitable foundations.

Chapter Review

1. What are the Luminous Mysteries?

2. What was the Transfiguration a sign of?

3. Describe the elites and the non-elites during the time of Jesus.

4. How are material poverty and poverty of heart related?

5. How are Adam's disobedience and Christ's obedience related?

6. How does the New Law of Christ purify our conscience?

7. What is the Commandment "You shall not commit adultery" meant to teach us? What deeper insight does the New Law give us in relation to this Commandment?

8. What are Christ's healings a sign of?

9. What did people in biblical times see as the causes of illness and disease?

Unit 3

God's Plan for Salvation Is Fulfilled

God's plan was fulfilled through the Passion, death, Resurrection, and Ascension of Jesus Christ—the events that are at the heart of the Paschal Mystery. These events stand "at the center of the Good News that the apostles, and the Church following them, are to proclaim to the world" (Catechism of the Catholic Church [CCC], 571). In previous chapters, we looked at everything that led up to these central events. In unit 3, we will look more closely at them and their meaning.

The people who put Jesus to death had political and religious reasons for doing so. But ultimately, as we see in this unit, Jesus died for us. When we were lost because of sin, God sent his Son to be our Redeemer to make it possible for us to enter into communion with him again. By rising from the dead, Jesus broke the power of sin and death once and for all. Sin and death can no longer hold us. God is more powerful than the consequences of sin that used to weigh us down.

However, the Resurrection was not the end of the Paschal Mystery. In this unit, we examine the Ascension: it revealed Jesus' glory, opened Heaven to all humanity, and made it possible for Jesus to be more present to us now than during his earthly life.

In the last chapter in this unit—chapter 8, "Redeemed by Christ: Our Eternal Destiny"—we recall that we have been saved by Jesus for joy and life with God, and we examine our judgment by God at the end of our own lives and at the end of time. Through our redemption in Christ, we can see once again our eternal destiny that has always been God's plan for us: full communion with him in Heaven for all eternity.

The enduring understandings and essential questions represent core concepts and questions that are explored throughout this unit. By studying the content of each chapter, you will gain a more complete understanding of the following:

Enduring Understandings
1. By his suffering and death, Jesus frees us from the power of sin and death.
2. The Resurrection of Jesus opens the way to our own resurrection.
3. The Ascension reveals Christ's authority, the possibility of eternal life with God, and how Jesus is present to us now.
4. The Paschal Mystery has implications for us and how we are called to live our life with Christ.

Essential Questions
1. How does Jesus' suffering and death show love for us?
2. How did the Resurrection continue the saving work Jesus began by his suffering and death?
3. How does Jesus' Ascension change how he is present to us?
4. If it happened so long ago, how does the Paschal Mystery affect our lives today?

Chapter
6
The Suffering and Death of Jesus

Introduction

We begin unit 3 by considering Christ's suffering and death. We must be careful not to take the meaning of these events for granted. As we walk through the events of Jesus' Passion and death, we can see how the Father's purpose was accomplished through the actions of the Jewish and Roman leaders. We come to understand that Jesus' death was not a senseless execution, but a supernatural event that freed all humanity from the bonds of death.

It might seem strange to non-Christians, and even sometimes to us, that we wear a cross as jewelry, as a sign of victory, when it originated as a method of execution and a sign of defeat. How have we come to revere a Savior who was tried as a criminal and executed? Who were the people behind the death of Jesus? What was the real reason he was executed? And how did his suffering and death free us from sin and death and restore us to original holiness and justice? In this chapter, we will uncover the answers to these questions and more.

Article 21: The Events of the Passion

In AD 30, a traveling Jewish rabbi made a decision that would change the world forever. For several years he had been traveling in Galilee and Samaria, teaching, healing, and forming a band of disciples to continue his mission after his departure. He knew his disciples were ready for the final challenge that lay ahead, even though they did not know what was in store. One of them had just announced that he believed the rabbi was the Messiah, the Son of the Living God. Then the rabbi—known as Jesus, son of Joseph the carpenter—made the decision to travel to Jerusalem, where he knew he would meet his death.

Catholic life includes visual reminders of the suffering and death of Jesus. We display crucifixes, which depict the dead body of Christ—called the corpus—even though most other Christians remember Jesus with empty crosses. We have the Stations of the Cross and the mysteries of the Rosary, two special prayer forms with visual elements that help us to reflect on the meaning of Jesus' death. On Good Friday we strip our churches bare to emphasize the emptiness and sorrow that Jesus and his disciples felt on that fateful day long ago. We take such care to commemorate these events because of what they mean for our salvation.

Each of the four Gospels gives the same account of the events leading to Jesus' death, with only small differences in details. The fact that these events are so important is clear when we consider how much of each Gospel is devoted to these accounts. Even though these events represent only one day of the three years of

Meeting Jesus on the way to his Crucifixion is one of the traditional seven sorrows of Mary. The feast day for Our Lady of Sorrows is September 15.

© jorisvo / Shutterstock.com

Jesus' public ministry, they take up two of Mark's sixteen chapters, for example. The Passion and Resurrection of Christ were at the center of the early Church's first preaching and teaching (see Acts 2:22–36, 3:11–15). Let's take a quick look at these events and who was involved. The following chart shows the corresponding biblical passages.

Day and Time	Event	Scripture Passages
Sunday	Jesus triumphantly entered Jerusalem.	Matthew 21:1–11, Mark 11:1–11, Luke 19:28–40, John 12:12–19
Thursday early evening	The Last Supper	Matthew 26:20–30, Mark 14:17–26, Luke 22:14–38, John 13:1–17:26
Thursday evening	Jesus prayed in the garden at Gethsemane and was soon arrested.	Matthew 26:36–56, Mark 14:32–52, Luke 22:39–53, John 18:1–13
Thursday night	Jesus faced his "trial" before the Sanhedrin. Peter denied Jesus.	Matthew 26:57–75, Mark 14:53–72, Luke 22:54–71, John 18:13–27
Friday morning (7 a.m.?)	Jesus faced his "trial" before Pilate and Herod.	Matthew 27:1–14, Mark 15:1–5, Luke 23:1–16, John 18:28–38
Friday morning (8 a.m.?)	Jesus was condemned, scourged, and led to Golgotha.	Matthew 27:15–32, Mark 15:6–21, Luke 23:18–32, John 18:38 –19:16
Friday morning (9 a.m.?)	Jesus was crucified.	Matthew 27:33–44, Mark 15:22–32, Luke 23:33–43, John 19:17–27
Friday afternoon (3 p.m.?)	Jesus died.	Matthew 27:45–56, Mark 15:33–41, Luke 23:44–49, John 19:28–37
Friday evening	Jesus was buried.	Matthew 27:57–61, Mark 15:42–47, Luke 23:50–56, John 19:38–42

Jesus' Triumphant Entry into Jerusalem

When Jesus decided to bring his mission to Jerusalem, tensions reached a breaking point, particularly with the **chief priests**. Jerusalem was the center of Jewish faith and worship, particularly during the annual commemoration of the Passover. Jesus' presence in the city was too direct a challenge to ignore. First, when Jesus arrived, crowds welcomed him as a triumphant king (see Matthew 21:1–11). Next Jesus went to the Temple, the very seat of the priests' and scribes' authority, and cast out the moneychangers (see Matthew 21:12–13). He did this to protest how the chief priests and scribes had let commerce and profit become intertwined with the practice of the Jewish faith. Mark and Luke both tell us that it was after this act that the religious leaders began looking for a way to kill Jesus (see Mark 11:18, Luke 19:47).

chief priests
These were Jewish priests of high rank in the Temple. They had administrative authority and presided over important Temple functions and were probably leaders in the Sanhedrin.

The Last Supper

Early Thursday evening Jesus gathered with his closest friends, the **Apostles**, for a final celebration of the Passover. During the meal Jesus washed their feet (see John 13:1–20) to show that true leadership is service. Because the meal was a Passover meal, Jesus identified himself with the Paschal Lamb whose blood was shed and flesh was eaten. He did this through the institution of the Eucharist (which we discussed in chapter 5, "The Redemptive Nature of Christ's Earthly Life"). When we celebrate the Eucharist, we commemorate and make present Christ's sacrifice.

© Jozef Sedmak / Shutterstock.com

Apostles
The general term *apostle* means "one who is sent" and can be used in reference to any missionary of the Church during the New Testament period. In reference to the twelve companions chosen by Jesus, also known as "the Twelve," the term refers to those special witnesses of Jesus on whose ministry the early Church was built and whose successors are the bishops.

Sanhedrin
An assembly of Jewish religious leaders—chief priests, scribes, and elders—who functioned as the supreme council and tribunal during the time of Jesus.

blasphemy
Speech or actions that show disrespect or irreverence for God; also, claiming to have the powers of God or to be God.

The Garden at Gethsemane

After the meal Jesus went with his Apostles to one of his favorite places to pray, the garden at Gethsemane. While Jesus was in prayer, accepting his Father's will, Judas led the Temple guards to Jesus so that they could arrest him and take him before the Jewish religious leaders. This event set up a wonderful biblical parallel. The first Adam disobeyed God in a garden, bringing sin and death into the world. In another garden, Jesus, the new Adam, now made a conscious choice to obey his Father, thus defeating sin and death (see Mark 14:36). And just as Satan tempted Adam and Eve to betray God in a garden, Satan also tempted Judas to betray the Son of God in a garden (see Mark 14:43).

The Trial Before the Sanhedrin

Jesus was brought before the **Sanhedrin**, the ruling group of Jewish religious leaders. They questioned Jesus, determined to find him guilty of a capital crime—meaning a crime that is punishable by death. The Gospels make it clear that the Sanhedrin had difficulty doing so (see Mark 14:55–59). The fact that the trial happened late at night seems to indicate that these leaders wanted to keep this trial out of public view and get it over with quickly. Because of Jesus' popularity with the non-elites, they were concerned that riots would break out if their treatment of Jesus became public. They found Jesus guilty of **blasphemy** when he confirmed that he is the Messiah (see Mark 14:61–62). According to the Law, the penalty for blasphemy is death by stoning. However, because they were then under Roman rule, the Jewish leaders did not have the authority to condemn someone to death.

The Trial Before Pilate

As early as possible the next morning, the Jewish leaders took Jesus to the Roman governor, Pontius Pilate, and made their case against Jesus. Because Pilate did not care about Jewish religious law, they had to accuse Jesus of treason rather than blasphemy. They charged Jesus with inciting rebellion against Rome, probably even with claiming to be the king of the Jews (see Mark 15:1–3), which was a capital offense in the Roman Empire. Though Luke and John indicate that Pilate thought Jesus was innocent, the reality is that only Pilate could have ordered Jesus to be crucified. That fact that he did so suggests that he believed Jesus' message was in some way a threat to Roman authority. The fact that Jesus said so little in his own defense (see Mark 15:4–5) is probably an indication that he knew he would be found guilty and that nothing he could say would change Pilate's decision.

The Scourging

Pilate ordered Jesus' execution, although some Gospel accounts indicate that he simply permitted it to happen, rather than specifically ordering Jesus to be killed. Then the Roman soldiers prepared Jesus to be executed.

A Roman execution was especially brutal. It was meant to be as horrible as possible to frighten people into obedience. First, Jesus was scourged, or whipped, with a leather lash that had pieces of bone and metal embedded in it. This type of lash was designed to tear the skin from a person's back. Condemned prisoners were sometimes whipped to hasten their death; at times people died from the whipping alone. Next, the soldiers sought to publicly humiliate Jesus by clothing him with a purple cloak and then crowning him with thorns. This humiliation was intended to mock his supposed claim to be a king. Finally, he had to carry on his bloody back the cross on which he would be crucified.

The Crucifixion

When Jesus reached the hill called Golgotha, the soldiers stripped him of his clothes to completely humiliate him and then they nailed him through his wrists to a crossbeam, which was lifted into place on a permanent post. His arms and feet were tied to the cross to keep his body from tearing free of the nails. People who were crucified often lived for days before dying from blood loss, exposure, or the inability to breathe. The Gospels provide details that show how the events of the Crucifixion were the fulfillment of many Old Testament prophecies. Jesus' final words on the cross indicated his suffering, his humanity, his forgiveness, his love for his Mother, and his trust in God.

Jesus' Death

According to the Gospel accounts, Jesus died in six hours or less, no doubt in part due to the blood he lost from the scourging. His death was accompanied by dramatic natural events: a solar eclipse and an earthquake (see Matthew 27:45,51). The earthquake split the veil of the Temple, the curtain that separated the Holy of Holies from the rest of the Temple. Only the high priest could go behind the veil. So the tearing of the Temple veil symbolically indicates that with the death of Christ, all

Did You Know?

Walking in Jesus' Footsteps

© Anilah/Shutterstock.com

For centuries people have traveled to Jerusalem to walk in the footsteps of Jesus by retracing the route of his Passion and death. People who travel for religious reasons are called *pilgrims*, and their journeys are called *pilgrimages*. But not everyone can make a pilgrimage to Jerusalem.

During the fourteenth century, a prayerful solution emerged. Parish churches began to display events from the Passion of Christ along the walls. These events were called stations, or stops. A local "pilgrim" could stop and pray at each one.

Today the Stations of the Cross are a fixture in most Catholic churches. Sometimes they are marked by a simple cross with a number on it. In other churches, they take the form of pictures, icons, or statues. The Stations of the Cross can be prayed privately. During Lent, members of the parish also assemble on a weekday evening to pray the Stations of the Cross together.

people, not just the high priest, have access to the presence of God.

Normally a convicted criminal's body would have been left on the cross to be further desecrated, eaten by birds and animals. But one follower of Jesus, Joseph of Arimathea, was an influential man. He was able to convince Pilate to let him take down Jesus' body and place it in his personal tomb (see Matthew 27:57–60). The Gospels are careful to mention that the location of the tomb was noted by the women disciples (see verse 61). Matthew also adds the detail that the tomb was watched over by guards (see verse 66). These details confirm that Jesus' death was real and that his body was not later stolen by his followers.

Jesus' Death Is the Real Thing

Some people think that because Jesus is God, his death was no big deal for him. After all, didn't he know how it would all turn out? Would someone divine really suffer at the hands of humans? But the Gospel stories take great care to show us that Jesus experienced doubt, pain, and fear as he was betrayed, put through a mock trial, tortured, and crucified. He was not saved from these human feelings because of his divine nature. His death was the real thing. The Son of God suffered, died, and was buried for the forgiveness of our sins so that we might experience full communion with God in this life and the next.

> **When you make a choice that causes you fear or pain, does it comfort you to know you did the right thing?**

Article 22: Who Killed Jesus?

The mystery of the Incarnation tells us that Jesus was both true God and true man. So we should not be surprised to learn that there are both human and divine reasons behind his death. To fully understand the importance of Jesus' death, we need to understand both sets of

Brooklyn Museum of Art, New York, USA / Bridgeman Images

reasons. Let's start by considering the human reasons.

The Nicene Creed states that Jesus Christ "was crucified under Pontius Pilate, he suffered death and was buried." This statement tells us that a Roman governor—Pontius Pilate—was involved in Jesus' death, but it doesn't mention the Jewish religious leaders. The Gospels make clear that both Jewish and Roman leaders wanted Jesus dead. But why?

The Jewish Leaders' Reasons

For the religious leaders of the Jewish community, the answer is fairly clear: Jesus challenged their authority to such an extent that they believed Jesus was undermining them with the common people. Consider some specific examples:

- Mark 2:23 – 3:6 The Pharisees and scribes taught that people could do absolutely no work on the Sabbath. Jesus' disciples plucked grain on the Sabbath, and Jesus healed on the Sabbath. He challenged the Pharisees and scribes' teaching by saying, "The sabbath was made for man, not man for the sabbath" (2:27).

- Mark 2:1–12 Jesus claimed to have the power to forgive sins. The Jewish religious leaders taught that this power belongs to God alone, and they did not recognize Jesus as the Divine Savior.

- Luke 16:19–31 Many of the religious leaders believed that having material wealth was a sign of being right with God. Jesus contradicted them by saying that God also blesses the poor. He even taught that being rich while ignoring the poor is a sin.

- Luke 15:1–10 The religious leaders avoided having anything to do with common sinners such as prostitutes and tax collectors. Yet Jesus freely associated with these people. He even scolded the Pharisees for avoiding them.

As you have already seen, things came to a head when Jesus brought his mission to Jerusalem and directly confronted the authority and power of the chief priests and scribes. However, the Jewish leaders could not put Jesus to death simply because he challenged their authority. So the crime they charged him with was blasphemy, the crime of speaking irreverently about God (see Matthew 26:63–66). The chief priests and scribes claimed that Jesus committed blasphemy when he claimed powers for himself that belonged to God alone. According to the Law of the Old Covenant, a person could be stoned to death for this. But because they were under Roman authority, only the Roman **procurator** could order a death sentence.

procurator
A word used to describe Roman governors, who had administrative and legal authority over a province or region of the Roman Empire.

The Roman Leaders' Reasons

The Roman leaders' reasons for executing Jesus are not completely clear if we just read the Gospel accounts. To understand their reasons, we need to understand how

Live It!
Jewish People Are Our Spiritual Brothers and Sisters

Throughout history many people have misinterpreted the Gospel accounts to conclude that all Jewish people are responsible for Jesus' death. This is simply not true. We must remember that most of the early disciples, the Apostles, Jesus' Mother, and even Jesus himself, were Jewish. Only the Jewish leaders who were alive at the time of Christ and who collaborated with the Roman Empire should be held accountable.

The Second Vatican Council states that "God holds the Jews most dear" and that "the Church, mindful of the patrimony she shares with the Jews . . . decries hatred, persecutions, displays of anti-Semitism, directed against Jews at any time" (Declaration on the Relation of the Church to Non-Christian Religions, 4). Both Jews and Christians call the same God "Father." All Jewish people are our spiritual brothers and sisters.

the Roman Empire stayed in power and, in particular, the role of the Roman procurator.

For all intents and purposes, a Roman procurator, or governor, held absolute power in the region he controlled. His power was enforced by the legions of soldiers under his command. The procurator was accountable to the Roman Emperor and the Roman Senate only, not to any local authorities or the local population. The procurator's main responsibilities were to send tax money regularly to Rome and to keep the peace, which generally meant stopping any rebellions against Rome. To help with these tasks, he sometimes appointed local people to positions of power. These local leaders were required to enforce Roman laws and taxes; if they did not do this, they were quickly replaced. They were also expected to report to the procurator regarding any suspicion that people were plotting against Rome. By the time of Jesus, the local ruling family in Israel, the Herodians, had been cooperating with the Roman Empire for several generations. And the Herodians appointed the high priest and chief priests of the Temple, until eventually the Romans took over that too.

The procurator at the time of Jesus' betrayal was Pontius Pilate. Why would he have ordered Jesus' Crucifixion? First, as procurator he tried everyone accused of treason against Rome and ordered the public execution of anyone he found guilty. Second, all he really needed to know was that the Jewish leaders who served him thought Jesus was a threat to Rome's authority (see Luke 23:5). We know from sources outside the Bible that Pontius Pilate was a ruthless and effective leader, responsible for the deaths of many Jewish citizens, even before Jesus' Crucifixion.

Yet the Gospel accounts portray Pilate as having ambivalent feelings towards Jesus. He was amazed with Jesus' composure in facing him (see Mark 15:4–5). He tested the crowd's conviction by allowing them to choose whether to release Jesus or a criminal named Barabbas (see Mark 15:6–15). In the Gospel of Luke, we read that

Pilate publicly declared Jesus innocent three times (see 23:4,14,22). But in the end, Pilate had his soldiers scourge and crucify Jesus. Regardless of whether Jesus was a revolutionary, he was a threat to the peace that Pilate was pledged to maintain. The bottom line is clear: Jesus would not have been crucified without the

Brooklyn Museum of Art, New York, USA / Bridgeman Images

approval of Pilate, acting on behalf of the Roman Empire.

Only Pilate had the authority to condemn Jesus to death. The Gospels present Pilate as being amazed at Jesus' composure before him.

The Irony of Jesus' Condemnations

When we consider why both the Jewish and Roman leaders sought to have Jesus executed, we discover at least two ironies in their human reasons behind Jesus' Passion and death. These ironies are not specifically mentioned in the Gospels, but the Evangelists certainly expected their readers to see them.

The first irony lies in the crime the Jewish leaders charged Jesus with. They charged him with blasphemy, for claiming to be the Messiah, the Son of God. The irony is that Jesus is indeed the Son of God, the Second Person of the Trinity. Jesus was not committing blasphemy. He was simply speaking the truth, one that the religious leaders of his time could not accept.

The second irony is that Pilate executed Jesus to eliminate a threat to the authority of the Roman Empire. He wanted to stop the spread of Jesus' message of a kingdom of justice marked by compassion for the poor and leaders who are first the servants of others. Jesus' message directly challenged the core values of the Roman Empire. The irony is that in executing Jesus, Pilate set in motion the events that brought the Kingdom of God to its fulfillment. Pilate's actions were unable to defeat God's purpose, proving that the Kingdom of God would triumph over all earthly empires despite their efforts to keep it from happening.

How does Jesus' message challenge the core values of our society today?

Article 23: The Meaning of the Cross

We now turn to the supernatural, or divine, reasons for Jesus Christ's Passion and death. His death was not merely the execution of a subversive leader. Saint Peter, in talking about the death of Jesus, said, "This man, delivered up by the set plan and foreknowledge of God, you killed" (Acts 2:23). The Father planned that his Son would take on the burden of sin for all humanity, dying so that we might be free from the sentence of death. "[Christ] himself bore our sins in his body upon the cross, so that, free from sin, we might live for righteousness. By his wounds you have been healed" (1 Peter 2:24). Salvation from sin and death for every person in every age comes through the death and Resurrection of Jesus Christ.

Does all this sound too fantastic to believe? Many people living at the time of Jesus thought so. Many of the speeches in the Acts of the Apostles and much of the teaching in the letters of the New Testament are devoted to explaining how Jesus' death frees us from sin. Their teaching tends to fall into three metaphors, or symbolic explanations: Jesus, the Suffering Servant; Jesus, the Paschal Lamb; and Jesus, the Ransom for Many. Because the symbols and the Scripture passages associated with these metaphors are important in Catholic liturgy and theology, we will look at each of them.

Jesus, the Suffering Servant

The first Christians, like Jesus himself, were Jews. Guided by the Holy Spirit, they looked to their sacred writings, the Jewish Scriptures (which contain most of the same books that are in the Old Testament), to understand the meaning of Jesus' death. No doubt they immediately thought of the "Suffering Servant" passages in Isaiah (see 42:1–4, 49:1–6, 50:4–9, and 52:13–53:12), which you encountered in chapter 3, "The Path to Restoration." These passages describe an unnamed servant of the Lord who suffers greatly—not as punishment for his own sins but to save the people from theirs. "He [the Suffering Servant] was pierced for our sins, / crushed for our iniquity. / He bore the punishment that makes us whole, / by his wounds we were healed" (Isaiah 53:5).

Can you see how these passages apply to the suffering and death of Jesus? In making this connection, the early Christians began to understand how Jesus' freely given obedience to the Father's will helped to explain how we have been freed from our sins. Saint Paul explains, "For just as through the disobedience of one person the many were made sinners, so through the obedience of one the many will be made righteous" (Romans 5:19).

One of Jesus' symbolic titles is the Lamb of God. What other symbols associated with Jesus are in this stained glass?

© Dave Bartruff / CORBIS

Jesus, the Paschal Lamb

Another event in the Old Testament that connects to Jesus' Passion is the account of the Paschal, or Passover, Lamb. This story ties all the way back to the time

Primary Sources

Christ's Suffering Is a Sign of Love

Julian of Norwich (1342–1416) was a medieval mystic who lived in England. In this passage, she explains how Jesus' willingness to suffer was a sign of his deep compassion and intimate care for us:

> At the same time as I saw this sight of the head bleeding, our good Lord showed a spiritual sight of his familiar love. I saw that he is to us everything which is good and comforting for our help. He is our clothing, who wraps and enfolds us for love, embraces us and shelters us, surrounds us for his love, which is so tender that he may never desert us. (*Showings*, chapter 5)

when the Israelites were slaves in Egypt. To convince Pharaoh to let the people go, God sent a series of ten plagues upon the Egyptian people. The last and most horrible plague was the death of the firstborn son of every family in the land. God told Moses to instruct the Israelites to kill a lamb and put its blood on their door-posts so the Lord would pass over their homes without killing their firstborn sons. After this plague Pharaoh let the people go, and they began their journey to the Promised Land.

The Gospel of John and the Book of Revelation refer to Jesus as "the Lamb of God, who takes away the sin of the world" (John 1:29). To make it perfectly clear, the Gospel of John tells us that Jesus was crucified on the Feast of the Passover—the same day the Paschal lambs

Faith in Action
Saint Paul of the Cross: God's Love Revealed

© Nomad_Soul/Shutterstock.com

Paul Daneo (1694–1775), born in Italy, could have been a successful merchant like his father. Instead he became a priest. In the midst of darkness and temptation, he found strength and peace in meditating on the Passion of Jesus Christ. At the same time, he noticed the fate of the ordinary people of his time who worked long hours, were left without hope when they fell ill, and were abandoned by society. Who would tell them of Christ's love and compassion? Who would assure them that suffering leads to resurrection?

To meet the needs of those who were poor and suffering, and also to make their needs known to both the Church and society, Father Paul (later known as Saint Paul of the Cross) founded the Congregation of the Passionists. Today the mission statement of the Passionists of Holy Cross Province in the United States announces: "We Passionists proclaim God's love for the world revealed through the Passion of Jesus Christ."

Saint Paul of the Cross also founded the Passionist nuns. They are devoted to a life of prayer and share the Passionist charism through prayerful meditation on the Paschal Mystery of Christ. With Mary, they stand at the foot of the cross and are especially mindful of praying for all those who suffer in any way.

were being slaughtered in the Temple. Just as the blood of the Paschal lambs liberated the Israelites from death and slavery, so too did Jesus' death and Resurrection save all humanity from death and from slavery to sin. You will sometimes hear Christians expressing this idea by saying, for example, "I've been washed in the blood of the Lamb." This is why we call the mystery of Jesus' Passion, death, Resurrection, and Ascension the Paschal Mystery.

Jesus, the Ransom for Many

In the Roman Empire, a ransom was the price paid to release a slave. The payment was made in front of a shrine to a local god, to indicate that the slave was now the property of that god and could no longer be owned by another person. Because they wanted to reach Gentiles (non-Jews) as well as Jews, the early Christians adapted this concept to explain the saving nature of Jesus' death to people throughout the Roman Empire. We see this particularly in the Gospel of Mark, where Jesus says, "For the Son of Man did not come to be served but to serve and to give his life as a ransom for many" (10:45). The idea of ransom helps us to understand that Jesus paid to God the price of our freedom so that we are no longer "owned" by sin and death.

All these explanations are important ways for us to understand what Catholics mean when we say Jesus died for our sins. We must be careful though to not interpret them too literally. If you take any of these metaphors to the extreme, God can begin to seem like an angry and cold-hearted accountant, demanding exact payment in blood before setting us free. This image is the exact opposite of Jesus' description of God as a loving and forgiving Father. What these three explanations help us to understand is that through God's initiative, the suffering and death of Jesus Christ has bridged the separation between God and humanity—a consequence of the Fall. This is God's great gift of love to us, the freely offered sacrifice of God himself, in the person of Jesus Christ.

Doctor of the Church
A title officially bestowed by the Church on saints who are highly esteemed for their theological writings, as well as their personal holiness.

A Hymn of the Cross

Saint Ephrem of Syria (306–373) used music to counter the Christological heresies prevalent in his time. He composed popular hymns that taught the true faith. The Church declared Ephrem a **Doctor of the Church** in 1920. This passage from one of his hymns helps us to understand how Jesus conquered death through his own death and Resurrection:

> Death slew [Christ] by means of the body which he had assumed, but that same body proved to be the weapon with which he conquered death. Concealed beneath the cloak of his manhood, his godhead engaged death in combat; but in slaying our Lord, death itself was slain. It was able to kill natural human life, but was itself killed by the life that is above the nature of man. . . .
>
> We give glory to you, Lord, who raised up your cross to span the jaws of death like a bridge by which souls might pass from the region of the dead to the land of the living. We give glory to you who put on the body of a single mortal man and made it the source of life for every other mortal man. You are incontestably alive. Your murderers

Pray It!

The Cross Is the Power of God

When we have to endure suffering, we remember that Jesus suffered too, and that his suffering was the path to our salvation. We pray:

Jesus,

You were obedient to your Father even though it meant that you would be abandoned by your friends, accused of being a criminal, beaten, and executed on a cross. You remind me to do the right thing despite the problems I might face. By putting all my faith in you, I know I can endure mockery, abandonment, rejection, or even worse.

Give me the strength to bear my crosses in life. In my most difficult moments, remind me that the cross is not the end, but the beginning. Give me the courage to let go of greed, hatred, lust, pride, and everything else that keeps me from doing your will. Remind me of Saint Paul's words: "The message of the cross is foolishness to those who are perishing, but to us who are being saved it is the power of God" (1 Corinthians 1:18). Amen.

sowed your living body in the earth as farmers sow grain, but it sprang up and yielded an abundant harvest of men raised from the dead.

Which of the metaphors in this section helps you to understand something new about the Paschal Mystery? Why?

Article 24: Why Did the Father Allow His Son to Suffer?

Some people ask why the Father required his Son to die for our sins. Why didn't he find some way to save his Son from such a torturous death? When confronted with questions

© Holy Transfiguration Monastery; Brookline, MA; used with permission

like these, we can find it helpful to remember some of the things we have learned in this chapter.

First, no action on the Father's part required the Son's redeeming death. Rather, our first parents' Original Sin necessitated Jesus' sacrifice. The Father allowed his Son's death in order to destroy the power of death and restore our friendship with God so that we might live eternally with him.

Second, the Father did not force his Son's sacrificial death. Jesus Christ freely accepted his Passion and death. As an innocent victim, he took upon himself all the sins and injustices of humanity to overcome them. Because Jesus is the Second Person of the Trinity, his Incarnation and his death were part of his divine mission in the work of salvation. Christ's Resurrection is proof that his death was necessary to overcome the power of sin and death. The suffering and death of Christ are not signs of God's weakness but of his strength. They do not show God's apathy but rather show the depth of his love.

How can a deeper understanding of Christ's suffering and death help you to feel God's strength and love more profoundly?

Saint Ephrem firmly believed that God's love is stronger than death. His faith gave him the courage and wisdom to proclaim this joyful news throughout his life.

Chapter Review

1. When did Jesus' conflict with the chief priests come to a head? Why?

2. What dramatic natural events occurred at the time of Jesus' death?

3. What were the Jewish leaders' reasons for wanting Jesus to be put to death?

4. How was Jesus a threat to the Roman Empire?

5. What are three metaphors used to communicate the supernatural meaning of Jesus' death?

6. If you were asked why God the Father would allow his Son to suffer and die as he did, what would your response be?

The Resurrection and Ascension of Jesus

Chapter 7

Introduction

In this chapter, we focus on Christ's Resurrection and Ascension, the glorious events that are the culmination of his saving work. God's plan was brought to fulfillment through Jesus Christ's Passion, death, Resurrection, and Ascension—the events that are at the heart of the Paschal Mystery. Without Christ's Resurrection we would have no basis to hope for our own resurrection and eternal life with God. Saint Paul explains: "If Christ has not been raised, your faith is vain; you are still in your sins. Then those who have fallen asleep in Christ have perished" (1 Corinthians 15:17–18).

But what is the Resurrection? How do we know it really happened? What is a resurrected body like? What does the Resurrection prove? Why did the resurrected Christ ascend into Heaven after forty days? This chapter explores these important questions. Above all, Christ's Resurrection should cause us to rejoice because God invites us to participate in this great mystery, the culmination of his saving plan. In the words of Saint Paul:

> For I handed on to you as of first importance what I also received: that Christ died for our sins in accordance with the scriptures; that he was buried; that he was raised on the third day in accordance with the scriptures; that he appeared to Cephas [Peter], then to the Twelve. After that, he appeared to more than five hundred brothers at once, most of whom are still living, though some have fallen asleep. (1 Corinthians 15:3–6)

Resurrection
The bodily rising of Jesus from the dead on the third day after his death on the cross; the heart of the Paschal Mystery and the basis of our hope in the resurrection from the dead.

Article 25: The Events of the Resurrection

Throughout the pages of history, we find great spiritual leaders: Moses, Confucius, the Buddha, and Mohammed, to name a few. Many great spiritual leaders taught their followers to live a moral life based on love of others. Many also taught belief in and love for God. What makes Jesus Christ different from these other spiritual leaders? Only Jesus Christ is the Son of God, the Second Divine Person of the Trinity, who was raised from the dead and now reigns in Heaven forever.

The **Resurrection** is, in fact, the work of all three Divine Persons of the Holy Trinity. We sometimes signify this by saying that the Father raised up his Son (see Acts 2:24, Romans 6:4). But the Son was not a passive participant. The Gospel of John tells us that Jesus says, "No one takes [my life] from me, but I lay it down on my own. I have power to lay it down, and power to take it up again" (10:18). And wherever the Father and the Son are

Did You Know?

Jewish Burial Customs

© Mordechai Meiri / Shutterstock.com

Jesus was buried according to traditional Jewish customs. The importance of burying the dead is emphasized throughout the Old Testament as the final act of care and respect owed to those who have died. (Tobit, the father of Tobiah in the Book of Tobit, courageously risked his life to bury the bodies of those who were executed by pagan rulers.) One important custom of Jewish Law was burying a body in the ground before sundown (placing a body in a tomb qualified as a burial) in a special area set aside for that purpose.

The traditional Jewish burial garment was a shroud. Even among many Jews today, a shroud made of pure, white linen is wrapped around the body of the deceased. The shroud is made without pockets. This symbolizes that we can take nothing with us when we leave this world, and that God judges us on our actions, not on material wealth.

at work, there we also find the Holy Spirit at work. The inseparable Persons of the Holy Trinity accomplish our salvation.

The Resurrection is closely related to Christ's Incarnation. He was able to save us from sin and death because he is true God and true man, the only mediator who can restore us to full communion with the Father, Son, and Holy Spirit. But the Resurrection provides us with proof for this truth. Without Christ's Resurrection all our claims about who Jesus is and what he did for us sound hollow and empty. Some people have come to believe that the Resurrection never happened; they argue that it is a big hoax. But the evidence for the Resurrection is compelling. Let's look at the accounts of the Resurrection and the evidence that it was an actual historical event.

The Gospel Accounts of the Resurrection

Each of the four Gospels gives us a slightly different account of what happens in the days after Jesus' death. The Gospel of Mark offers the fewest clues. Mark's Gospel originally ended with his account of when several women discover an empty tomb, and an angel tells the women that Jesus has been raised. A longer ending was later added to this Gospel, describing how Jesus appears to Mary Magdalene and the other disciples. The Gospel of Luke also tells us that several women are the first to discover the empty tomb and that they learn of Jesus' Resurrection from "two men in dazzling garments" who appear before them (24:4). In the Gospel of Matthew, we read that Pilate places a guard at the tomb to keep the disciples from stealing Jesus' body, but an angel rolls away the stone. The resurrected Jesus meets the disciples on a mountain in Galilee, where he gives them a mission to "make disciples of all nations" (Matthew 28:19). The Gospel of John takes the prize for the most Resurrection stories, with four separate accounts of Jesus' appearing to different people.

The following chart describes the Resurrection appearances. Because of differences between details in the four Gospel accounts, it is difficult to tell whether some of these details refer to the same event or different events. These potentially different accounts are indicated with brackets.

Appearance	Scripture Passages
Several women (Mary Magdalene, Mary, the mother of James, Salome, and Joanna) saw an angel and witnessed the empty tomb.	Matthew 28:1–8, Mark 16:1–8, Luke 24:1–10, John 20:1–10
Jesus appeared to Mary Magdalene.	[Matthew 28:9–10], Mark 16:9, John 20:11–18
Jesus appeared to two disciples walking away from Jerusalem.	Mark 16:12–13, Luke 24:13–35
Jesus commissioned the eleven Apostles.	Matthew 28:16–20, Mark 16:14–18, Luke 24:36–49, [John 20:19–23]
Jesus appeared to the Apostles, including Thomas.	John 20:24–29
Jesus appeared to Peter and six other disciples in Galilee.	John 21:1–23
Jesus ascended to Heaven.	Mark 16:19, Luke 24:50–53, Acts 1:6–12
Jesus appeared to Saul (later Paul).	Acts 9:1–6

Despite their differences, the Gospel accounts of the Resurrection have these points in common:

- First some women disciples, and then some of the men, went to the tomb and discovered that the body of Jesus is no longer there.
- The women who went to the tomb found out from angels that Jesus was no longer dead but alive and that he would reveal himself to the disciples soon.
- Jesus revealed himself to Mary Magdalene at the tomb (and to the other Mary in Matthew's account).

- Later Jesus appeared to groups of disciples to wish them peace and charge them with continuing his mission. Often the disciples' initial reaction was shock and fear. But soon they experienced Jesus in such striking ways that they could not doubt that it is he— alive again, and yet somehow different from the way he was before his death.

The Risen Jesus specifically appeared to Mary Magdalene in almost all of the Gospel accounts. We know that Jesus had cast seven demons out of Mary (see Luke 8:2 and Mark 16:9) and that after her healing she became one of Jesus' disciples, following him from village to village where he proclaimed the Good News of the Kingdom (see Luke 8:1–2 and Mark 15:40–41). Mary Magdalene had courage. She was present at the cross when most of the men who followed Jesus had run away (see John 18:25). At daybreak on the day of Jesus' Resurrection, Mary Magdalene, with Mary the mother of James, went to the tomb where Jesus had been buried. On seeing the empty tomb, they were fearful yet overjoyed. As they hurry to tell the other disciples, Jesus met them and greeted them, saying, "Do not be afraid" (Matthew 28:10).

Put yourself in Mary's place as she recognized the Risen Christ. Can you imagine the surprise, the joy, the awe she must have felt? Make Mary Magdalene your model of courage and trust as you follow Jesus.

This is a painting of Mary Magdalene meeting Jesus after his Resurrection. Why do you think the artist chose to render most of the scene in darkness?

Morris Museum of Art, Augusta, Georgia / Bridgeman Images

Evidence for the Truth of the Resurrection

But how do we know the Gospel accounts are all true? What if the Gospel writers simply made it all up? These are valid questions we must directly consider if we are to be honest about what we believe. Several good arguments show us that it is reasonable for us to believe in the Resurrection of Jesus as a historically valid event. Let's explore some of those arguments.

One argument asserts that we can trust the historical validity of the New Testament books and letters. Although we do not have original copies of the New Testament books or letters, we have copies that can be traced back to within a few centuries of Jesus' earthly life. And we have lots of different ancient copies of the New Testament books and letters from different parts of the ancient world. For historians and biblical scholars, these facts provide us with greater proof for the authenticity of the New Testament books than for any other ancient writing.

Another argument relies on the fact that the Resurrection was a consistent belief in the early Church. We can find it in all four Gospels, in the letters of Saint Paul, and in the speeches contained in the Acts of the Apostles. In fact, experiencing the Risen Jesus was considered a key qualification for being accepted as one of the Apostles (see Acts 1:15–22). In this we find clear evidence that the earliest Christians accepted it as fact.

We can also examine the argument of the empty tomb. If the tomb was not empty, surely the Romans or the Jewish religious leaders would have produced the corpse to end the rumors of Jesus' Resurrection right away. No evidence has been found that they tried to do this. But you might ask, "Couldn't the disciples have stolen Jesus' corpse and then claimed that he had risen?" The problem with this question is that so many disciples died as martyrs rather than deny their faith in the resurrected Jesus. Why would they have chosen to die for a hoax?

And we can argue that the Resurrection appearances of Jesus caused a profound change in his followers. This may be the most important evidence of all. After Jesus' death his disciples were beaten, discouraged, and afraid for their lives. Yet somehow they found the courage to go out in public and continue Jesus' mission, facing ridicule, persecution, and even death. With total conviction they preached that Jesus had risen. What reasonable explanation could there be for this change other than their encounter with the Risen Christ?

Christ's Resurrection was a real event. It was historically attested to by the disciples, who truly encountered the Risen One. The empty tomb signified that by God's power, Christ's body escaped the bonds of death. The empty tomb prepared the disciples to encounter and believe in the Risen Lord.

Let's bring this to a personal level. The most important question you will ever face is this: Do you believe that Jesus Christ was raised from the dead? Why is this such an important question? It is important because how you answer that question will determine how seriously you live out your belief in Jesus. If you answer, "I believe in the Resurrection!" how can you not make Jesus Christ the center of your life?

© jgroup / istockphoto.com

Do you personally believe that Jesus Christ was raised from the dead? Why or why not?

Article 26: What Does *Resurrection* Mean?

Most people want to know what the resurrected Jesus was like. The fact that the Gospel accounts are purposefully vague gives us one clue: the resurrected Jesus cannot easily be explained in human terms. He showed up without warning and disappeared just as suddenly. The disciples knew he wasn't a ghost, because they could touch him and he ate with them. He was different enough that some people did not recognize him immediately. Yet when they did recognize him, he was still the same person they

Gnosticism
A group of heretical religious movements that claimed salvation comes from secret knowledge available only to the elite initiated in that religion.

knew from before. Being in Jesus' risen presence gave them peace and hope.

In the Nicene Creed, we state our belief in the resurrection of the body. In his First Letter to the Corinthians, Saint Paul explains that at the Second Coming of Jesus, "The trumpet will sound, the dead will be raised incorruptible [meaning "without decay"], and we shall be changed" (15:52). But what do we really mean when we talk about the resurrection of the body? No one can tell you exactly what it means to be resurrected or what it will be like to experience it. This is a mystery of faith that we will only fully understand after our death. However, God does reveal to us what we need to know. You will find the most direct biblical explanation of this question in chapter 15 of Saint Paul's First Letter to the Corinthians. Take a few minutes to read that chapter right now if you can. Then return to this section for some help in interpreting what Saint Paul is saying.

First Corinthians, Chapter 15

In interpreting First Corinthians, chapter 15, we have to consider what we know about literary forms and biblical cultures. We must first ask why Saint Paul wrote his letters. Clearly he wrote them to respond to specific questions or concerns that developed in the Christian communities he was associated with. What question or concern did Saint Paul address in First Corinthians, chapter 15? It seems that some people in the Corinthian community were claiming that there is no such thing as bodily resurrection from the dead. Why would they make such a claim despite all the evidence they had for Christ's Resurrection? Their argument probably reflects the influence of a widespread cultural belief system called **Gnosticism.**

Many Gnostics believe that the human person is composed of two parts: body and spirit (or soul). But rather than believe that both body and spirit are good and necessary, they believe that the body is bad and the spirit is good. According to the Gnostics, the body keeps the soul captive and holds it back from its full potential. As a result, many Gnostics believe that the goal of a full human life is to leave behind "bodily" concerns and focus primarily on the spiritual. For them, eternal life means that we will live forever as pure spirit, shedding our bodies forever.

Saint Paul was writing to counter this false belief by explaining what resurrection truly is. He makes his argument in three steps.

Step 1: The Resurrection Really Happened

In the first twelve verses of chapter 15, Saint Paul reminds the Corinthians that the Resurrection was a real event. He emphasizes the fact that the Risen Christ appeared to over five hundred believers. Notice Saint Paul's wording: he emphasizes that Christ *appeared*, not that people simply *saw* him. Here he establishes the Resurrection as an objective event, not simply a subjective event.

This information was passed on to Saint Paul from eyewitnesses, but he also had his own experience of the Risen Christ. Saint Paul defends himself as an Apostle in response to those who attacked his credibility. By mentioning the fact that he persecuted the Church at first, he subtly suggests that it would take something pretty impressive to make him change sides. All of this implies that Christ was resurrected, body and soul, for how could human beings experience him otherwise?

Can you identify the three different groups near the empty tomb? Only the Gospel of Matthew has the account of guards posted at the tomb who were later paid to say that the disciples stole Jesus' body.

© Agnew's, London, UK / The Bridgeman Art Library International

Second, Christ's Resurrection is proof of our resurrection.

In verses 20–24, Saint Paul makes the point that Christ's Resurrection is the guarantee that we too will experience the **resurrection of the dead** when Christ comes again in glory. He says that if we deny Christ's Resurrection, we deny any hope for our own resurrection after death. He goes on to say that in God's saving plan, Christ will be the first to be resurrected so that we might all be resurrected: "Since death came through a human being, the resurrection of the dead came also through a human being" (verse 21). To emphasize this point, Saint Paul likens Christ's Resurrection to the "firstfruits," meaning the first fruits, vegetables, and stalks of grain that ripen at the end of the growing season. When the firstfruits ripen, we know that the remaining fruit will also ripen shortly and be ready for harvest.

Saint Paul says that there is an order to God's plan: First, Christ was raised. Then all those who belong to (or

Live It!
Be a Farsighted Traveler

Being nearsighted means you have trouble seeing things at a distance, or that you are do not look toward the future to see what is coming. Near-sighted travelers going on a month-long jungle safari would bring things for the airplane and the hotel only. They would be ill-prepared for the main event. Being a Christian means being a farsighted traveler. Because of Christ's Resurrection, we know that our lives do not end at death. We stay focused on our ultimate destiny, Heaven, in the following ways:

1. We pray for guidance daily.
2. We trust that following God's directions will get us to our destination, even if the road is sometimes challenging.
3. If we get detoured and end up on the wrong path, we turn around.
4. We use the road maps, the Bible and Tradition.

The journey continues. Our trip won't always be easy, but we have God's promise of a destination worth the cost—Heaven!

have faith in) Christ will be raised when Christ comes again. When their resurrection is complete, Christ will have conquered sin and death forever, and the Kingdom of God will be fully restored: "When everything is subjected to him, then the Son himself will [also] be subjected to the one who subjected everything to him, so that God may be all in all" (verse 28). Paul concludes this section by listing all the Christian practices (such as Baptism) that would be useless if there were no resurrection of the dead.

Step 3: A Resurrected Body Is a Transformed Body

In the third and longest section, verses 35–58, Saint Paul attempts to explain what a resurrected body is. He can do this through analogy only. His first analogy likens our earthly body to a seed. For a seed to become what it is destined to be, it must first "die" by being buried in the ground. Only then can it grow into a plant. The plant looks nothing like the seed, but they are the same being, and one is a continuation of the other. So it is with our earthly body and our resurrected body.

Though Saint Paul cannot tell us exactly what a resurrected body is, he does paint a picture of its qualities by contrasting certain qualities of our earthly body with qualities of our resurrected body.

Earthly Body	Resurrected Body
corruptible	incorruptible
dishonorable	honorable
weak	powerful
natural body	spiritual body

When we put all these things together, the following picture emerges: Our resurrected bodies will never die and cannot be damaged by illness or disease—in other words, they will not be **corruptible**. Our resurrected bodies will not be subject to the temptations of sin and will not be

resurrection of the dead
The raising of the righteous on the last day, to live forever with the Risen Christ. The resurrection of the dead means that not only our immortal souls will live on after death, but also our transformed bodies.

corruptible
Something that can be spoiled, contaminated or made rotten, especially to be made morally perverted.

limited by the physical constraints of time and space as we are now.

A resurrected body is not a reanimated corpse. Jesus was truly transformed by the Resurrection, just as we will be after our death. At our death our soul will live on, and at the end of the world God will join our soul to our resurrected body. We will still be the same person, but we will have an utterly new kind of existence. Beyond that we do not know much more, but we can trust that it will be truly glorious.

> **Would you find it easy or hard to explain Christ's Resurrection in your own words to a friend?**

Article 27: The Significance of Christ's Resurrection

Why do we naturally root for the good people to win in books and movies? Why are we sad and sickened when someone dies tragically or at a young age? Why do medical professionals work so tirelessly to save people with life-threatening illnesses or injuries? The answer is a simple one. God created us for eternal life—a life in which there is no hatred, pain, or injustice. Even many people who do not believe in God do not easily accept dying and death.

When we look more closely at the religious significance of Christ's Resurrection, we can identify what Christ's Resurrection confirms and what it makes possible for us.

The Resurrection Confirms Revealed Truths

Many truths that God has revealed become crystal clear because of the Resurrection. The following are some of those revealed truths.

Jesus Is the Son of God

For the first disciples, seeing the resurrected Jesus was clear proof that he was more than just another human being. Jesus himself predicted this, as we read in the Gospel of John: "When you lift up the Son of Man, then you will realize that I AM" (8:28). The story of doubting Thomas says it very clearly. When Thomas saw the resurrected Jesus for the first time, he declared, "My Lord and my God!" (20:28). Belief in Jesus' Resurrection and belief in the Incarnation go hand in hand. Throughout the centuries people have believed in the divinity of Jesus Christ because they first believed in his Resurrection.

© Scala / Art Resource, NY

All Jesus' Teachings Are True

If the Resurrection reveals the truth of Jesus' divinity, then it also reveals that all his other teachings are true. If we believe that Jesus was raised from the dead, how can we not also believe that Jesus spoke the truth in his teachings, which include the following:

Can you identify with the doubts of Thomas the Apostle? Remember, he was also one of the first to declare Jesus' divinity (see John 20:28).

- that God's love for us has no limits
- that we find fulfillment only by first loving and serving God and then by loving and serving others
- that forgiveness is more powerful and Godlike than revenge
- that those who are rich must share with those who are poor
- that we must refuse to accept the human-made prejudices that separate us from one another

The Resurrection is a guarantee that all these teachings—and many other things Jesus taught that are not on this list—are true beyond a doubt.

The Resurrection Opens the Way to New Life

The Paschal Mystery has two aspects: by his death, Christ liberates us from sin; by his Resurrection, he opens for us the way to a new life. This new life is above all justification that

biblical exegesis
The critical interpretation and explanation of Sacred Scripture.

reinstates us in God's grace, "so that as Christ was raised from the dead by the glory of the Father, we too might walk in newness of life."[1] (Catechism of the Catholic Church [CCC], 654)

Christ's Resurrection does more than just confirm the truths he taught and the truth that he is the Son of God. His Resurrection "is the principle and source of our future resurrection" (CCC, 655). Because of the Resurrection, death is not the end; rather, death is our doorway into new and eternal life in full communion with God and with one another. We know that the life we live now is not all there is, as some people claim. We live in hope because the Risen Christ lives in our hearts. We can endure the sufferings and pain of this life because we know that something better and glorious is yet to come.

Saint Melito of Sardis (d. ca. 180) was a bishop of Sardis in the second century. He was known for his

Pray It!

Life after Death

Death leads to new life. Jesus even used the natural world to demonstrate this point: "I say to you, unless a grain of wheat falls to the ground and dies, it remains just a grain of wheat; but if it dies, it produces much fruit" (John 12:24). We experience many smaller deaths before we reach the end of our lives: graduation marks the end of an era, friendships end, maybe we outgrow our youthful dreams. In the midst of suffering and loss, it is sometimes difficult to see resurrection ahead. So we pray:

Lord Jesus,
Most of your friends left you.
You were falsely accused of a crime;
And you were beaten and humiliated in public.
Yet you trusted that your Father would make all things right.
Give me the courage to trust you.
Remind me that beyond the small deaths I experience,
There is resurrection,
There is new life.
There is the joy and happiness that you alone provide.
Amen.

biblical exegesis and theological writings. Most of his writings have been lost, but we do have some of his sermons. In his Easter sermon, he depicted Christ speaking for himself about the triumph of the Resurrection. Here is an excerpt:

> I have destroyed death, triumphed over the enemy, trampled hell underfoot, bound the strong one, and taken men up to the heights of heaven: I am the Christ. Come, then, all you nations of men, receive forgiveness for the sins that defile you. I am your forgiveness. I am the Passover that brings salvation. I am the lamb who was immolated for you. I am your ransom, your life, your resurrection, your light, I am your salvation and your king. I will bring you to the heights of heaven. With my own right hand I will raise you up, and I will show you the eternal Father. *(Liturgy of the Hours)*

> **Saint Melito of Sardis assigned Jesus many roles and titles. Which one helps you to understand Christ in a new way? Why?**

Article 28: The Ascension

After the Resurrection the Risen Jesus continued to appear to his followers for forty days. In Sacred Scripture, we read that Jesus did two things during his appearances. First, he taught his disciples how to interpret Scripture in relation to his life, death, and Resurrection (see Luke 24:44–48). Second, he directed them to continue his mission: "Go, therefore, and make disciples of all nations, baptizing them in the name of the Father, and of the Son, and of the holy Spirit, teaching them to observe all that I have commanded you. And behold, I am with you always, until the end of the age" (Matthew 28:19–20).

And then Jesus left them. Or did he? Let's look more closely at the Ascension, starting with an important related event: Christ's descent into Hell.

Christ's Descent into Hell

After his death but before his Resurrection, Jesus Christ descended into Hell. We find a passing reference to this event in the Letter to the Ephesians: "What does 'he ascended' mean except that he also descended into the

righteous
To be sinless and without guilt; those who are in such standing before God.

Ascension
The "going up" into Heaven of the Risen Christ forty days after his Resurrection.

lower [regions] of the earth? The one who descended is also the one who ascended far above all the heavens, that he might fill all things" (4:9–10). In other words, Jesus experienced death as completely as we do. He too experienced the complete loss of physical life that comes with death.

Then, after his death, Jesus went to the realm of the dead, where the souls of all those who had died before him awaited his judgment. Sacred Scripture calls the realm of the dead Hell (*Sheol* in Hebrew, *Hades* in Greek). Hell is essentially the absence of God. The immediate implication of Christ's descent into Hell is that he brought salvation to all the righteous souls who died before his own Resurrection.

But the full significance of this event is that Christ's death and Resurrection brought salvation to the righteous of all times and all places. Those who are **righteous** are now brought into Heaven, and the unrighteous are condemned to remain in Hell, separated from God for all eternity. By descending into Hell, Jesus completely established his power over all creation—on earth, in Heaven, and in Hell.

© Scala / Art Resource, NY

This image of Jesus' descent into the world of the dead is filled with symbols. Who has Jesus crushed? Who has been waiting for his arrival?

Christ's Ascension into Heaven

We proclaim the truth of the **Ascension** in the Nicene Creed when we say, "He ascended into Heaven and is seated at the right hand of the Father." The Gospel writers had a hard time describing this event in words. Matthew and John do not mention it at all. Mark's Gospel simply says, "So then the Lord Jesus, after he spoke to them, was taken up into heaven and took his seat at the right hand of God" (16:19). Luke says, "As he blessed them he parted from them and was taken up to heaven" (24:51). The author of Luke gives us a slightly longer version of the Ascension at the beginning of Acts of the Apostles, sometimes called the second volume of Luke's Gospel (see 1:6–12).

These Gospel accounts are trying to describe an event that is beyond our human comprehension. Many people in the ancient world believed that a layer of water covered the sky and was the physical boundary of the universe. Once you got past those waters, you were in Heaven. In Sacred Scripture, approaching God is often associated with ascending, or going up to a high place. For example, Solomon built the Temple on the highest

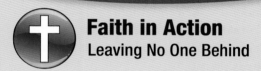

Faith in Action
Leaving No One Behind

© ipm / Alamy Stock Photo

The mystery of the Ascension seems to imply that Jesus, in going back to the Father, leaves the rest of us "behind." Nothing could be further from the truth. In the Ascension, Jesus breaks the boundaries between earth and Heaven, and is present to each of us, through the Holy Spirit. Jesus leaves no one behind!

This is also the spirit and practice of Ascension Health, a Catholic health ministry founded by five religious congregations in 1999. The motto of this ministry is, "Healthcare that leaves no one behind." This ministry began in Saint Louis but has now spread to fifteen hundred locations in twenty-three states and the District of Columbia.

Ascension Health works through its 113,000 associates who provide leadership in healthcare in Catholic hospitals, clinics, or other outreach organizations. Ascension Health provides a formation program for willing participants to participate fully in their own faith journey while identifying more closely with the mission of Ascension Health: to provide "spiritually centered, holistic care, which sustains and improves the health of individuals and communities." Six terms summarize the values that Ascension Health seeks to incorporate into the ministry of each associate: *service of the poor, reverence, integrity, wisdom, creativity,* and *dedication.*

Ascension Health is particularly aware of expanding the role of the laity to ensure that Catholic health ministry remains a vibrant presence in our society, now and into the future.

hilltop in Jerusalem. Psalm 24 asks, "Who may go up the mountain of the Lord? / Who can stand in his holy place?" (verse 3). The prophets frequently referred to God's "holy mountain." The prophet Elijah encountered God in a tiny whispering sound on a mountain. So for the sacred human writers, it made sense to think that for Jesus to join his Father in Heaven, he would have to rise into the sky and travel past the layer of water.

We know, of course, that God is present everywhere and that *up* and *down* are relative terms. So what are some other reasons the sacred human writers associate God's presence with ascending to high places? One reason is that high places are more visible and that God seeks to be known by all people. Jesus said, "A city set on a mountain cannot be hidden" (Matthew 5:14). Another possible reason is that going uphill takes more work than going downhill. So approaching God takes some effort; it is not always the easiest path.

Today we know that there is no layer of water over the sky and that Heaven doesn't lie just outside our atmosphere. However, these scientific facts don't change the reality the Gospel writers were trying to address when they described the Ascension. Namely, after spending time with some of his faithful followers after his Resurrection, Jesus left this world to be with his Father in Heaven. He left this world to open wide Heaven's doors for us and to be more present to us through the power of the Holy Spirit.

Mary and the Apostles witness Jesus' Ascension into Heaven. Notice the variety of reactions by those on earth and in Heaven.

© Réunion des Musées Nationaux / Art Resource, NY

The Ascension Reveals Christ's Glory

We celebrate Christ's Ascension forty days after Easter. Because the date for Easter varies from year to year, so does the date of the Feast of the Ascension. It always falls on a Thursday, because Easter is always on a Sunday. But many dioceses celebrate the Ascension on the following Sunday.

Some Catholics and other Christians do not see why we should celebrate the Ascension. Most likely they do not understand its importance. Indeed Christ's Ascension is a very important part of God's plan of salvation. Once you understand how the Ascension reveals Christ's glory, you will want to celebrate it every year.

We have already seen that the Incarnation and the Resurrection are closely linked. Similarly, the Incarnation and the Ascension are also closely linked. These two events form a kind of symmetry. In the Incarnation, the Son of God left Heaven to come to earth, where he humbly assumed a human nature. In the Ascension, the Son of God left earth to return to Heaven, where his full glory continues to be revealed. But here's the amazing thing. Jesus Christ did not leave his human nature behind when he returned to Heaven. For the rest of eternity, he remains true God and true man. Let's examine three implications of this great mystery.

Jesus Has Full Authority

First, this mystery means that Jesus Christ now has full authority over Heaven, earth, and even Hell. He is now

Primary Sources

Here He Is

If the Risen Christ never ascended into Heaven, we would look for him outside ourselves rather than recognize him in our heart. We would look for a person rather than find him in everyone we meet. In his book *The Confessions*, Saint Augustine reflects on the Ascension of Christ: "He left our sight so that we might return to our heart and find him there. He went away, and look: here he is."

paradox
A statement that seems contradictory or opposed to common sense and yet is true.

free from the limits he humbly accepted during his time on earth. His authority is signified by the fact that he is seated at the right hand of the Father. He demonstrated his authority by his descent into Hell, his Resurrection from the dead, and his Ascension into Heaven. The reverence we should have for him is expressed in an early Christian hymn, quoted by Saint Paul: "At the name of Jesus / every knee should bend, / of those in heaven and on earth and under the earth, / and every tongue confess that / Jesus Christ is Lord" (Philippians 2:10–11).

Jesus Opened Heaven to Humanity

Second, the Ascension means that all humanity now enjoys the possibility of spending eternity with God in Heaven. After his Ascension into Heaven, Jesus remained fully God and fully man—he did not give up his human nature even though his mission had been accomplished. Thus he honors our human nature and has opened the doors to Heaven for all humanity, overcoming the final barriers separating us from God. In Heaven, Jesus' resurrected body assumes its full glory, as will ours.

Jesus Is More Present to Us

Third, the Ascension means that in a **paradoxical** way, by leaving the earth physically, Jesus can be more present to us now than before his Ascension. Before his final Ascension, Jesus was still somehow limited by time and space. We see hints of this in Jesus' mysterious words to Mary Magdalene: "Stop holding on to me, for I have not yet ascended to the Father" (John 20:17).

Jesus' presence to us, even after his Ascension, is connected to two promises he made in the Gospels. The Gospel of Matthew tells us that he promised, "I am with you always, until the end of the age" (28:20). His second promise was to send the Holy Spirit: "And I will ask the Father, and he will give you another Advocate to be with you always, the Spirit of truth, which the world cannot accept, because it neither sees nor knows it. But you know it, because it remains with you, and will be in you. I will not leave you orphans; I will come to you" (John

14:16–18). By sending his Spirit, Jesus is now with us in a new way. From the beginning until the end of time, the mission of the Son and the Spirit are linked and insepa- rable. Wherever one is sent, the other is also present.

So Jesus never really left us, even though he ascended into Heaven. How is he present to us now? First and foremost he is present to us in the Sacra- ment of the Eucharist, in his sacred Body and Blood. But he is also present to us in Sacred Scripture, in our private prayer, in the liturgy, through our friends and family, and in our service to others. Because of his Ascension, Jesus is no longer limited to being in one place at one particular time. He is free to be everywhere, with everyone, for all time.

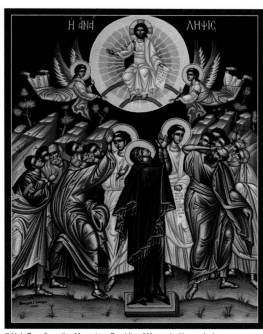

© Holy Transfiguration Monastery; Brookline, MA; used with permission

Think of all the ways Christ is present to us after his Ascension. Which one makes you feel most con- nected to the Risen Christ? Why?

How does this icon symbolize Jesus' "location" after the Ascension? Notice that he is sitting as if on a throne. What does this symbolize? Notice that the Apostles below are in different poses, some looking up, some looking around. What might this mean?

Chapter Review

1. Describe several of Jesus' Resurrection appearances.

2. Give one argument for believing in the Resurrection as a historically validated event.

3. What question or concern was Saint Paul addressing in First Corinthians, chapter 15?

4. How will our resurrected body be different from our earthly body?

5. What revealed truths are confirmed by the Resurrection?

6. Why does Christ's Resurrection give us hope for our own resurrection?

7. Why did Christ have to descend into Hell?

8. Describe three things that are results of Christ's Ascension.

Redeemed by Christ: Our Eternal Destiny

Introduction

God has a plan, and you are a part of it! You might be thinking, "That's a nice thought, but it really doesn't affect my daily life in any meaningful way."

The reality is that the Paschal Mystery has everything to do with us and our lives. Christ suffered, died, was buried, and rose so that we might be saved from sin and saved for a full and glorious life, both now and for all eternity. God wants us to accept this truth and base our lives on it. This is the most important choice we will face throughout our lives. In the rest of this book, we will explore what this means for us: how to live our lives with Christ.

We begin by looking at what we have been saved *from* and what we have been saved *for*. We will see that through God's grace, we share in Christ's death and Resurrection. In this chapter, we will also learn about the judgment we face at our death and about God's plan for us to enjoy eternal happiness with him in Heaven.

Article 29: Saved from What?

Saint Augustine of Hippo (354–430) is well known for many reasons, but one theme stands out in many of his writings: the human desire for God. This Church Father is famous for saying, "You have made us for yourself, O Lord, and our heart is restless until it rests in you." Here is an excerpt from one of his writings on this topic:

> The entire life of a good Christian is in fact an exercise of holy desire. You do not yet see what you long for, but the very act of desiring prepares you, so that when he comes you may see and be utterly satisfied. . . . By desiring Heaven we exercise the powers of our soul. Now this exercise will be effective only to the extent that we free ourselves from desires leading to infatuation with this world. Let me return to the example I have already used, of filling an empty container. God means to fill each of you with what is good; so cast out what is bad! If he wishes to fill you with honey and you are full of sour wine, where is the honey to go? The vessel must be emptied of its contents and then be cleansed. Yes, it must be cleansed even if you have to work hard and scour it. It must be made fit for the new thing, whatever it may be. (From the *Tractates on the First Letter of John*)

Augustine's words remind us that through the Paschal Mystery, Christ is saving us *from* something and he is also saving us *for* something. We need to be saved from the things that fill our lives with lies and empty promises. We must allow Christ to "empty" our lives of these things. Let's look more closely at some of the things the Paschal Mystery saves us from: namely, sin and the consequences of sin.

The source of Augustine's inspiration is symbolized in this painting. His mind is influenced by God's truth (*veritas*) and by compassion.

© 2009 Museum Associates / LACMA / Art Resource, NY

Saved from Sin and the Consequences of Sin

Human history, the stories you hear in songs and movies, and your own experiences testify that sin is the most fundamental thing we need to be saved from. We all sin, and every time we do, we damage our relationship with God. What's more, we are unable to keep from sinning on our own power. We need God's grace to save us from sin. The Paschal Mystery saves us from both Original Sin and personal sin.

The Paschal Mystery also saves us from the consequences of sin by providing the means for us to reconcile with God in this life and experience loving communion with him in Heaven. What are some of these consequences of sin?

- **Guilt and shame** Sin causes us to feel guilt and shame. Sometimes we don't recognize that we're feeling guilty or shameful; we just know we're feeling bad. At other times we completely deny or repress those feelings because we do not want to face them. Unless we deal directly with these feelings through our honest sorrow and repentance in the Sacrament of Penance and Reconciliation, they will do further damage to us. We will eventually feel depressed and unlovable, unable to experience the love and communion God has waiting for us.

- **Loneliness, despair, and the feeling of being unloved** It is natural to feel lonely at times, especially when we are separated from close friends and family members. But we can experience a deeper loneliness caused by the shame that is the result of sin. Shame causes us to doubt our own goodness; we forget that we are made in the image of God. We fall into despair and start to believe that no one could love us—neither God nor other people. We end up isolated, separated from God and from the people who would love us. We can feel this kind of loneliness and despair even in a crowd of friendly people.

- **Addictions and attachment to things** When we feel guilt and shame, when we feel lonely and unloved, we look for ways to ease these negative and painful feelings. One way many people try to do this is by using things that lead to a momentary high, such as alcohol,

venial sin
A less serious offense against the will of God that diminishes one's personal character and weakens but does not rupture one's relationship with God.

mortal sin
An action so contrary to the will of God that it results in complete separation from God and his grace. As a consequence of that separation, the person is condemned to eternal death. For a sin to be a mortal sin, three conditions must be met: the act must involve a grave matter, the person must have full knowledge of the evil of the act, and the person must give his or her full consent in committing the act.

drugs, or sex. Even television, gaming, or food can easily become the focus of obsessive behaviors or active addictions. Another way we try to ease the pain is by accumulating money and things, believing that possessions will fill the emptiness we feel. But all these things are dead ends. They do not deal with the real problem: our separation from God caused by Original Sin and our own personal sin.

- **Death** Saint Paul warned us, "For the wages of sin is death" (Romans 6:23). Death is the ultimate separation from God, the natural outcome of Original Sin and our personal sins. But for those who have been baptized, who live lives of faith, and who die free of mortal sin, physical death is just a passing over into new and eternal life because of the Paschal Mystery. For those who do not accept God's grace, however, physical death is the beginning of eternal separation from God, who is the source of all love and goodness.

What negative influences and impulses can you eliminate from your life, as Saint Augustine recommends, so that God can fill you with what is good?

Article 30: Saved for What?

Christ's Passion, death, Resurrection, and Ascension do not just save us from bad things. In fact, sometimes Christians focus too much on these things and can come across as very somber and unhappy people. When we study the Paschal Mystery, we must always keep in mind what we are saved for: a new and glorious life in loving communion with God and with one another.

The Paschal Mystery Saves Us for Eternal Life

So what does the Paschal Mystery save us for? Ultimately we are saved for eternal life in full communion with God in Heaven. But the process begins in this life, as we are also saved from sin and its effects. In many ways, the things we are saved for are the opposite of what we are saved from. Christ empties us of sin, shame, loneliness, despair, and unhealthy attachments so that he can fill us with his wonderful presence.

- **Forgiveness and healing** Our life with Christ is marked by the forgiveness of sins. The Gospels tell us that Jesus constantly taught about the importance of forgiveness. In fact, when some people came to him for physical healing, he first focused his attention on forgiving their sins. Christ's teaching and example are why the forgiveness of sins is so central to the sacramental life of the Church. In Baptism the mark of Original Sin is removed, and any personal sins we have committed are forgiven. The Eucharist wipes away **venial sins** and preserves us from future **mortal sins**. The Sacrament of Penance and Reconciliation frees us from all personal sins, both venial and mortal. Hopefully you will often know the joy and the freedom that come from being forgiven and from forgiving others.

- **Freedom** "For freedom Christ set us free; so stand firm and do not submit again to the yoke of slavery" (Galatians 5:1). In this passage, Saint Paul is not talking about being enslaved to other people. He is teaching us that through the Paschal Mystery, Christ set us free from all things that enslave us. We are freed from the guilt and shame of sin. We are freed from

© osari / istockphoto.com

despair and from feeling unlovable. We are freed from attachment to things, attachment that brings us false joy. We are freed from the fear of God's punishment and death. We are free to experience all the joy and love God wants us to have.

What things in your life keep you captive, keep you from experiencing a life full of forgiveness, freedom, joy, and love?

- **Joy** Saint Paul writes, "For the kingdom of God is not a matter of food and drink, but of righteousness, peace, and joy in the holy Spirit" (Romans 14:17). The great Christian author C. S. Lewis wrote a book titled

Beatific Vision
Directly encountering and seeing God in the glory of Heaven.

Surprised by Joy in which he tells of his journey from being an atheist to being a fully committed Christian. He tells how his whole life was a search for joy and explains that he never truly found it until he accepted the source of all joy: God. Lewis discovered what you hopefully know already—that our life in Christ is a joyful life because we have been freed from those things that separate us from God, and we are now filled with the love of God. That is why saints still have joy in situations that people would otherwise find painful and disheartening.

- **Loving communion** Saint Paul also explains, "The love of God has been poured out into our hearts through the holy Spirit that has been given to us" (Romans 5:5). Christ suffered, died, rose again, and ascended into Heaven so that our original holiness and justice that were lost through Adam's sin would be restored. We are no longer separated from God, one another, and creation by Original Sin. Baptism restores our ability to experience the full measure of God's love and friendship. In this earthly life, we experience God's love and friendship only in partial ways, although at times we may experience a glimpse of the **Beatific Vision** the saints enjoy in Heaven.

- **Eternal life** "Amen, I say to you, there is no one who has given up house or wife or brothers or parents or children for the sake of the kingdom of God who will not receive [back] an overabundant return in this present age and eternal life in the age to come" (Luke 18:29–30). Ultimately, the Passion, death, Resurrection, and Ascension of Christ save us for eternal life in Heaven. There we will enjoy the Beatific Vision; that is, we will be in full communion with the Holy Trinity and we will know God face-to-face. Words cannot describe what this will be like, but the Book of Revelation gives us a hint: "God's dwelling is with the human race. He will dwell with them and they will be his people and God himself will always be with them [as their God]. He will wipe every tear from their eyes, and there shall be no more death or mourning, wailing or pain, [for] the old order has passed away" (21:3–4).

We Already Share in Christ's Death and Resurrection

All salvation comes from Jesus Christ, the Head, through the Church, which is his Body. Our salvation depends on our faith in Christ and on the Church. Through Baptism we enter the Church and become participants in Christ's death and Resurrection. We are on our journey to salvation. In the waters of Baptism, we die to sin and are raised to new life in Christ. This means all our sins are forgiven by God—including Original Sin and our personal sins. Nothing remains to keep us from entering the Kingdom of Heaven. Nothing separates us from God. We are "a new creation," an adopted child of God, and we "share in the divine nature" (2 Corinthians 5:17, 2 Peter 1:4).

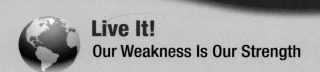

Live It!
Our Weakness Is Our Strength

"For I do not do what I want, but I do what I hate" (Romans 7:15). Saint Paul is describing the guilt we feel after doing something wrong. Afterward we ask, "Why did I do it?" Sometimes we make things worse by avoiding responsibility or even blaming others.

But Christ calls us to a higher path. We must admit our sin and examine our weakness. Ask yourself: "Did I do it because I'm lonely and want others to like me? Because I did not want to look scared? Because I feel empty inside?" Answering these questions can be painful because we must face the dark places in ourselves that we need to be saved from.

Our weakness in the face of temptation is what makes us reach out to God and rely on him alone. Reach out to God and rely on his grace instead of your own power. This is what makes us strong and able to resist temptation. Because Saint Paul knew this, he could say, "For when I am weak, then I am strong" (2 Corinthians 12:10).

sanctifying grace
The grace that heals our human nature wounded by sin and restores us to friendship with God by giving us a share in the divine life of the Trinity. It is a supernatural gift of God, infused into our souls by the Holy Spirit, that continues the work of making us holy.

Yet obstacles remain for us. Though the mark of Original Sin has been removed from our soul, its effects linger; we experience weakness of will, we are affected by illness and other frailties, and we are still tempted to sin. The inclination to sin is called concupiscence. And though we are a new creation, we will not experience the resurrection of the body until after our death. We live in a kind of in-between state, which some have called the "already but not yet" time. We are already citizens of the Kingdom of God, but we are not yet in a state of perfect grace.

As you can see, between our Baptism and our death, each of us is on a journey to become "perfect, just as your heavenly Father is perfect" (Matthew 5:48). Do not worry! We are not expected to achieve perfection on our own. To assist us on this journey, we receive the gift of **sanctifying grace** at Baptism. This grace enables us to practice the **theological virtues**: to have complete faith in God, to put all our hope in God, and to love God with all our strength. Sanctifying grace also helps us to follow the lead of the Holy Spirit in our lives by using his gifts. And this grace helps us to grow in goodness by living out the moral virtues. The Sacraments of the Church aid us on our journey toward Heaven, starting with Baptism.

Faith

God

Hope

Love

When you are strongly tempted to sin, what helps you to resist the temptation?

Article 31: Our Judgment by God

As a student you are used to being tested and judged. You have tests or assessments in all of your classes. You may have to be judged in order to qualify for a team or be cast in a play. So if the thought of being tested or judged does not excite you, that's not surprising. Being judged is not most people's idea of a good time. But let's keep in mind that the one judgment that really counts, the one that should be our ultimate concern, is our judgment by Christ at the end of our lives. God does not want us to fear this judgment, but he does call us to prepare for it with the utmost seriousness. Saint John of the Cross reassures us: "At the evening of life, you shall be examined in love."

Our Particular Judgment

The New Testament reveals that each of us will face two times of judgment: our **Particular Judgment** and the Final Judgment. Immediately after death each person undergoes a personal Particular Judgment by Christ. Our soul will be rewarded according to our faith and works. The Parable of the Rich Man and Lazarus (see Luke 16:19–31) and the words of Christ to the repentant thief (see 23:43) affirm this immediate judgment that determines our soul's ultimate destiny: Heaven or Hell.

So if the Particular Judgment is kind of like our life's final exam, what will we be judged on? Because the Gospel of John talks about eternal life more than the other three Gospels, let's consider what John's Gospel says about the requirements for inheriting eternal life:

theological virtues
The name for the God-given virtues of faith, hope, and love. These virtues enable us to know God as God and lead us to union with him in mind and heart.

Particular Judgment
The judgment that occurs immediately at the time of our death, when our immortal souls will be judged as worthy or unworthy of Heaven.

Primary Sources

Be a Worthy Sharer in Christ's Glory

In Dogmatic Constitution on the Church (Lumen Gentium, 1964), Vatican Council II described how we can work toward holiness in this life so that we can experience eternal happiness with the Holy Trinity in the next:

> The classes and duties of life are many, but holiness is one—that sanctity which is cultivated by all who are moved by the Spirit of God, and who obey the voice of the Father and worship God the Father in spirit and in truth. These people follow the poor Christ, the humble and cross-bearing Christ in order to be worthy of being sharers in His glory. Every person must walk unhesitatingly according to his own personal gifts and duties in the path of living faith, which arouses hope and works through charity. (41)

- Believe in the Son of Man, God's only Son (see 3:15–16).
- Obey Jesus (see 3:36).
- Hear Jesus and believe the One who sent him (see 5:24, 17:3).
- Eat Jesus' flesh and drink his blood (see 6:54).
- Don't be attached to the things of this world (see 12:25).

In addition to these things, we should also consider Jesus' description of the Last Judgment in Matthew 25:31–46. In this passage, Jesus says that those who will inherit Heaven are those who have fed the hungry, given drink to the thirsty, welcomed strangers, clothed the naked, cared for the ill, and visited those in prison.

The Final Judgment

Christ will return in his glory, and all the dead will be raised. We call this time the last day or the Final Judgment. Saint Paul tries to explain that moment in the First Letter to the Thessalonians:

> Indeed, we tell you this, on the word of the Lord, that we who are alive, who are left until the coming of the Lord, will surely not precede those who have fallen asleep. For the Lord himself, with a word of command, with the voice of an archangel and with the trumpet of God, will come down from heaven, and the dead in Christ will rise first. Then we who are alive, who are left, will be caught up together with them in the clouds to meet the Lord in the air. Thus we shall always be with the Lord. (4:15–17)

Jesus himself foretold of his coming again, as we learn in several Gospel passages, such as Mark 13:24–27: "Then they will see 'the Son of Man coming in the clouds' with great power and glory" (verse 26). This event is called the Second Coming or, to use a more Catholic term, Christ's Parousia. (*Parousia* is a Greek word meaning "arrival.") The Parousia will signal a final judgment of all humanity.

Matthew 25:31–46 is the clearest biblical teaching we have about the Final Judgment. This passage tells how

Jesus will gather all humanity together to face a final judgment. Acting as supreme judge, Christ will reveal the secret character of each person's heart. He will separate those who have followed his will by caring for others from those who did not follow his will because they lived only for themselves. Every person will be held accountable for his or her own deeds. Those who have followed the will of God and accepted his grace will be welcomed into his eternal, heavenly kingdom, which has been prepared for them from the beginning of the world. Those who have refused his grace and failed to serve Christ in needy and suffering people will be sent into eternal punishment.

Thus at the end of time, the Kingdom of God will come into its perfection. The Book of Revelation teaches us that at that time all creation will be transformed, and there will be "a new heaven and a new earth" (21:1). The just will reign

© Wallraf Richartz Museum / The Bridgeman Art Library

with God in Heaven for eternity, their soul united with their glorified, resurrected body. God will be all in all because the whole of creation will be in perfect communion with its creator.

This image of the Final Judgment is based on Matthew 25:31–46. What do you think the artist is trying to communicate about God's judgment?

Who Can Be Saved?

The Church has always taught that the Sacrament of Baptism is necessary for our salvation. Jesus himself says this in the Gospel of John: "Amen, amen, I say to you, no one can enter the kingdom of God without being born of water and Spirit" (3:5). Does this mean that people in non-Christian religions, who have been raised in them all their lives and have never heard the truth of Christ presented in a convincing way, will all go to Hell?

Such a statement would be contrary to God's mercy and love. That is why the *Catechism of the Catholic Church* teaches that "every man who is ignorant of the Gospel of Christ and of his Church, but seeks the truth and does the will of God in accordance with his understanding of it, can be saved. It may be supposed that such persons would have *desired Baptism explicitly* if they had known its necessity" (1260). This teaching is why you sometimes hear people say that non-Christians can be saved through the Baptism of desire.

When Will Christ Return?

Jesus Christ did not return for the Final Judgment during Paul's lifetime. Throughout the centuries that followed, the Church has pondered the question, When will Christ return again? And the answer has always been this: Only God knows the time. Human history could well go on for

Did You Know?

Children Who Die without Baptism

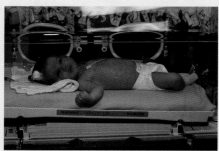

© Rick's Photography / Shutterstock.com

The death of a child is always a tragedy. As they grieve, parents and loved ones may also worry about what happens to a child who died before he or she was baptized. In the funeral rites for such children, the Church entrusts them to the mercy of God. This is entirely fitting, for Jesus himself said, "Let the children come to me; do not prevent them, for the kingdom of God belongs to such as these" (Mark 10:14).

The rate of infant mortality (death at birth or soon after) used to be much higher than it is today. For that reason, a baby was baptized as soon as possible. Today better medical care for both mother and baby has made infant deaths increasingly rare in the developed world. Thus Baptisms can be celebrated for infants within a few months of birth. Yet the Church does urgently call for infants to be baptized and welcomed into the family of God. The grace of Baptism begins a child's walk with God in her or his family of origin and in the family of the Church.

thousands or millions of years. Or Christ could return tomorrow. Some Christian leaders have tried to predict the time of the Second Coming, but Catholics have learned from the first Christians that every effort to do so misses the real point of this teaching—that we should follow God's will every day, because we do not know which day will be our last.

Christ does not want us to fear his judgment. He wants us to trust his love and his mercy and then to follow him as completely as we can. If we do this, we have nothing to fear. We do not save ourselves. It is only through the love, mercy, and power of the Holy Trinity that we are brought into eternal life. Saint Paul believed in this so strongly that he looked forward to his death. He wrote: "For to me life is Christ, and death is gain. If I go on living in the flesh, that means fruitful labor for me. . . . I am caught between the two. I long to depart this life and be with Christ, [for] that is far better" (Philippians 1:21–23).

> **If Christ returns tomorrow, are you ready? What can you start doing today to follow him more completely?**

Article 32: Where Do We Go after Death?

Most of us would rather not think too much about our own death. Yet every once in a while, because of an accident, a serious illness, or the death of someone close to us, we have to face the possibility of our own death. In these times, the thought that races through most people's minds is, "What will happen to me when I die?" To find an answer, many people turn to religious beliefs and faith.

It may surprise you to know that the Old Testament books rarely refer to an afterlife. In the Book of Ecclesiastes, we read: "The dead no longer know anything. There is no further recompense for them, because all memory of them is lost" (9:5). This passage suggests that a common view among many of Jesus' ancestors was that nothingness followed death. Nevertheless, we also find evidence that a concept of life after death did emerge among the Jewish people. We know this because two of the last Old Testament books to be written—a couple of centuries before the birth of Jesus—contain references to life after death (see 2 Maccabees 7:23, Daniel 12:1–3).

As Christians, however, we know what happens to us when we die, because the person who supplied us with the answers actually died and rose from the dead.

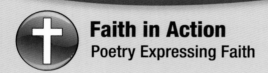

Faith in Action
Poetry Expressing Faith

© duncan1890 / istockphoto.com

Expressing faith through the arts has been the vocation of many people through the ages. One of the most famous poets who expressed his faith through his writings was Dante Alighieri (ca. 1265–1321), popularly known as Dante.

Dante was a native of Florence, Italy. His greatest work is called the *Divine Comedy*. In Dante's time, *comedy* did not mean something funny. It meant a work of art (a poem or play) with a happy ending. The opposite of comedy was tragedy—a work that explored the darker aspects of human life and perhaps taught a moral lesson as well.

In his great poem, Dante portrays himself as guided through "life after death": that is, Hell, Purgatory, and Heaven. The *Divine Comedy* is divided into three sections: *"Inferno"* ("Hell"), *"Purgatorio"* ("Purgatory"), and *"Paradiso"* ("Paradise"). Dante describes each in detail. He even assigns biblical people, mythical figures, and the famous people of his time (popes, rulers, military leaders) to various levels of Hell, Purgatory, or Heaven.

In his own life, Dante lived in political exile from Florence, and this separation gave him a perspective from which he could evaluate his society. The *Divine Comedy* is both an act of faith and a critique of Dante's social surroundings.

The poem begins on Good Friday and ends on Easter Sunday, when the literary persona of Dante is rewarded with a vision of God. He now understands that God is at work in everything and is "the Love that moves the sun and all the other stars" (*Paradiso*, Canto XXXIII, line 145).

After death our soul will be judged, and those who have remained faithful to God will be united with him in Heaven. Those who separated themselves from God in this life will be separated from him for all eternity in Hell. Believing in Jesus' promise that we shall rise to new life does not completely take away the sting of a loved one's death, but our faith does help us to understand that death is not an end but a new and glorious beginning.

Heaven

What exactly is **Heaven**? Neither the Bible nor Sacred Tradition gives us a definitive description of Heaven. What we do know is that in Heaven the relationship between God and humanity that was broken by Original Sin will be restored. In Heaven we will know the joy of being in perfect communion with the Holy Trinity, the relationship that God has intended for us from the beginning of time.

Think of a moment when you were with a group of good friends and you had just done something really great and exciting—maybe you won an important game or finished a retreat or a big service project. Everyone was content and joyful and excited. That experience is a little bit like what Heaven will be like, except in Heaven it won't be just a moment—it will last for all eternity. Saint Ignatius of Antioch (ca. 35–107) anticipated the joy of Heaven in a letter he wrote while traveling to his death: "It is better for me to die in behalf of Jesus Christ, than to reign over all the ends of the earth. . . . Allow me to obtain pure light: when I have gone there, I shall indeed be a man of God."

Even though we generally refer to Heaven as being "up" and Hell as being "down," they are not physical places as we experience time and space. Thus we can describe them only through metaphors and analogies. For example, when speaking of Heaven, Jesus used the metaphor of a mansion: "In my Father's house there are many dwelling places. If there were not, would I have told you that I am going to prepare a place for you?"

Heaven
A state of eternal life and union with God in which one experiences full happiness and the satisfaction of the deepest human longings.

(John 14:2). In addition, some of the most powerful descriptions of Heaven come from the Book of Revelation. Consider these examples:

> I heard a loud voice from the throne saying, "Behold, God's dwelling is with the human race. He will dwell with them and they will be his people and God himself will always be with them [as their God]. He will wipe every tear from their eyes, and there shall be no more death or mourning, wailing or pain, [for] the old order has passed away." (21:3–4)

The title of this painting is *Heaven and Hell*. How do you see the title reflected in the elements of the painting?

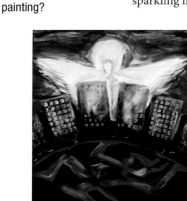

© Renphoto / istockphoto.com

> Then the angel showed me the river of life-giving water, sparkling like crystal, flowing from the throne of God and of the Lamb down the middle of its street. On either side of the river grew the tree of life that produces fruit twelve times a year, once each month; the leaves of the trees serve as medicine for the nations. Nothing accursed will be found there anymore. The throne of God and of the Lamb will be in it, and his servants will worship him. They will look upon his face, and his name will be on their foreheads. Night will be no more, nor will they need light from lamp or sun, for the Lord God shall give them light, and they shall reign forever and ever. (22:1–5)

Hell

Hell

The state of permanent separation from God, reserved for those who die in a state of mortal sin, that is, who freely and consciously choose to reject God to the very end of their lives.

Hell is the opposite of Heaven. It is the eternal punishment of separation from God, reserved for those who die in mortal sin without repenting and accepting God's merciful love. In describing the Final Judgment, Jesus said, "Depart from me, you accursed, into the eternal fire prepared for the devil and his angels" (Matthew 25:41). And the Book of Revelation says this: "Then Death and Hades were thrown into the pool of fire. (This pool of fire is the second death.) Anyone whose name was not found written in the book of life was thrown into the pool of fire" (20:14–15). Some scholars think the inspiration for describing Hell as a place of fire came from the garbage pit outside Jerusalem. The pit was often burning, full of things that no longer filled their purpose.

Popular images of Hell usually include burning pits and demons with pitchforks, who torture the unfortunate souls who end up there for eternity. Hell is indeed a painful reality. But the principal punishment isn't physical torture; it is the spiritual anguish of being separated from God. Think of Hell as the natural and logical consequence for a person who has already decided to separate herself or himself from God here on earth. Once on this journey, unless there is a change of heart, the person drifts farther and farther into sin and away from the One who is the source of all life and happiness. At death that separation becomes complete.

Pray It!

Praying for the Dead

Saint Cyril of Jerusalem (ca. 313–386) said, "We pray . . . for all who have fallen asleep before us, in the belief that it is a great benefit to [their] souls." Quite often on the night before a funeral, we take part in a rite called the Vigil for the Deceased to pray for the person who has died. The opening prayer of this rite acknowledges our pain in losing a loved one and celebrates the hope of eternal life:

Lord our God,
[Death reminds us of] our human condition
and the brevity of our lives on earth.
But for those who believe in your love
death is not the end,
nor does it destroy the bonds
that you forge in our lives.
We share the faith of your Son's disciples
and the hope of the children of God.
Bring the light of Christ's resurrection
to this time of testing and pain
as we pray for [the deceased] and for those who love him/her,
through Christ our Lord.
Amen.

(*Order of Christian Funerals,* 72)

Purgatory
A state of final purification or cleansing, which one may need to enter following death and before entering Heaven.

Purgatory

But the reality is that when most of us die, we are neither perfect saints nor perfect sinners. We believe in God and desire God's grace, yet different areas of our lives might need to be purged of selfishness and sin. All who die in God's grace and friendship, but who are not perfectly purified, undergo a purification in order to achieve the holiness necessary to enter into the full glory of God in Heaven. This state of final purification is called **Purgatory**.

Whether a soul is in need of Purgatory is something known to God alone. Souls in Purgatory are assured of entering Heaven once their purification is complete. This belief is part of the truth God has revealed in Sacred Tradition and in Sacred Scripture. In both the Old and New Testaments, we encounter references to the idea of purification after death. For example, in the Second Book of Maccabees, we read about our need to atone for the dead in order to free them from sin (see 12:46). In the First Letter to the Corinthians, Saint Paul speaks of a person's being saved through a purifying fire (see 3:15).

© Lisa F. Young / istockphoto.com

Catholics believe our prayers for the dead honor them and can aid in their final purification.

What questions did you have about Heaven, Hell, and Purgatory before this chapter? Do you understand Heaven, Hell, and Purgatory better now? In what ways?

Chapter Review

1. Name four things the Paschal Mystery saves us *from*, and then briefly describe them.

2. How would you describe the meaning of death for those who die in God's grace?

3. Name four things the Paschal Mystery saves us *for*, and then briefly describe them.

4. How do we already share in Christ's death and Resurrection?

5. Describe the difference between our Particular Judgment and the Final Judgment.

6. What is the Parousia?

7. What is the main difference between Heaven and Hell?

8. How would you describe Purgatory to someone who had never heard of it?

Unit
4

The Paschal Mystery and Your Life

The first three units of this book describe God's plan of salvation, which culminated in the Paschal Mystery. Now we will explore what the Paschal Mystery means for our lives. We are part of God's plan for salvation—not just as watchers, but as active participants.

God calls us to be holy people. What does it mean to be holy? Someone holy reveals God and shares in God's own life. A holy person is consecrated to God, as we are consecrated through Baptism, and is free from impurity. Being holy is not easy, but God helps us. As part of our baptismal call, we share in Christ's mission as priest, prophet, and king. In this unit, we will learn how we participate in God's work of salvation by living out these roles.

The Paschal Mystery also helps us to understand the role of suffering in our lives. Through the lens of the Paschal Mystery, we see that suffering and sacrifice, though difficult, are part of our salvation. Jesus' example shows us that accepting suffering to do the will of God takes courage and strength found only in God. We participate in Christ's saving work especially when we unite our suffering and sacrifice, great or small, to Christ's. We are not left alone to suffer. God is always with us. His gift of fortitude guides and strengthens us. And we know that suffering is not the end; we are bound for eternal life in Heaven.

By answering our call to holiness and uniting our suffering to Christ's sacrifice, we participate in the Paschal Mystery every day.

The enduring understandings and essential questions represent core concepts and questions that are explored throughout this unit. By studying the content of each chapter, you will gain a more complete understanding of the following:

Enduring Understandings

1. We are all called to holiness, which is a lifelong commitment and challenge.
2. Through Baptism we share in Jesus' mission as priest, prophet, and king.
3. When we unite our suffering to Christ's suffering, we are participating in God's saving work.
4. When viewed through the eyes of faith, suffering presents us with a unique opportunity to see and experience God's grace.

Essential Questions

1. How are we able to live out the call to holiness?
2. How do we share in Jesus' ministry and saving work?
3. Why are we called to accept suffering if it was not part of God's original plan for us?
4. How can suffering help us to grow in faith?

Chapter

9

Living as a Disciple

Introduction

Through the Paschal Mystery, God calls us and strengthens us to be active participants in his plan. This means he calls us to become perfect in our love for him, our love for other people, and our love for all creation. In other words, we are called to be holy people.

Through our Baptism, God gives us the grace to live out our call to holiness. But that doesn't mean we can be holy without trying. On the contrary, holiness requires effort on our part. We need to exercise spiritual and moral discipline because we are in a spiritual battle, fighting against our own conflicting inner desires and fighting against the pull of a world still affected by Satan's influence. But we are not alone. In this chapter, we will discover many gifts that God freely gives us to help us answer the call to holiness. As disciples of Jesus Christ, we turn to him for strength and guidance. He is the source of our salvation and our model for a holy life. We unite our lives to Christ's life by following his example. In particular, we are called to participate in Christ's threefold ministry of priest, prophet, and king. In this chapter, we will explore what life as a disciple of Christ means for us today.

Article 33: Our Call to Holiness

You are called to be holy. What do you think when you hear this? Does it seem like an impossible goal? Does holiness seem like something that should be expected of clergy and consecrated religious only? Does the idea conjure up images of people who are at church all the time, attending every event offered by your parish?

There is some truth in each of these, but also some misunderstanding. Yes, being holy is a lifelong commitment and challenge, but it is not an impossible goal. Clergy and consecrated religious should be examples of holiness—but so should every Christian. The Church does help us to live holy lives, but we are also called to bring our holiness into the world, to help our families, our schools, and our workplaces become holy. Don't let questions or doubts become an excuse to avoid your own call to be a holy person.

What Is Holiness?

Holiness is difficult to describe because it has many dimensions and meanings. Let's consider three of these dimensions to help you understand your own call to be holy.

First, something is holy because it somehow reveals God and shares in God's own life. In a general sense, therefore, all creation is holy. But in a particular sense, every human being is holy in a special way. Each of us is made in God's own image and likeness. So each of us reveals God and is in communion with God in a way no other part of creation is. Simply put, we are holy because we are made in the image of God.

Second, something is holy when it has been **consecrated** to God; that is, it has been solemnly designated or set aside for service to God. In the account of the Last Supper in the Gospel of John, we read that Jesus said, "I consecrate myself for them, so that they also may be consecrated in truth" (17:19). Jesus completely dedicated himself to his Father's purpose. In Baptism we too have been solemnly designated for service to God.

holiness
The state of being holy. This means to be set apart for God's service, to live a morally good life, to be a person of prayer, and to reveal God's love to the world through acts of loving service.

consecrate
To declare or set apart as sacred or to solemnly dedicate to God's service; to make holy.

We are holy because we have been consecrated to God through our Baptism. Christ now lives in us, and we share in his holiness.

Third, in the Bible something is holy because it is considered clean, free from anything that would make it impure. Thus the animals brought as sacrifices to God had to be healthy, strong, and free from blemish or physical defects. Similarly, we must be morally clean, free from the impurity of sin. We are holy because we have a clean heart and a clean conscience. We are holy when we are not burdened with unrepented sin and when we avoid immoral behavior that would give scandal to the Gospel of Jesus Christ.

So what does it mean to be holy? We could summarize it like this: We are holy from the moment of our conception because we are made in the image and likeness of

Live It!
Daily Schedule for a Holy Teenager

6:30	Rise and say morning prayers.
6:40	Shower, dress, and eat breakfast.
7:45	Go to school.
3:00	Attend extracurricular activities.
6:00	Eat dinner.
7:00	Do homework and chat online.
10:30	Say night prayers and go to bed.

Are you surprised by this schedule? Did you think it would include church meetings and prayer groups? Being a holy person is not so much about *what* you do, but rather *how* you do it. Prayer is an essential element, but this does not mean you have to sit alone and pray for hours. Short prayers before, during, and after daily activities are appropriate to a young person's life.

Besides prayer, living a holy life means many things. You can help a friend to study for a test. Be honest in school and in your relationships. Feed your body, mind, and soul with good things. Treat yourself and everyone around you as children of God. As Saint Teresa of Calcutta said, "You have to be holy where you are—wherever God has put you."

God. Our holiness is corrupted, however, because of Original Sin. Baptism restores our original holiness and consecrates us to God's service. As baptized people we perfect our holiness by avoiding sin and dedicating our lives to the service of others, following the example of Jesus.

Aids to Holiness

In the Sermon on the Mount, Jesus says, "So be perfect, just as your heavenly Father is perfect" (Matthew 5:48). Jesus isn't talking about being a perfect athlete or a perfect student or a perfect musician, of course. In the context of the Sermon on the Mount, he is clearly talking about perfection in living a life of holiness. This is not an easy task. The *Catechism of the Catholic Church (CCC)* says: "The way of perfection passes by the way of the Cross. There is no holiness without renunciation and spiritual battle"[1] (2015). Being holy means, among other things, having to say no to things other people are saying yes to. And it will be a struggle.

We are not without help, however. God provides us with many aids to guide us and strengthen us on our path to holiness. You have heard of these gifts, but it helps to be reminded of them. As you read the list that follows, consider how each of these gifts can help you to become holy.

Intellect and Free Will

Every human being is born with intellect and free will. Our intellect helps us to see and understand the natural order God has created. It helps us to weigh decisions and evaluate potential outcomes in order to make good moral choices. In turn, our free will allows us to act on those good choices, sometimes even if no one else does.

Grace

Grace is God's supernatural gift to help us respond to his love, to restore us to original holiness and justice, and to help us live holy lives. Through grace we participate in

grace
The free and undeserved gift that God gives us to empower us to respond to his call and to live as his adopted sons and daughters. Grace restores our loving communion with the Holy Trinity, lost through sin.

interiority
The practice of developing a life of self-reflection and self-examination to attend to our spiritual life and call to holiness.

the life of the Holy Trinity with God as our Father, Jesus as our brother, and the Holy Spirit as the one who lives within us and gives us strength and guidance.

Various kinds of grace assist us on our way to perfection. At Baptism we receive sanctifying grace, which gives us a share in the divine life, orients us toward God, and helps us to live in keeping with his call. Actual grace is God's intervention and support for us in the everyday moments of our lives. This type of grace is important for our continuing growth in holiness. Sacramental graces are the gifts specific to each of the Seven Sacraments. Special graces, also called charisms, are associated with one's state in life and are intended to build up the Body of Christ.

© Mika Heittola / Shutterstock.com

Taking time for self-reflection is an important tool for growing in holiness. When and where do you take time to reflect?

Self-Reflection

God has given us the ability—and the responsibility—to engage in self-reflection, sometimes called **interiority**. This gift encourages us to remove ourselves from the noise and distractions of everyday life. In the silence of our hearts, we can then look at the direction our lives are heading, examine the choices we've made, and listen for and follow the voice of our conscience.

The Church

The Church is certainly God's greatest gift to help us live a holy life. The Church's sacramental life unites us to Christ and provides us with the gifts and guidance of the Holy Spirit. As the Body of Christ, the members of the Church give strength, hope, and support to one another in our common goal of becoming holy people. The Church provides us with opportunities for education, prayer, community, and service to the world. Christ has given the Church the gift of holiness. As members of the Church, we share in that gift.

How Can You Answer God's Call?

You can answer God's call to become a holy person! Take time away from the rush and noise of the world to meet Jesus in the silence of your heart. Then go out into the world and let Christ's holiness shine through you to bring God's love to others. God has forgiven you your sins. Now let his forgiveness touch the hearts of others through you. Let your positive moral choices influence others to make the right choices. Let your acts of humble and loving service show others that they are not alone— they are loved by God. "Be perfect, just as your heavenly Father is perfect" (Matthew 5:48).

laity
All members of the Church with the exception of those who are ordained as bishops, priests, or deacons. The laity share in Christ's role as priest, prophet, and king, witnessing to God's love and power in the world.

> **How do you already answer God's call to holiness? What can you start to do today?**

Article 34: Our Call to Participate in Christ's Priestly, Prophetic, and Kingly Ministry

Would you be surprised to learn that you are called to serve others as priest, prophet, and king? In the *Dogmatic Constitution on the Church (Lumen Gentium, 1964)*, the Second Vatican Council describes the role of the **laity** in the Church by using the images of priest, prophet, and king. These titles, all biblical in origin, refer to offices in which people are established through anointing. These titles are given to Jesus Christ, the Anointed One, to describe his saving work in the world. But the bishops of the world teach us that these titles describe our Christian identity too, because we are called to participate in Christ's mission through our Baptism. The *Catechism* says: "Jesus Christ is the one whom the Father anointed with the Holy Spirit and established as priest, prophet, and king. The whole People of God participates in these three offices of Christ and bears the responsibilities for the mission and service that flow from them"[2] (783).

Still, you might say: "I'm not a priest, a prophet, or a king. How can these roles apply to me?" This is a good question. We are familiar with the role of priest, but prophet and king are not roles we hear about too often in our time. We will take a closer look at each of these titles in the next sections and explore what they mean for us.

Article 35: Participating in Christ's Priestly Ministry

When you think of a priest, you are probably most familiar with parish priests and ordained chaplains, men whom God calls to the vocation of ministerial priesthood. The Sacrament of Holy Orders confers a sacred power on men called to ministerial priesthood. They represent Christ to the community, serving the faithful in the name and person of Christ.

But did you know that all of us are called to participate in a different kind of priestly ministry by virtue of our Baptism? This kind of priesthood is called the common priesthood of the faithful. Through the graces of Baptism and Confirmation, we are united with Christ in serving the world, fulfilling our call to holiness. Just as the ordained priest offers the sacrifice of the Mass to God, we too can offer our daily work, studies, family life, and leisure activities—if they are done in the Holy Spirit—as a spiritual sacrifice to the Father. We can

Primary Sources

The Priesthood of the Laity

This excerpt from *Dogmatic Constitution on the Church (Lumen Gentium, 1964)* shows how the bishops of the Second Vatican Council called on the laity to fully live out their priestly mission:

All the disciples of Christ, persevering in prayer and praising God, should present themselves as a living sacrifice, holy and pleasing to God. . . . They live in the ordinary circumstances of family and social life. . . . They are called there by God . . . [so that] they may work for the sanctification of the world from within . . . [and] make Christ known to others, especially by the testimony of a life resplendent in faith, hope and charity. (10, 31)

also take time to develop our prayer life, offer prayers for the needs of others, and participate regularly in the Sacraments.

Christ's Priestly Ministry

At the time of Jesus' earthly life, a Jewish priest had one principal role: to lead the worship in the Temple. This primarily meant offering animal sacrifice. The priests were divided into twenty-four divisions, and each division worked in the Temple one week out of every twenty-four. When they were not on duty in the Temple, priests served as judges, teachers of the Torah (Scripture), and scribes (copying texts or writing up legal documents).

By now you know that Jesus was not a priest in this sense. As far as we know, he never offered animal sacrifice in the Temple. Yet the author of the Letter to the Hebrews repeatedly calls Jesus a high priest, because Jesus perfectly fulfilled the sacrificial role of the Jewish priests. The Jewish priests offered animal sacrifice for the forgiveness of the people's sins, but their sacrifice had to be repeated regularly. Jesus offered a single sacrifice for the forgiveness of all sin, and his one sacrifice was sufficient for all people for all time.

As our high priest, Jesus' sacrifice makes possible our salvation. We follow his example of prayer, sacrifice, and worship.

His sacrifice was his own body and blood. So Jesus, our great high priest, teaches us how to pray, sacrifice, and worship.

Jesus has a lot to teach us about prayer. He was committed to personal prayer, often rising early in the morning to pray alone (see Mark 1:35). He was also committed to communal prayer, joining others in local synagogues on the Sabbath to read Scripture and pray together (see Luke 4:16). His prayer included prayers of praise and thanksgiving (see 10:21) and also prayers of petition and

© Roy Pedersen / Shutterstock

supplication (see John, chapter 17). (These prayer forms will be explained in chapter 11, "The Fundamentals of Prayer.") Jesus taught us that our prayer should be humble and honest (see Luke 18:10–14). It is not too emphatic to say that Jesus despised prayer that was showy and hypocritical.

Jesus also taught us how to sacrifice. Suffering and sacrifice will be covered more completely in chapter 10, "Suffering and the Paschal Mystery." For now, simply remember how Jesus dedicated his life for the good of others and called his disciples to do the same. In doing so, he sacrificed human comforts and luxuries: "Foxes have dens and birds of the sky have nests, but the Son of Man has nowhere to rest his head" (Matthew 8:20). He made it clear that he expected his disciples to do the same: "Whoever wishes to come after me must deny himself, take up his cross, and follow me" (16:24).

By teaching us how to dedicate our lives as sacrifice, Jesus also gave us guidance about how to worship. Worship isn't something we do for an hour on Sunday only, before we go back to our regular lives. Nor is it something we do passively, sitting in a congregation. When we go through our daily routine, we are called to bring the Holy Spirit into every task, every moment of leisure, and every interaction with others. In this way, we can actively make every moment of our lives into an opportunity for holiness. The *Catechism* states: "In the celebration of the Eucharist these [moments] may most fittingly be offered to the Father along with the body of the Lord. And so, worshipping everywhere by their holy actions, the laity consecrate the world itself to God, everywhere offering worship by the holiness of their lives"[3] (901).

An Example of Priestly Ministry: Saint Benedict the Moor (1524–1589)

Benedict Manasseri was the child of Ethiopian parents who were taken as slaves to Italy in the early 1500s. His parents had converted to Christianity before his birth. From childhood Benedict worked alongside his family for meager wages, showing his willingness to sacrifice by giving what he had earned to those with greater needs and to the sick. He never learned to read and write.

When Benedict was twenty-one years old, he was publicly insulted because of his darker skin color. Some Franciscans noticed this and invited him to join their order. Benedict agreed and showed his devotion to a

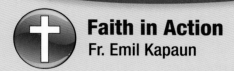

Faith in Action
Fr. Emil Kapaun

U.S. Army Courtesy Photo

The Medal of Honor is the highest military honor given by the United States of America. It is awarded for personal acts of valor above and beyond the call of duty and is usually presented by the president.

In April 2013, Fr. Emil Kapaun (1916–1951), a U.S. Army chaplain, was awarded the Medal of Honor posthumously (after death) for his courage and valor in caring for his fellow prisoners of war during the Korean War. To supplement their meager rations, he foraged in nearby fields and brought back rice and potatoes. He found pots and boiled clean water to cleanse his comrades' wounds. At night he would sneak from hut to hut to lead prisoners in prayer, administer the Sacraments, and offer these words: "God bless you." In the midst of despair, Father Kapaun brought hope.

When Father Kapaun's health failed, the guards took him to a dirty and unheated "hospital," a place of certain death. President Barack Obama told the rest of Father Kapaun's story at the medal ceremony:

And yet, even then, his faith held firm. "I'm going to where I've always wanted to go," he told his brothers. "And when I get up there, I'll say a prayer for all of you." And then, as he was taken away, he did something remarkable—he blessed the guards. "Forgive them," he said, "for they know not what they do." Two days later, in that house of death, Father Kapaun breathed his last breath. His body was taken away, his grave unmarked, his remains unrecovered to this day.

In 1993, Father Kapaun was declared "Servant of God," the first step on the road to sainthood.

Mateus Hidalgo

private life of prayer by becoming a **hermit**. But God had other things in store for him. Benedict was asked to join a Franciscan community, where he started as cook. But he was promoted, despite his own reluctance, to be the community superior, even though he was illiterate and was a lay brother (meaning he had not taken vows). Later in his life, he chose to return to his position as a humble cook for the community, but his reputation as a healer and spiritual counselor led many of the faithful to visit him through the end of his life. Saint Benedict the Moor is a wonderful example of full participation in the priestly ministry of Christ. His feast day is April 4, and he is the patron saint of African Americans and of missions in Africa.

How You Can Participate

Because we have been united to Christ through Baptism and Confirmation, all laypeople share in Christ's priesthood. God calls us to exhibit the graces we receive in the Sacraments in all the dimensions of our lives: with our family, with our school and work, with our church family, with our community and nation. In doing this, we fulfill our call to holiness.

Perhaps ideas on how you can participate in Christ's priestly ministry are already coming to you. Here are some foundations for making his priestly ministry an integral part of your life:

- **Take time to pray daily.** Your prayer time doesn't have to be long or heavily structured. Just take a few minutes of private, quiet time every morning to recognize the presence of God and ask his help to make the day a holy day. You could read a few verses from Sacred Scripture, reflect on a short spiritual reading, or say a prayer that focuses your mind and heart on your call to be a disciple.

- **Attend Mass every week.** Jesus attended the synagogue every Sabbath because reflecting on Scripture and worshipping his Father with other faithful believers is important for strengthening faith. The same is even truer for us. At every Eucharist, we receive Christ through his Word and through his sacred Body and Blood. This is not just a nice thing to do; it is central to our faith because the Eucharist is the foundation of Christian life. Attending Sunday Eucharist, a precept of the Church and a requirement of the Third Commandment, is such an important obligation that if we miss Sunday Mass through our own fault, we commit a mortal sin and must receive absolution in the Sacrament of Penance and Reconciliation before receiving Communion again.

- **Participate regularly in the Sacrament of Penance and Reconciliation**. You already know the importance of regular participation in the Eucharist. It is just as important to celebrate the one other Sacrament that we are called to participate in regularly throughout our lives: Penance and Reconciliation. Through our repentance and God's forgiveness of our sins, we grow in holiness and prevent sin from leading us away from God.

- **Sacrifice time and comfort to share God's love**. We sometimes find that sacrificing time and comfort is not an easy thing to do. We live in a culture that in many ways tells us we deserve whatever we want, whenever we want it. But that attitude will not ultimately make us happy or holy people. When we make sacrifices to help others—whether those sacrifices involve our time, our money, or our comforts—we will know the true peace and joy that come from uniting ourselves with Jesus Christ.

You may be able to think of many other ways to participate in the priestly ministry of Christ. Devote yourself

hermit
A person who lives a solitary life in order to commit himself or herself more fully to prayer and in some cases to be completely free for service to others.

to becoming a person of prayer and sacrifice, and your holiness will grow, day by day.

> **How do you already participate in Christ's priestly ministry? What can you start doing today?**

Article 36: Participating in Christ's Prophetic Ministry

Do you know someone who likes to speak out for important causes, someone who encourages other people to do the right thing? Maybe you know someone who is committed to a matter of justice like ending abortion or providing affordable housing for all people. Maybe you have seen people who share with others their faith in Jesus. Maybe *you* are a person like this.

Christians who do these things are participating in the prophetic ministry of Christ. As prophets we witness to Christ through our words and actions. We witness to him to every group and in every circumstance we find ourselves. As laypeople we witness in places where clergy are often not found: work, politics, sports, family, and so on. Our witnessing is also called *evangelization*, a word that literally means "to announce good news." By calling for greater love and justice in the world, we are sharing God's desire that all people know his love and justice.

Christ's Prophetic Ministry

Jesus perfectly fulfills the role of prophet. A prophet gives voice to God's Word, proclaiming it to those who need to hear it. Because Jesus is God, his every word and action during his earthly life proclaimed the divine Word to the world. The Gospel of John tells us that Jesus made very clear that his words and actions revealed his Father: "If you know me, then you will also know my Father. . . . Whoever has seen me has seen the Father" (14:7,9). Ultimately, Jesus' prophetic ministry has one primary focus: to lead people to the one, true God.

Given that all of Jesus' words and actions are pro-phetic, we can find it difficult or maybe even misleading to identify the fulfillment of his prophetic ministry with a particular teaching or action. However, we can see how his words and actions were consistent with the tradition of the prophets of the Old Testament. Here is a chart of some of those parallels:

Old Testament Prophetic Themes	Parallels in Jesus' Words and Actions
The prophets called the people to reject idolatry, the worship of false gods (for example, see Isaiah 10:10–11, Jeremiah 32:34–35, Hosea 13:2).	Jesus called for an end to the worship of money and possessions, a form of idolatry (for example, see Matthew 6:19–24, Luke 12:13–34).
The prophets called for the care of the most vulnerable in society, particularly the widow, the orphan, and the stranger (for example, see Isaiah 1:17, Jeremiah 7:6, Zechariah 7:10).	Jesus healed the most vulnerable people of his time. He said that in the Final Judgment we would be judged by our service to the most vulnerable people (see Matthew 25:31–46).
The prophets called for an end to societal injustice. They called for the powerful to protect the poor and vulnerable (for example, see Micah 3:1–4, Amos 2:6–8).	Jesus called on the wealthy to practice justice by sharing their wealth with those in need (see Luke 12:33, 14:7–14, 16:19–31). He said true leaders were the servants of others (see Mark 10:43–44).
The prophets called for an end to hypocritical worship of God (for example, see Isaiah 1:11–15, Jeremiah 6:20). They called people to worship God with a pure heart.	Jesus disrupted the moneychangers and sale of sacrificial animals in the Temple, a hypocritical practice (see Matthew 21:12–13). He called for authentic worship (see John 4:23–24).

However, we must always keep in mind that although Jesus followed in the tradition of the Old Testament prophets, he is the Second Divine Person of the Trinity—far more than just a prophet.

An Example of Prophetic Ministry: Saint Martin de Porres (1579–1639)

Martin de Porres was born in Lima, Peru, the illegitimate son of a Spanish nobleman and a freed black slave. He grew up in poverty, and at age fifteen he joined a Domin-ican friary as a servant. Although the friary had a rule against blacks becoming full members, they swayed the

Gianni Dagli Orti / The Art Archive at Art Resource, NY

rule when they saw Martin's great piety. He eventually became a full brother and was placed in charge of the infirmary.

Saint Martin had a great commitment to justice for slaves and for the poor. He established an orphanage and a children's hospital for the poor. He collected alms, which he used to feed hundreds of poor people regularly. Miraculous cures were attributed to him; he sometimes brought healing with just a cup of water. When an epidemic struck the city, Martin tirelessly cared for those taken ill, risking his own life and health. Saint Martin de Porres is an inspirational example of full participation in the prophetic ministry of Christ. His feast day is November 3. He is the patron saint of people of mixed race and also the patron saint of social justice.

Pray It!

Fellow Prophets, Pray for Us

As Christians we are all called to be prophets. It can be a difficult job (see Matthew 5:12), and we cannot do it without relying on God's help. We can get some guidance by looking to the example and the support of the prophets who have gone before us. Let us call on them to pray for us.

Lord,

We need your help. As we go into the world to care for those who are oppressed and needy, to speak out against injustice, and to proclaim the Good News, grant us the gifts of the prophets before us.

Give us courage. Oscar Romero, pray for us.

Give us humility. Saint Teresa of Calcutta, pray for us.

Give us strength. Saint Thomas More, pray for us.

Give us trust. Jeremiah, pray for us.

Give us goodness. Pope Saint John XXIII, pray for us.

Give us concern for the poor. Dorothy Day, pray for us.

Give us selflessness. Saint Maximilian Kolbe, pray for us.

All you holy people, pray for us! Amen.

How You Can Participate

The world needs the prophetic ministry of Christ in many ways. Be open to whatever way God is calling you to be a prophet. There are big things and small things you can do, and all of them are important. Here are just some things young people have already done:

- **Speak out for the unborn.** Join the fight against abortion by letting others know that abortion, the murder of an unborn child, is a sin against God's Law. Help others to understand that it also causes emotional and spiritual harm to the mother and those connected to her and to her unborn child, especially her other children and the father of the child. Write to your legislators, asking them to vote to limit and end abortions and to work to reduce the poverty that makes some pregnant women feel that abortion is their only option. Collect baby items and hold fundraisers for groups that help to support pregnant women who are in need.

- **Speak out against violence in your community.** Jesus warned us against the evil of violence and revenge. Teens like you have organized campaigns against bullying and other violence in schools, communities, and social groups. Violence flourishes when people ignore it or turn the other way. Make sure the leaders in your community know about the presence of violence in families, schools, or neighborhoods.

By organizing and participating in works of service, we share in Christ's prophetic and kingly ministry. How do you serve others?

- **Organize to help people in need.** Jesus spent much of his time helping those in his community who were in greatest need. Young people have helped others to experience God's love by organizing food drives, clothing drives, hunger walks, Christmas collections, and many other efforts. You can

© Ariel Skelley / Blend Images / Corbis

catechesis, catechists
Catechesis is the process by which Christians of all ages are taught the essentials of Christian doctrine and are formed as disciples of Christ. Catechists instruct others in Christian doctrine and for entry into the Church.

volunteer to help build homes for people who need them or to clean up after a natural disaster. You don't have to be rich or skilled in some trade. You just have to be willing and committed to helping in whatever way you can.

- **Share your love of God with others.** So many people in our world need to hear that God loves them. Young people have shared the love of God by becoming **catechists** of younger children and volunteering on retreat teams and mission trips. You can talk about God with others when using social networks. You can watch for friends and classmates who are troubled or hurting and offer a kind heart and a listening ear.

These are only some of the many ways you can participate in the prophetic ministry of Christ. Pray for the courage and commitment to live your faith publicly and for the willingness to share your faith with others.

How do you already participate in Christ's prophetic ministry? What can you start doing today?

Article 37: Participating in Christ's Kingly Ministry

That man is rightly called a king who makes his own body an obedient subject and, by governing himself with suitable rigor, refuses to let his passions breed rebellion in his soul, for he exercises a kind of royal power over himself.

—Saint Ambrose (ca. 340–397)

Only one who devotes himself to a cause with his whole strength and soul can be a true master. For this reason mastery demands all of a person.

—Albert Einstein

If a king is honestly for the rights of the poor,
    his throne stands firm forever.

—Proverbs 29:14

You have royal blood in you, for you are an adopted son or daughter of God. What does it mean to be kingly—to be a leader from God's point of view? The preceding quotations suggest that it starts with the self-discipline to consistently choose what is good and right. It continues with our commitment to follow God's call with all our strength and soul for our entire lives. And it means always serving those most in need.

Christ's Kingly Ministry

What do you think of when you imagine a king? Christ's kingly ministry is unlike most earthly versions of kings and rulers that probably come to mind. To understand his kingship, we need to clear our mind of images of kings and leaders who seek their own fame or their own gain. In answer to Pilate's question, "Are you the king of the Jews?" Jesus answered, "My kingdom does not belong to this world" (John 18:33,36). Jesus did not deny that he is a king, but he would not allow Pilate or any earthly authority to define what his kingship means.

In chapter 3, "The Path to Restoration," we established that the Kingdom of God is the fulfillment of the promise, or covenant, that God made with David: "Your house and your kingdom are firm forever before me; your throne shall be firmly established forever" (2 Samuel 7:16). Jesus Christ is the King of Kings whose Kingdom will last forever. But we have to carefully examine Jesus' words and actions in the Gospels to understand what his kingship truly is. Three key passages will help to make this clearer.

The first passage describes Jesus' temptation in the desert at the beginning of his ministry. In the second temptation, the Devil showed Jesus all the kingdoms of the world and promised to make him the ruler of all of them if Jesus would only worship the Devil. Jesus quoted Deuteronomy 6:13 in his response: "You shall worship the Lord, your God, / and him alone shall you serve" (Luke 4:8). Jesus refused to become a ruler through any compromise with evil. Jesus' leadership was completely rooted in obedience and service to God. It was a leadership that is fully committed to doing the right thing. Jesus knew that a good end can never be achieved through sinful means. Even when his commitment to doing the right thing resulted in personal suffering and apparent failure, Jesus never veered from the holy and moral path.

The second passage tells us how two of Jesus' Apostles asked if they could sit in places of honor, at his left side and his right side, when he came into his glory. Their request understandably upset the other Apostles. Jesus used this as a teaching moment: "You know that those who are recognized as rulers over the Gentiles lord it over them, and their great ones make their authority over them felt. But it shall not be so among you. Rather, whoever wishes to be great among you will be your servant; whoever wishes to be first among you will be the slave of all" (Mark 10:42–44). Jesus was referring to the Romans' use of power and entitlement in order to maintain control over the population. Jesus made clear that this is not true leadership. In the Kingdom of God, those who lead are first the servants of others. Jesus led by his example of love and concern for others.

© Stefan Holm / Shutterstock.com

The third passage is a parable Jesus told about a king or a prominent man who throws a banquet but whose invited guests refuse to attend. And so the king tells his servants, "Go out, therefore, into the main roads and invite to the feast whomever you find" (Matthew 22:9). In Luke's version of this parable, the king says, "Go out quickly into the streets and alleys of the town and bring in here the poor and the crippled, the blind and the lame" (14:21). Jesus was teaching that leaders in the Kingdom of God will not focus just on people who can return favors. Rather, leaders in the Kingdom of God will reach out to all people, especially the people whom worldly leaders overlook.

These passages help us to understand Jesus' example of kingly ministry. It is leadership that is based in a moral life committed to personal holiness. It is leadership that does not focus on our own fame or gain but instead on being of service to others. It is leadership that reaches out to all people, especially the people overlooked by others. You are called to share in Jesus' kingly ministry, to be this kind of leader for the Kingdom of God.

An Example of Kingly Ministry: Saint Katharine Drexel (1858–1955)

Katharine Drexel was born in Philadelphia, the daughter of a wealthy banker. As a young woman, she was moved by the needs of African Americans and Native Americans. She used her family's wealth to build schools for their education. She even visited Pope Leo XIII to ask for missionaries to staff her schools. In response, he suggested that she become a missionary herself. So in 1891 she founded the Sisters of the Blessed Sacrament for Indians and Colored People and became the order's first mother superior.

From the age of thirty-three until her death at age ninety-six, Katharine dedicated her personal wealth to her ministry. She herself lived a life of voluntary poverty, even wearing the same pair of shoes every day for ten years. Her crowning achievement was the building of Xavier University in New Orleans in 1915. Xavier University was the first college in the country to be built for African Americans. At the time of Katherine's death, more than five hundred sisters were teaching in sixty-three schools. For all these reasons, Saint Katharine Drexel is an inspirational example of participation in the kingly ministry of Christ. She was canonized by Pope John Paul II in 2000, only the second recognized American-born saint. Her feast day is March 3.

© ASSOCIATED PRESS

How You Can Participate

You may have noticed that the characteristics of Jesus Christ's threefold ministry of priest, prophet, and king overlap to some degree. These three ministerial roles do not have sharp distinctions. They are three ways to describe the same reality: what it means to be a disciple of Christ. So some of the ways already mentioned for participating in Christ's priestly and prophetic ministry can also be ways for you to participate in his kingly ministry. The important focus in Christ's kingly ministry is the attitude we bring to our words and actions.

- **Be outstanding in your personal morality.** You must be committed to living a morally pure life. Avoid sin and temptation. Participate frequently in the Sacrament of the Eucharist and the Sacrament of Penance

Did You Know?

The Meaning of *Disciple*

© Shots Studio / Shutterstock

The word *disciple* has deep meaning. We usually think of this word as meaning "follower," but it means much more than that. At its Greek root, it means "a pupil of a teacher or an apprentice to a master craftsman." The Latin word *discipulus* means "a learner" or "a student." Yet being a disciple involves more than learning facts from a book, a teacher, or a computer screen. It involves learning from God. The prophet Isaiah wrote about his relationship with God in terms that involve being a disciple as follows:

> Morning after morning
>> he wakens my ear to hear as disciples do.
>> (Isaiah 50:4)

Being a disciple involves listening to God, being willing to hear his Word, and being determined to carry it out in one's life. As Jesus said, "When fully trained, every disciple will be like his teacher" (Luke 6:40).

The goal of discipleship is to become like Jesus.

and Reconciliation to strengthen yourself with God's graces. Do not succumb to the temptation of trying to achieve a good result if it means lying, cheating, intentionally hurting someone, denying your faith, or taking any other moral shortcut.

- **Find work or service that in some way helps others.** Commit to making a difference in the world. Ask God to lead you to wherever you are needed—and then be ready to go there. It may take some time to find a service opportunity that really fits, so be willing to try different things.

- **Be humble.** Being a holy leader will have its own spiritual rewards, but these will not come if your primary reason for volunteering is to call attention to yourself or to seek some kind of personal gain. Always examine your motives as a leader. Be humble and acknowledge that your gifts for leadership and service come from God and are to be used for the good of others.

- **Have a servant attitude.** Let your first thought be, "How can I help?" Don't get caught up in wanting to do only the "important" tasks. Remember that Jesus washed the feet of his disciples to show that no act of service is unimportant. A holy leader does whatever is needed to help build the Kingdom of God.

Each Christian is called to participate in Christ's kingship in some way, to be a holy leader. Our world desperately needs such leaders, but it is not an easy path to take. Often the world models leadership that is built on moral compromise, personal ego, or financial gain. Frequently ask the Holy Spirit to strengthen you and guide you in being a servant leader in your home, school, and community.

> **How do you already participate in Christ's kingly ministry? What can you start doing today?**

Chapter Review

1. What are three ways to describe what it means to be holy?

2. What is one aid to holiness that God has given us? Describe how this aid helps us to be holy.

3. How can we say that Jesus Christ has a priestly ministry even though he was never a Jewish priest?

4. What are two ways you can participate in Christ's priestly ministry?

5. How does Jesus' prophetic ministry follow the tradition of the Old Testament prophets?

6. What are two ways you can participate in Christ's prophetic ministry?

7. What are some of the characteristics of Jesus' kingly ministry?

8. What are two ways you can participate in Christ's kingly ministry?

Chapter 10

Suffering and the Paschal Mystery

Introduction

Suffering is an essential part of the Paschal Mystery. By now you know that the Paschal Mystery refers to the Passion (suffering), death, Resurrection, and Ascension of Jesus Christ. Note that suffering is the first stage of the Paschal Mystery, a reality we often do not want to face. But as we will see in this chapter, we cannot escape suffering. It is an inevitable part of being human. We all experience both physical pain and emotional pain. We even experience spiritual suffering, the pain of separation from full communion with God.

Throughout history Christians have participated in the Paschal Mystery by accepting suffering and sacrifice as inevitable parts of life and as necessary consequences that come with following Christ. But there is good news. The Gospel proclaims that suffering is not our ultimate end; it is only a step on our path toward Heaven and eternal life. What's more, when we join our suffering to Christ's suffering, we participate in God's saving work. This chapter introduces this spiritual reality, which you will encounter again and again throughout your life.

Article 38: Making Sense of Suffering

We want life to make sense and to be fair, so we sometimes struggle with the reality of suffering. It does not seem rational to us that God—who is all good—would allow suffering to exist. Furthermore it seems so unfair that "good" people are just as prone to suffering as "bad" people. The Book of Job, in the Old Testament, is essentially a debate over this very issue. Job was a good man who had some bad things happen to him. His friends thought Job must be guilty of some kind of sin, so they kept arguing that things would get better if he would just admit his sin. But Job maintained his innocence and demanded an audience with God to plead his case.

Where do you see suffering in the world today? In the story of Job, we learn that suffering is a mystery we cannot fully understand because we do not see things from God's perspective.

After many chapters Job got his wish. God appeared before him and proceeded to overwhelm him with questions about the mysteries of the universe that no human being could answer. At the end Job responded to God: "I know that you can do all things, / and that no purpose of yours can be hindered . . . / I have spoken but did not understand; / things too marvelous for me, which I did not know" (42:2–3).

What does Job's response mean? He was saying that as human beings we are limited in what we can know and understand in God's great plan of salvation. Suffering is a mystery we can never fully understand, because we simply do not see things from God's perspective. This does not mean, however, that the mystery of suffering is completely incomprehensible. When we apply what we know about the history of salvation and the Paschal Mystery, we can begin to comprehend a part of this mystery.

© Musee Bonnat, Bayonne, France / Lauros / Giraudon / The Bridgeman Art Library International

Keys to Understanding Suffering

One key to understanding suffering is the fact that it is due to Original Sin. Because of Adam and Eve's Fall, experiences that previously would not have caused human beings pain and suffering—symbolized by pain during childbirth and the hard labor required to raise food (see Genesis 3:16–19)—now *do* cause pain and suffering. Suffering was not a part of God's original plan for us. To save us from meaningless suffering and death, the Father sent his only begotten Son into the world. By assuming a human nature, Jesus made our suffering his own: "He took away our infirmities / and bore our diseases" (Matthew 8:17).

Another key to understanding suffering lies in knowing that suffering and sacrifice are the pathway to redemption and salvation. Sacrifice is simply suffering that we freely accept. You may have heard the saying "No

Pray It!

Trust in God

We must have one thing to make it through times of suffering: trust in God. Like Job, when we are lost and in the shadow of death, we must place our trust in God, knowing that he is with us in our pain and confusion.

Dear heavenly Father,
Life has been challenging for me lately.
The path before me is dark and uncertain.
I feel alone, even though I have people who care for me.
I feel anxious and afraid, even though Jesus tells us not to be.
I feel like I'm walking "through a dark valley" (Psalm 23:4)
that has no end.
But I choose to place my trust in you,
believing that you love me and want the best for me.
I will trust you to guide me in the right path
even though I'm not sure right now what it is.
I will trust that you are with me
even though I do not feel your presence at this moment.
And I will trust that this dark time will pass
because you have given us the promise of eternal life.

pain, no gain." In one way, this reflects a deep spiritual truth: God can and will transform suffering and sacrifice into healing and new life. The animal sacrifices of the Chosen People recognized this spiritual truth. But those sacrifices were imperfect and insufficient. It is only through Christ's perfect sacrifice of himself that death was destroyed and the doors to Heaven were opened, restoring the possibility of our full communion with God for all eternity.

Following Christ's example we too must accept suffering and make sacrifices as we work out our salvation. Jesus himself tells us that we need to do this: "You will be hated by all because of my name, but whoever endures to the end will be saved. . . . Whoever does not take up his cross and follow after me is not worthy of me" (Matthew 10:22,38; for more on persecution, suffering, and discipleship, read all of Matthew, chapter 10). Uniting our personal sufferings and sacrifices with Christ's is part of our priestly ministry as Christians. We do this not only because of our hope and faith in our eternal reward in Heaven but also to make up in some small way for the hurt and harm caused by our own personal sins.

Practical Examples of Everyday Sacrifice

Perhaps you might be saying, "I don't understand when and where I would possibly accept suffering as part of my life as a disciple." Consider these practical examples:

- You choose to spend time with a sick classmate or family member instead of attending a fun activity with friends.

- You choose to sacrifice personal popularity because you would feel pressured to participate in immoral activities.

- You prayerfully connect your experiences of illness and pain with the sufferings of Christ and accept them without becoming bitter and resentful.

- You willingly donate money and time to people in need, instead of spending it on yourself.
- You sacrifice time and comfort to use less energy, conserve and recycle natural resources, and protect the environment.
- You make your faith known publicly, even when it leads to ridicule and sarcastic comments, or worse.
- You make the choice to remain a virgin until you are married, even if it means sacrificing short-term pleasure and relationships.

Such sacrifices might seem to be impossible—no one could do all these things. But Christians make these sacrifices every day and accept the suffering that comes with them. Not only have they discovered that the Holy Spirit provides the strength they need, but they have also discovered, paradoxically, that their lives are more meaningful and more joyful than before.

Suffering in the Bible

The question of suffering is a theme that runs throughout the books of the Bible. The passages in the following chart offer just a few examples of how doing God's will helped someone to find meaning in suffering. Read through some of these examples. You will also notice that those who suffer in these passages are supported and strengthened by God.

Passage	Theme
Job, chapters 1, 6, 11, 40, 42	The Book of Job is a long debate about why we suffer. The chapters selected will give you a taste of the argument.
2 Maccabees 6:18–31	A Jewish martyr accepted death by torture rather than deny his faith.
Isaiah 52:13–53:12	The Suffering Servant gave his life as an offering for sin.
Matthew, chapter 10	Jesus warned his disciples that they would be persecuted and would need to sacrifice if they followed him.
John 15:18–16:15	Jesus promised his disciples that even though they would be persecuted, he would send the Holy Spirit to guide and strengthen them.

Passage	Theme
2 Corinthians 1:3–11	Saint Paul shared his conviction that God is with us and that he encourages us in our afflictions and sufferings.
1 Peter 3:13– 4:6	The author reminds us to be willing to suffer for what is right, just as Christ suffered.

Accepting suffering can make life more meaningful and joyful. Have you found this to be true? How?

Article 39: Is Accepting Suffering a Sign of Weakness?

By this point in your life, you probably know firsthand that our most common reaction to suffering is to try to avoid it. In fact, many people would consider the willingness to sacrifice time, money, and worldly success to be foolish, a sign of personal weakness. This reaction isn't

Did You Know?

The Sacrifice of Martyrdom

© Zvonimir Atletic / Shutterstock.com

The word *martyr* comes from a Greek word meaning "witness." By their willingness to die for the truth of faith, martyrs witness to the presence of God in the world and to the hope of eternal life. The first martyr was Saint Stephen (d. ca. 34), and his witness is described in the New Testament, in Acts of the Apostles, chapter 7. Today martyrs are still witnessing to their faith throughout the world.

Martyrs also witness to the great gift of human life. To give up this precious gift requires the greatest love. Jesus himself speaks of this gift of love in the Gospel of John: "No one has greater love than this, to lay down one's life for one's friends" (15:13). A true martyr does not seek death for its own sake, or for the fame it might bring, or even for the reward that is promised in Heaven. A true martyr accepts death as the price of "living the truth in love" (Ephesians 4:15).

a new phenomenon; even the early Christians struggled with it. In his First Letter to the Corinthians, Saint Paul addresses the accusation that Christians are foolish to believe that salvation comes through Christ's suffering on the cross:

> The message of the cross is foolishness to those who are perishing, but to us who are being saved it is the power of God.
> . . . For the foolishness of God is wiser than human wisdom, and the weakness of God is stronger than human strength.
> . . . God chose the lowly and despised of the world, those who count for nothing, to reduce to nothing those who are something. (1:18,25,28)

The Example of Jesus

The example of Jesus shows us that the willingness to accept suffering takes a great deal of courage and strength. We see this most clearly in Jesus' last days. He could have avoided his torturous death if he had chosen to. He prayed to his Father to allow him to avoid this suffering if possible. Yet in the end, Jesus accepted the necessity of doing his Father's will with courage and strength. All four Gospels testify to Jesus' struggle and his ultimate acceptance of the Father's will.

Jesus' Passion and death are not the only times he demonstrated the strength and courage required for sacrificial love. He taught it in his Parable of the Prodigal Son and his Parable of the Lost Sheep. He taught it in his sayings about forgiveness and love of enemies. He demonstrated it by embracing a life of poverty and simplicity. He asked others to exercise moral courage by challenging wealthy and powerful people to give away their wealth and serve those in need.

Read the Parable of the Prodigal Son (Luke 15:11–32). How is the forgiving Father in this parable a sign of sacrificial love?

Brooklyn Museum of Art, New York, USA / Bridgeman Images

Deep down, every human heart knows that it is only through courage and sacrifice that we can truly achieve something worthwhile. But we must add one more thing. **We must sacrifice for the right thing: to build the Kingdom of God.** Some people make tremendous sacrifices to achieve personal fame and fortune. But when they have achieved their success, they still feel like they are missing something. And they are! They are missing the love and joy that come from letting Christ live in our

Faith in Action
Saint Joan of Arc

© CSLD/Shutterstock.com

Saint Joan of Arc (1412–1431) was born in a small village in France. When she was a young girl, Saint Michael the Archangel, Saint Catherine of Alexandria (ca. 282–305), and Saint Margaret the Virgin (d. 304) spoke to her. They told her that she had been chosen to drive the English out of France and to bring the heir to the throne (the dauphin) to Reims to be crowned king.

At that time France was devastated by what historians now call the Hundred Years' War. British raids had left the fields of France barren and the people poor and hungry. In the midst of this chaos, seventeen-year-old Joan managed to meet the dauphin and offer her help. Joan was placed at the head of the French army, and after several military successes, she led the dauphin, Charles VII, into Reims.

Eventually Joan was captured by the English and tried for heresy. She confounded the court with her simple yet profound understanding of her faith. But, after refusing to retract her statement that God and the saints had commanded her actions, she was sentenced to be burned at the stake. She was nineteen years old.

After her death the Church opened a retrial and, on July 7, 1456, declared that Joan was an innocent woman and a martyr. The Church found that the original trial had been unfair, illegal, and politically motivated.

In listening to God and to the saints, Saint Joan, like Jesus, was obedient to death. Her feast day is May 30, the anniversary of her entrance into Heaven. Joan of Arc is the patron saint of soldiers and of France.

heart, from joining our lives to his life, from participating in his mission to bring God's love to others. This love and joy requires a sacrifice that people simply cannot understand without God's help—it seems foolish. This is why we have to act as God's hands and voice, to show by our lives the wisdom of the cross.

The Example of Saint Damien of Molokai

Fr. Damien de Veuster (1840–1889) is today known as Saint Damien of Molokai, the "apostle to the lepers." Saint Damien's life was living proof that the willingness to endure suffering for the sake of following Christ is not a sign of weakness. Born in Belgium, he became a missionary priest who ministered in the Hawaiian Islands. He later volunteered to minister to the leper colony on the island of Molokai, an assignment no one wanted for fear of contracting the disease. When Father Damien arrived, the colony was a wretched place. He acted as pastor, counselor, builder, and undertaker. Conditions in the colony improved immensely.

Primary Sources

"Press On, Young People!"

Pope Francis was elected Pope just before Holy Week in 2013. In his first Good Friday address as Pope, he reminded us that Jesus' sacrifice on the cross is God's answer to evil and suffering in the world:

> One word should suffice this evening, that is the Cross itself. The Cross is the word through which God has responded to evil in the world. Sometimes it may seem as though God does not react to evil, as if he is silent. And yet, God has spoken, he has replied, and his answer is the Cross of Christ: a word which is love, mercy, forgiveness. It also reveals a judgment, namely that God, in judging us, loves us. Let us remember this: God judges us by loving us. If I embrace his love then I am saved, if I refuse it, then I am condemned, not by him, but my own self, because God never condemns, he only loves and saves. ("Address of Pope Francis, Way of the Cross at the Colosseum")

© Dan Leeth / Alamy

Saint Damien served God despite many hardships. He knew that serving others and building God's Kingdom was worth sacrificing his comfort and health.

After twelve years on the island, Father Damien himself was diagnosed with **leprosy**. At first he was upset, wondering why God had not protected him from the disease. He worried about who would continue his work after his death. But he soon accepted his condition, describing himself as the "happiest missionary in the world." Help poured in from around the globe, and four new missionaries arrived at the island. Father Damien died in 1889 and was canonized on October 11, 2009, by Pope Benedict XVI. Saint Damien is the patron saint of lepers and of people with HIV/AIDS.

How can Jesus' example of accepting the Father's will in the face of suffering help you through a difficult time?

Article 40: Finding Strength in Times of Suffering

Knowing that sacrifice and suffering have an important role in God's plan of salvation does not automatically make it easier for us to accept and endure suffering in our own lives. To go from knowing this truth to living this truth is a spiritual journey we must all make. You may know from personal experience that this journey is not an easy one. You would even be right to ask, "How can any person be expected to willingly sacrifice his or her own comfort and safety, even if it is for a greater good?"

The answer is that such sacrifice is impossible for us if we are acting on our own. We can do it only by being empowered by our loving and compassionate God, who desires to help us on this journey. Let's look at three key spiritual truths that have encouraged and strengthened Christians through the centuries in their journey to accept the sacrifices necessary for the Kingdom of God and to unite their sufferings with the suffering of Christ.

Keys to Finding Hope and Strength

We Do Not Suffer Alone

First, and perhaps most important, we have the gift of knowing that we do not suffer alone. For some people the anguish caused by pain and suffering is multiplied by the feeling that they are alone in their pain. But Christians have the comfort of knowing that God is with us in our suffering. He is not aloof or removed from our suffering. Our God and Savior suffered greatly in his Passion, and he has promised to be with us in everything we experience. The Gospel of John gives us Jesus' final speech, when he offered us these words of comfort: "I will not leave you orphans; I will come to you. In a little while the world will no longer see me, but you will see me, because I live and you will live. On that day you will realize that I am in my Father and you are in me and I in you" (14:18–20). He continued: "As the Father loves me, so I also love you. Remain in my love. If you keep my commandments, you will remain in my love, just as I have kept my Father's commandments and remain in his love" (15:9–10).

leprosy
An infectious disease resulting in numbness, paralysis, and physical deformities; also called Hansen's disease. Effective treatment was not developed until the late 1930s.

Live It!
Suffering Binds Us Together

In September 2008, Hurricane Ike battered Texas. Many houses were damaged or even totally destroyed. People lost electricity for weeks. But in the wake of the destruction, neighbors helped one another by sharing chainsaws, generators, ice coolers, and so on.

We often strive to be strong and independent, and in some ways those are good qualities. But if you were totally self-sufficient, why would you need anyone? Why would you need God? When we suffer, God wants us to support one another. Asking for other people's support not only helps us, but it also allows the helpers to live out their Christian mission. Similarly, when other people ask us for assistance and support, we have an opportunity to live out our Christian mission. Helping and supporting one another during times of suffering helps to bind us together as the Body of Christ. What support can you offer to a friend, classmate, teacher, or family member today? What support do you need from others today?

fortitude

Also called strength or courage, the virtue that enables one to maintain sound moral judgment and behavior in the face of difficulties and challenges; one of the four Cardinal Virtues.

virtue

A habitual and firm disposition to do good.

One of the primary ways we experience God's caring presence is through the Church. In his familiar analogy of the Body of Christ, Paul says, "If [one] part suffers, all the parts suffer with it" (1 Corinthians 12:26). Christians come to one another's aid in times of suffering. We spend time with the sick, and we support the brokenhearted. We help those who have experienced disaster, and we provide for those who are going through financial difficulties. None of this means that the support of the Church will make everything right or that your hardship will just disappear. But if you are part of an active faith community, you will find people to support you. Just be sure to make your needs known.

We Receive Courage through the Holy Spirit

The gift of **fortitude**, or courage, is a second key to finding hope and strength in times of suffering. Fortitude is one of the Seven Gifts of the Holy Spirit that we receive through Baptism and that are strengthened at our Confirmation. You have only to ask for fortitude when you need it, so ask often. Even the great Saint Paul speaks about his need for courage: "After we had suffered and been insolently treated, as you know, in Philippi, we drew courage through our God to speak to you the gospel of God with much struggle" (1 Thessalonians 2:2).

Fortitude is also a human **virtue** we must cultivate in our lives. It is one of the four Cardinal Virtues—prudence, justice, fortitude, and temperance—that are pivotal or essential for full Christian living. These virtues guide our actions in accordance with reason and faith so that we become persons of good moral character. They help us to control our passions so that we don't act impulsively or react immorally. So even though courage is a gift, it is also a virtue that grows through education, deliberate choices, and perseverance. God's grace will then purify and strengthen our courage. In this way, courage becomes more and more a natural response when we are faced with fearful and painful situations.

Suffering Is Not the End of the Story

A final key to hope and strength is in knowing that suffering is not the end of the story. We know that the Paschal Mystery ends with Christ's Resurrection and Ascension into Heaven. The Paschal Mystery is God's promise that we too shall experience resurrection and eternal life with God in Heaven if we are faithful in following Christ. We must look beyond our suffering to the joy and peace of Heaven, which will be ours for all eternity.

Keys to Hope and Strength
- Trust God is with you
- Suffering is not the end of the story
- Ask for fortitude

The Example of Saint Kateri Tekakwitha

Saint Kateri Tekakwitha (1656–1680) was born in present-day Auriesville, New York, to a Christian Algonquin mother and a non-Christian Mohawk chief. When she was four years old, smallpox killed her parents and left her disfigured and partially blind. In later childhood, Kateri met Jesuit missionaries, and through their influence she was baptized into the Church in 1676.

Kateri's new life made it difficult for her to remain in her village. The other members of her tribe resented her new way of life as a follower of Christ, so they persecuted her. Kateri eventually left her village and settled in a Christian village 200 miles away, near Montreal. Having made a vow not to marry, she dedicated her life to praying and fasting, teaching others about Christ, and serving those in need.

Kateri trusted God to care for all her needs and believed that he would be her source of strength when she faced hardship and suffering. Speaking of the poverty she might face because of the life she had chosen, she said: "I am not my own; I have given myself to Jesus. He must be my only love. The state of helpless poverty that may befall me if I do not marry does not frighten me. . . . If I should

ST KATERI TEKAKWITHA

© Bill Wittman / www.wpwittman.com

become sick and unable to work, then I shall be like the Lord on the cross. He will have mercy on me and help me, I am sure." Kateri died at age twenty-four. She is the first Native American saint. We celebrate her feast day on July 14.

> **Do you find it difficult to trust God to care for all your needs, as Saint Kateri Tekakwitha did? Explain.**

Article 41: The Promise of the Paschal Mystery in Times of Suffering

This chapter does not intend to minimize the sacrifice and suffering many people experience. In fact, we have a responsibility to help wherever and however we can to lessen and eliminate suffering. Much suffering in the world is the result of human violence and injustice, and we must challenge these sins just as Jesus did. But just as he did not eliminate suffering on earth, neither can we hope to eliminate it. We accept that suffering is a part of every human life and that sacrifice is a part of every Christian's life, trusting that in the end God will make all things right. This is the promise of the Paschal Mystery, a promise you can bet your life on.

> **In the end God will make all things right. How can this truth help you the next time you experience suffering or difficulty?**

Chapter Review

1. How does God's response to Job help us to understand suffering?

2. What is the deep spiritual truth about suffering and sacrifice that disciples of Christ accept?

3. Describe three biblical passages that address the topic of suffering.

4. How does the example of Jesus Christ show us that the willingness to accept sacrifice and suffering is not foolish or a sign of weakness?

5. What are three keys that help us to develop the hope and strength necessary to accept sacrifice and unite our suffering with the Passion of Christ?

6. What is the gift of fortitude?

Unit 5
Prayer and the Paschal Mystery

The unity of our Christian faith shows itself in the natural connections between the truths revealed by God and our practice of the faith. This course started with an overview of God's great plan of salvation that began at Creation and is leading to the Final Judgment. The heart of this plan is the Paschal Mystery: the Passion, death, Resurrection, and Ascension of Jesus Christ. As disciples of Jesus Christ, we are called to unite our own lives to his and to participate in his priestly, prophetic, and kingly ministry.

In this final unit, we will take it one step farther. How do we join our efforts to Christ's saving work? How do we move from the theory of Christianity to the practice of Christian living? How do we move from knowing about God to knowing God, to developing an intimate relationship with the Father, the Son, and the Holy Spirit? The answers to these questions lie in the unity of faith that connects the Paschal Mystery to prayer. We can think of prayer as simply a way of conversing with God. Whether we pray to ask God for help, to thank him for a blessing, or simply to praise him as our Creator, we become more open to his love and his saving plan for us.

Every Eucharist makes the Paschal Mystery real and immediate for us. We particularly enter into the Paschal Mystery during the Easter Triduum—Holy Thursday, Good Friday, and the Easter Vigil. During the Easter Triduum, we prayerfully commemorate the Last Supper, Jesus' Passion and Crucifixion, and his glorious Resurrection.

The enduring understandings and essential questions represent core concepts and questions that are explored throughout this unit. By studying the content of each chapter, you will gain a more complete understanding of the following:

Enduring Understandings

1. We are all called to prayer as a way to grow in holiness and communion with God.
2. Developing a consistent and regular prayer life involves confronting various obstacles and challenges.
3. In the Church's liturgy, especially the liturgies of the Triduum, we enter into the mysteries of Jesus' suffering, death, and Resurrection more deeply.

Essential Questions

1. Why is prayer important in the life of a disciple?
2. How should we respond to difficulties and obstacles in prayer?
3. How does the Church's liturgy, especially the Sacred Triduum, draw us into the events of the Paschal Mystery?

Chapter
11

The Fundamentals of Prayer

Introduction

Through prayer God is continually calling every human being into relationship. Salvation history can be thought of as the unfolding of a relationship of prayer: God calls us into full communion with him, and we call out to God in search of his love and truth.

We begin this chapter by considering what prayer is and why we pray. Simply put, prayer is a conversation with God. When we regularly talk with God in prayer, we deepen our relationship with him, open up fully to his will and love, and become more loving in all our other relationships. We will look at the five basic forms of prayer: blessing, petition, intercession, thanksgiving, and praise. We will also look at three ways in which we can express prayer: vocal prayer, meditation, and contemplation.

Do you find it difficult to develop a consistent and regular habit of personal prayer? If so, be assured that you are not alone. Anyone can face obstacles that make it difficult to pray, sometimes for a day, sometimes for a longer stretch of time. We will look at common misunderstandings and difficulties that make it hard for us to pray—and discuss ways to overcome these difficulties so we can continue to grow in our relationship with God through prayer.

Article 42: Why We Pray

If you made a list of ways to develop good friendships, what would you include? Many people would include points like these:

- making time for your friends
- talking about things that are important, such as hopes and dreams
- doing things together, or just hanging out
- listening to your friends
- seeking reconciliation and forgiveness when a conflict has damaged a friendship

These and other ways to make and keep strong friendships also apply to another important relationship—the deep, personal relationship we develop with God through prayer.

Prayer Defined

When you were young, you learned to talk by imitating others. Sounds and words gradually became yours, and you gradually learned to string them into phrases and then sentences to express thoughts. We often follow a similar process when we learn to pray. The family should be the first place we learn to pray. You probably first learned to talk to God using prayers you were taught. These memorized prayers helped you to express a child's faith. As you have grown older, you have most likely expanded the ways in which you pray. Maybe you now use your own words in prayer to express who you are, what you think, how you feel, and what you need. But prayer is more than talking to God. We must also spend time in silence to hear God's voice in our lives.

Words are an important part of **prayer**. But just as relationships are more than words, so prayer is also more than words. A classic definition of *prayer* says that "'prayer is the raising of one's mind and heart to God or the requesting of good things from God' (Saint John Damascene, *De fide orth.* 3, 24: J. P. Migne, ed., Patrologia

prayer
Lifting up of one's mind and heart to God or the requesting of good things from him. The five basic forms of prayer are blessing, praise, petition, thanksgiving, and intercession. In prayer we communicate with God in a relationship of love.

Graeca [Paris, 1857–1866] 94, 1089C)" (*Catechism of the Catholic Church* [*CCC*], 2590). Prayer involves your mind and heart. It includes insight and affection, just like a good friendship does. Sometimes when you pray, you might experience insight, like a bright light bulb turning on in your head. More often, when you regularly raise your mind to God in prayer, your intellect is shaped so gradually and gently that you notice the change only over time—much like you come to appreciate, years later, the way a good friend or teacher has influenced your thinking.

Prayer is also a matter of the heart. An important aspect of prayer is the willingness to open up fully to God. He knows our real self and, knowing everything about us, loves us fully and freely. We may or may not love ourselves fully, but because of God's freely given love, we always have the ability and opportunity to bring our whole self to God in prayer. God loves us. He wants to save us from sin and help us to grow in virtue.

Primary Sources

Being Prayerful Means More Than Saying Prayers

Saint John Chrysostom (347–407), a Doctor of the Church, was a great preacher and theologian in the eastern part of the Roman Empire. Br. David Steindl-Rast is a modern theologian and member of the Benedictine order. These two men were born nearly sixteen hundred years apart, but they both spent time as hermits and developed deep insights into prayer. In these passages, they remind us that we don't need memorized prayers or a quiet corner to pray. We can talk with God anytime, anywhere, during any activity:

It is possible to offer fervent prayer even while walking in public or strolling alone, or seated in your shop . . . while buying or selling . . . or even while cooking. (Saint John Chrysostom)

If prayer is simply communication with God, it can go on continually . . . There is no reason why we should not be able to communicate with God in and through everything we do. (Br. David Steindl-Rast, OSB)

The more we learn to love ourselves as God has created us, the more we have to offer to others and God. Prayer can be self-reflection in the loving presence of God, enabling us to give fully of ourselves in our relationships with God and others. When we allow our hearts to open in friendship to God, we will find ourselves experiencing God's love in many different ways. When this happens, we experience the power of prayer to heal us and to help us become more loving in all our relationships.

Everyone Is Called to Prayer

When you really want to get to know someone, you may find that it's easy to get caught up in worrying about saying the right words and doing the right things. You can probably think of a time when you tried to impress someone else, but you ended up neither getting to know the person nor feeling like yourself. Hopefully you have learned that the best person to be when you are making friends is yourself.

The same is true in prayer. It is far less about the right words and techniques and far more about being who God made you to be: a person who desires to be in relationship with the One who called you into existence. Everyone is called to prayer. The desire for God is built into all people; prayer is a response to God, who first and tirelessly calls everyone to encounter him. Prayer is like picking up the phone to call a friend and finding your friend already on the line, having called you first. In prayer God reveals himself to you, and you learn about yourself. This reciprocal call between God and humankind has been going on throughout salvation history. Prayer is the central way God has revealed himself to humankind and shown us who we are.

The Church offers us many opportunities to pray and to learn

"I say to you, if two of you agree on earth about anything for which they are to pray, it shall be granted to them by my heavenly Father. For where two or three are gathered together in my name, there am I in the midst of them" (Matthew 18:19–20).

© Christopher Futcher / istockphoto.com

about prayer. We are invited to pray regularly through daily prayers, the Liturgy of the Hours, the Sunday Eucharist, and the feasts of the liturgical year. Many parishes have prayer groups, and prayer is a regular part of parish committee meetings and activities. Use these opportunities to make prayer a regular part of your life as you seek to grow in holiness and in communion with God.

What is one thing you can start doing to make time for regular prayer?

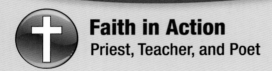

Faith in Action
Priest, Teacher, and Poet

© Associated Sulpicians of the United States Archives, Associated Archives at St. Mary's Seminary & University

The life of Fr. John Banister Tabb reminds us that a prayerful life is one in which our gifts—whatever they are, great or small—are offered to God. Father Tabb was born in 1845 to one of the wealthiest families in Virginia. Like many young men of his generation, he volunteered to fight in the Civil War. He became a blockade runner for the Confederacy but was captured in the last year of the war. Upon his release from the Union prison, he found himself penniless, but he was able to secure a teaching position at Saint Paul's Episcopal School in Baltimore. He was befriended by an Episcopal priest who later entered the Catholic Church, and John himself converted to Catholicism in 1872.

John began studying for the priesthood a few years later, and his seminary asked him to teach English to other seminarians. Ordained in 1884, he continued to teach English at the seminary until shortly before his death in 1909. Always plagued by poor eyesight, he was completely blind by the end of his life.

Father Tabb considered himself first of all a teacher, and he is remembered today for a grammar book he wrote, called *Bone Rules, or Skeleton of English Grammar*. His book dedication reads, "To my Pupils, active and passive; perfect and imperfect; past, present, and future, by their loving Father Tabb." He was especially known for his sensitive poetry, which was widely published in the popular magazines of the day. In 1936, the Tabb Monument in Amelia County, Virginia, was dedicated to his memory. It is maintained as a state park by the Commonwealth of Virginia.

Article 43: The Forms of Prayer

Friendships can be based on many things, and you would probably agree that different friends bring out different aspects of your personality. Although each friendship brings out a part of you, you probably aren't comfortable sharing everything about yourself with everyone.

blessing
A prayer asking God to care for a particular person, place, or activity.

The really wonderful thing about prayer is that it is *the* relationship in which you can share all of yourself and know you are loved. No part of you is out of range of the Holy Spirit. God wants to be in relationship with you in every aspect of your life—in all your concerns, gifts, faults, and feelings. The Holy Spirit instructs the Church in the life of prayer, inspiring new expressions of the same basic prayer forms: blessing (and adoration), petition, intercession, thanksgiving, and praise. These five different forms of prayer connect to different times and situations in your life. Let's look more closely at each of these prayer forms.

Blessing and Adoration

A **blessing** is a two-step form of prayer. First God gives us a gift, and then we respond with joy and gratitude. If you have ever watched the loving exchange between a parent and an infant, you have glimpsed the basic rhythm of blessing. The parent, who provides for the baby's every need, pours care and devotion over the child. The infant, rejoicing in a love that it can barely fathom, coos and squeals with delight. Like a baby's delight, our prayers of blessing in response to God's many gifts ascend to the Father through Christ, in the Holy Spirit.

"Blessed is he who comes in the name of the Lord. Hosanna in the highest" is an example of a blessing we pray at Mass. "I will bless the Lord at all times; / his praise shall be always in my mouth" is a blessing from the Psalms (34:2). Just remember that it is because God first blesses us that the human heart can in return bless the One who is the source of every blessing.

Adoration is closely related to blessing. When we adore God, we acknowledge that we are creatures before

People have things blessed that are an important part of their lives. We thank God for these things and pray that his power and love will protect them.

© HENRY ROMERO / Reuters / Landov

the One who created us. Adoration, which is reserved for God alone (see Exodus 20:2–7), can take the form of joyful song (see Psalm 95:1) or respectful, humbled silence.

In some blessings, you or someone else actually invokes God's power and care for another person, place, thing, or undertaking. The gesture or touch that often accompanies these blessings symbolizes the bestowal of God's grace on the receiver. In Numbers 6:22–27, we read that God instructed Aaron to bless the Israelites. The blessing at the end of the Mass, the familiar Irish blessing, and the blessing of animals on the Feast of Saint Francis are other examples of this kind of blessing.

Petition

A **petition** is a prayer form that asks God for something we need. At some level most of us know this. We make petitions, the most common form of prayer, dozens of times a day without even realizing it. "Help me pass this test!" "Give me a break, Lord!" "God, forgive me!" "Lord, tell me what to say!" Petition is prayer's most common form because it is the most spontaneous. It arises naturally from the depths of our heart, where we are aware of our relationship with God, where we know we depend on our Creator. In this prayer form, which is also called supplication, we ask, beseech, plead, invoke, cry out, even struggle in prayer.

Perhaps you know how difficult it is to have an honest conversation with a friend when you've had an argument. This uneasiness often spills over into other relationships, making them uncomfortable as well. Jesus knew this. In the Sermon on the Mount, he tells us to be reconciled with others before we pray (see Matthew 5:22–24). Therefore the first movement of petition is always asking forgiveness: acknowledging our shortcomings and turning back to God. The *Kyrie eleison* ("Lord have mercy, Christ have mercy, Lord have mercy"),

which is said at the Mass, is an example of this call to forgiveness as a prerequisite to prayer.

Even when things are going great with our relationships, we can find it awkward to ask for things. Jesus had something to say about that too. Right after he taught his disciples the Lord's Prayer, he told two parables about prayer that he summarized by saying, "Ask and you will receive; seek and you will find; knock, and the door will be opened to you" (Luke 11:9). Pray with confidence and perseverance, he says, and the Father will give you all you need, and the Holy Spirit above all. One example of perseverance is a novena, a prayer for a particular intention. These devotions, which span nine consecutive days or nine weeks, are based on the number of days Mary and the Apostles waited for the coming of the Holy Spirit, from the Ascension to Pentecost.

adoration
The prayerful acknowledgment that God is God and Creator of all that is.

petition
A prayer form in which one asks God for help and forgiveness.

intercession
A prayer on behalf of another person or group.

Intercession

"Put in a good word for me!" In the ordinary circumstances of life, you might speak a supportive word on behalf of a friend to a possible employer, a secret crush, a teacher, or a coach. **Intercession** is a form of prayer in which you do something very similar. You ask God's help for another person. A prayer of intercession is similar to a prayer of petition, except that intercession prays on behalf of another, whereas a petition usually asks God for something on your own behalf.

Intercessory prayer has great power. When we offer a prayer of intercession, we join our love for another person with God's love for the person we are praying for. If you have ever played with a magnifying glass on a sunny day, you know you can intensify a ray of sunlight by passing it through the glass. Intercessory prayer works in a similar way. You allow your heart to become like a magnifying glass, channeling God's love in a way that will forever change you and the person you are praying for.

Just as putting in a good word for a friend comes quite naturally, it is easy to pray for those who are closest to you. Intercession invites you to broaden your circle

thanksgiving
A prayer of gratitude for the gift of life and the gifts of life. Thanksgiving characterizes the prayer of the Church which, in celebrating the Eucharist, offers perfect thanks to the Father through, with, and in Christ, in the unity of the Holy Spirit.

of concern, to see yourself as part of something much greater. In prayers that reach out on behalf of Church and world leaders, and on behalf of the lonely, sick, and forgotten people throughout the world, every baptized person can work for the coming of the Kingdom. These more expansive prayers are also the basis for the prayers of intercession during Mass (also called the Prayer of the Faithful).

But what about Jesus' command to pray for our enemies and those who persecute us (see Matthew 5:43–44)? These can be the hardest prayers to offer with a sincere heart. When we stretch ourselves to pray for someone we are in conflict with, or for someone who has hurt us, we affirm our belief that no person or concern is outside the love and care of God.

Thanksgiving

In a prayer of **thanksgiving**, we remember that we are creatures and that God is our Creator. The more we pray in thanksgiving, the more we grow in awareness that all we have comes to us as a gift from God's abundant love. The Greek word *eucharist* means "thanksgiving." Early Christians prayed with a grateful spirit in the "breaking of bread" (see Acts of the Apostles 2:42–47). At the Mass, Catholics join with Christ in this prayer of thanksgiving and offer back to the Father all he has accomplished in Christ. Many people offer their personal prayers with the prayer of the Church by spending the quiet moments after the Communion Rite in thanksgiving.

Saint Paul tells us the real test of a grateful heart is this: "In all circumstances give thanks" (1 Thessalonians 5:18). This may sound a little phony to you, but Paul isn't telling you to put on a false front. What he means is that you can have confidence that God is loving you even in the middle of difficulties—even when you can't see the purpose for your suffering, even when no end is in sight. Such gratitude involves deep faith in the Paschal Mystery: the mystery that life and growth come through death and suffering. Through the lens of the Paschal Mystery, broken friendships, addictions, illness, and death become windows into the vastness of God's abiding love, and the Christian heart wells up in gratitude.

Praise

praise
A prayer of acknowledgment that God is God, giving God glory not for what he does, but simply because he is.

Praise embraces all other forms of prayer and carries them to God, who is our source and goal. Praise is the form of prayer that expresses our love for God simply because God *is*. You know if you have felt this natural, self-forgetful kind of love for God welling up in you for no particular reason. When you experience this kind of love, the Holy Spirit is working in you to inspire you to glorify God. Saint Paul tells us to "be filled with the Spirit, addressing one another [in] psalms and hymns and spiritual songs, singing and playing to the Lord in your hearts" (Ephesians 5:18–19).

Praise often finds its expression in music. The *Gloria* we sing at the Mass echoes the angels' song of praise that

Pray It!

The Divine Praises

The divine praises are a form of adoration. These praises name some of the wonderful blessings of our faith. Pray them from time to time as part of your adoration of God.

Blessed be God.
Blessed be his holy name.
Blessed be Jesus Christ, true God and true man.
Blessed be the name of Jesus.
Blessed be his most sacred heart.
Blessed be his Most Precious Blood.
Blessed be Jesus in the most holy sacrament of the altar.
Blessed be the Holy Spirit, the Paraclete.
Blessed be the great mother of God, Mary most holy.
Blessed be her holy and immaculate conception.
Blessed be her glorious assumption.
Blessed be the name of Mary, virgin and mother.
Blessed be Saint Joseph, her most chaste spouse.
Blessed be God in his angels and in his saints.

doxology
Christian prayer that gives glory and praise to God, often in a special way to the three Divine Persons of the Trinity.

beckoned the shepherds to worship the newborn Jesus. In this hymn of praise, we sing, "We praise you, we bless you, we adore you, we glorify you, we give you thanks for your great glory." The praise we offer in the *Gloria* is not for what God has done but simply because he exists and is so glorious. Many other traditional prayers express praise. *Alleluia* literally means "praise the Lord." This word comes to us from our Jewish roots and has been the Easter cry of the Church from the time the first Christians celebrated Christ's victory over death. Many of the Psalms are also prayers of praise. **Doxology** is a word for a Christian prayer of praise that is usually directed to the Trinity.

© Deddeda / Design Pics / Corbis

How is praise a part of your prayer life? When and where do you offer your praise and thanksgiving to God?

Do you feel like you can bring your whole self to God? Why or why not? What would help you to open more fully to God's love and grace?

Article 44: Three Expressions of Prayer

In chapter 9, "Living as a Disciple," we reflected on Jesus' prayer life and what he taught us about prayer. Usually we address our prayer to the Father. We pray to our Father in the name of Jesus, the Divine Son, and our prayer is guided by and empowered by the Holy Spirit. Through Sacred Tradition, the living transmission of our faith, the Holy Spirit teaches us how to pray. Tradition guides us to the many sources available for prayer: Sacred Scripture, the liturgy of the Church, and the theological virtues of faith, hope, and charity.

Sacred Tradition also teaches us about the three major expressions of prayer: vocal prayer, meditation, and contemplation. We might compare these three expressions to the way communication develops in courtship and marriage. At first the man and woman share all the things that are happening in their lives; they talk about their values, their goals, their day-to-day thoughts. As the friendship deepens, they also begin to reflect on their relationship. They have greater awareness of each other and of their love for each other. At some point in their life together, they simply enjoy each other's presence, their love connecting them without the need for words. The three expressions of prayer are similarly built upon an open and sincere heart as we deepen our relationship with God.

vocal prayer
A prayer that is spoken aloud or silently, such as the Lord's Prayer.

Vocal Prayer

When you want to get to know someone, you might strike up a conversation. At first you usually focus on simple things, like school, music, and sports. As you get to know each other better, you begin to share about topics of greater importance: your beliefs, your worries, your dreams for the future. **Vocal prayer**, which uses words either spoken aloud or recited silently, is similar to this kind of sharing because you focus on your conversation with God, which grows over time. Memorized prayer is the first way most people learn to pray vocally. Children usually learn these traditional prayers in their families and in religious education classes. The traditional prayers of the Church serve us throughout our lifetime and are important and appropriate at every stage of our spiritual development.

Creating a space to pray, however large or small, in your home is a reminder to make prayer a regular part of your life.

You will probably also find it helpful to pray to God in your own words. God wants us to share our joys and trials, hopes and frustrations. We can be angry with God, confused, or just plain goofy. The Gospels show that Jesus shouted at God both in joy (see Matthew 11:25–26) and in agony (see Mark 15:37). Praying memorized prayers

meditation
A form of prayer involving a variety of methods and techniques, in which one engages the mind, imagination, and emotions to focus on a particular truth, Scripture passage, or other spiritual matter.

contemplation
A form of wordless prayer in which one is fully focused on the presence of God; sometimes defined as "resting in God."

mysticism
An intense experience of the presence and power of God, resulting in a deeper sense of union with God; those who regularly experience such union are called mystics.

and praying in our own words are both important forms of vocal prayer.

Meditation

Meditation is a term we often hear used broadly and somewhat loosely. The word goes back to a Greek root meaning "care, study, and exercise." You can tell by these meanings that in its truest sense, meditation involves real activity. The *Catechism* uses the active word *mobilize* to describe the use of thoughts, imagination, emotions, and desires in meditation. When you meditate, you use these faculties to ponder God's presence and activity in your life and in the world. You discover the movements that stir your heart, and you say, "Lord, I want you to be the focus of my life."

There are many and varied methods of meditation. Catholics and other Christians often use Sacred Scripture as a springboard to meditation, as in *lectio divina*, a form of meditative prayer that focuses on a Scripture passage through repetitive readings and periods of reflection. Liturgical texts of the day or season, holy writings, the Rosary, icons, and all creation are other doors through which you can enter into meditation. Regardless of how you enter though, Christian meditation is not the same thing as Zen or Eastern meditation, relaxation exercises, or mere psychological activity. Christian meditation is a path to the knowledge of the love of Christ and union with him.

Contemplative Prayer

Like *meditation*, the word **contemplation** has held different meanings throughout the history of spirituality. This kind of union, or awareness of oneness, is the central element of **mysticism**, another term used to describe experiences of profound union with God. What is consistent in descriptions of contemplation is that it always involves deep awareness of the presence of God. We arrive at this awareness not by rational thought but by love. Contemplation is the experience of oneness with God that Jesus speaks about in the Gospel of John, saying, "Remain in me" (15:4) and "I in them" (17:26). Contemplation is union with the indwelling Christ that takes place in the heart at prayer.

You might be thinking, "Okay, really holy people can do this, but not me!" Remember, we are all called to holiness in the ordinary events of our everyday lives. It doesn't take holiness to pray, but prayer will make us holier. We should try not to think of contemplation as something we have to do. Rather, it is a way of being. God loves us and draws near to us. Contemplation is God's gift to us, and we can accept it only in humility. The Psalms offer an image that conveys the truly simple nature of contemplative prayer. We should think of it as climbing into God's lap, like a child rests in his or her mother's arms (see Psalm 131). Contemplation is simply dwelling in God's love.

> **Do you find it easier to pray with memorized prayers or in your own words? Why?**

Article 45: Overcoming Obstacles to Prayer

If prayer is so essential, it should also be easy, right? Prayer can seem easy, but developing a consistent and regular prayer life is often challenging. Like any good habit, it can be difficult to get going, but once we develop the habit, it is easy to maintain. Prayer brings God's peace and joy into our lives, and once we have had a taste, we will want to keep coming back for more.

But we all know that even good habits can die out over time. Those who do seek to develop the habit of prayer will sooner or later face other difficulties. These can include misconceptions about what prayer is supposed to be, as well as the challenges of distraction, periods of dryness, and even times of darkness. When this happens to us, we must take heart. Those great saints who said that prayer is a battle learned to fight the battle well, and they left advice for how to handle these difficulties. We consider some of that advice in this section. We must always remember that we are not alone. The Holy Spirit prays with us and will see us through.

Misconceptions about Prayer

A lot of misconceptions exist about prayer. Just as having the wrong idea about a person hinders us from getting to know him or her, having the wrong idea about prayer works against us. Perhaps you have heard some of these common misconceptions, such as the idea that prayer is merely a psychological activity or that it requires us to rattle off memorized words. Neither idea is part of healthy human relationships, and neither is true prayer. Another misconception is that prayer is something that requires expertise. But there are no black belts, no *summa cum laude* honors, no gold stars in prayer. Anyone can pray, and you probably already do.

For example, do you ever sit in your room listening to music, caught up in the rhythm and how the verses express your own thoughts and feelings about your

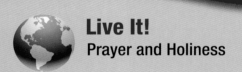

Live It!
Prayer and Holiness

For the Israelites, being holy meant more than just being good. It also meant being set apart for service to God. When things are important to us, we set aside a special place or time for them. Perhaps you set aside time for sports practice or music lessons. So if holiness is important to you, might you also set aside special times for prayer?

Most saints have found that growth in holiness is strongly tied to having regular times to pray. Sunday is a holy day for Christians, a day we set apart so that we can gather to pray as a community. In our personal lives, it is also important to set aside times for prayer. The morning, before you start the day's activities, is a good time to pray. So is the evening, before you close out your day. With friends and family, you might begin meals by giving thanks for God's gifts. Make yourself more open to the work of God's grace by setting aside time for prayer every day.

relationship with God? Do you ever look at a tiny infant or a beautiful sunset and think, "Way to go, God!" When you are caught in a difficult situation, do you turn to God and ask for help? If you do any of these things, you are already praying. Most people pray at some level, even if it is only occasional and unplanned. What God wants us to do is to be more disciplined and consistent in our prayer—to make him a regular part of our lives.

Another misconception centers on Saint Paul's command to "pray without ceasing" (1 Thessalonians 5:17). Saint Paul did not mean that every Christian should join a monastery and spend every waking moment in prayer. Rather, this command means that our whole life should be a prayer, a sign of our communion with God. We do this by remembering that it is always possible to pray, no matter what life may throw at us. We do it by remembering that prayer is a necessity. Without prayer we lose our connection to God and we fall back into a life of sin and unhappiness. And we make our whole life prayerful by remembering that prayer and Christian action are two sides of the same coin. Origen, an early Christian thinker, said it like this: "He 'prays without ceasing' who unites his prayer to works and good works to prayer. Only in this way can we consider as realizable the principle of praying without ceasing."

© Bill Wittman / www.wpwittman.com

People in monastic life pray the Liturgy of the Hours together several times a day as one way of "praying without ceasing." How can your life be a living prayer to God?

Difficulties in Prayer: Distractions, Dryness, and Darkness

Sometimes even when we understand what true prayer is, we experience difficulties that can interfere with our efforts to develop and maintain a habit of praying. Such difficulties can range from common distractions, to frustrating periods of dryness, to disturbing times of spiritual darkness.

Distractions in prayer are similar to what happens when you try to carry on a conversation and keep getting interrupted. Some days it seems the moment you bow your head in prayer, a dozen alarms go off in your head at once, all calling you away from the relationship of prayer: "Oh, no! I forgot to call Liz!" "I wonder what I should wear to the dance." "I've got to get that research paper done by tomorrow." The moment you quiet one distraction, another one pops up, like a mental jack-in-the-box.

Spiritual guides tell us that these distractions reveal our preferences and attachments and therefore which master we serve (see Matthew 6:21,24). They advise us against hunting down our distractions because that is precisely the trap—to get us chasing around instead of praying. Respond just as you would to interruptions in conversation. Turn your focus back to the Lord, with whom you want to be. In doing so you demonstrate which master you choose to serve. This requires vigilance: constantly seeking God instead of allowing other things to draw you away.

Another kind of difficulty, dryness, is like those times in even the best friendship when the spark seems to have faded. You feel like you're growing apart from your friend, and you no longer have as much fun when you are together. Remaining faithful to your friend and exploring new activities together are important if you do not want the friendship to die. In prayer, dryness is experienced as feeling separated from God. When we feel separated, the strength, joy, and peace of prayer run dry, and nothing seems to change the situation. Sometimes these periods of dryness are actually the gift and work of God, liberating you from imperfections and attachments. If this is the case, keeping faith will see you through.

At other times, dryness is the result of a lack of devotion to the relationship. In marriage, for example, couples can focus too much on other things—raising children, earning money, spending time with other friends—and grow lax in devotion to each other. The couple has to radically reorient their priorities to mend their marriage. If our prayer is dry because of lax practice or carelessness of heart, the remedy is conversion. Conversion involves a radical change of heart, turning away from the things that draw us away from God, and returning to God.

But sometimes our difficulty in prayer goes deeper than distractions or even dryness. We can sometimes experience periods of spiritual darkness. Spiritual darkness can begin with dryness due to carelessness, or it can be as profound as feeling that we have been abandoned by God, perhaps during a time of suffering or sorrow. If you have experienced this darkness, however, you are not alone. Many of our greatest saints went through dark periods of feeling abandoned by God. Saint John of the Cross (1542–1592), a Spanish mystic and spiritual poet, knew the meaning of sacrifice and suffering firsthand. But instead of turning bitter about his experiences, he devoted his life to teaching others to find God through love and prayer. In one of his books of poetry, *Dark Night of the Soul*, he offers encouragement to Christians who are struggling with spiritual darkness. Saint John suggests that we see these moments as times when our love for God is being purified. Rather than being a negative experience, the "dark night" can be a blessing in disguise, drawing us into closer communion with God.

All this talk of difficulties may have you feeling somewhat discouraged. Consider this

Saint John knew that God never leaves us, even when we cannot feel God's presence. In these times, our faith in God and in his love sustains us.

© The Crosiers / Gene Plaisted, OSC

spirituality
In general, the values, actions, attitudes, and behaviors that characterize a person's relationship with God and others. In particular, it refers to different schools of Christian prayer and action.

modern-day parable: The Devil takes a man on a tour of hell and proudly shows off all his storehouses brimming with the seeds of sin. There are lust and jealousy, anger and envy, and so on—a large storehouse for each big sin. But the man points out another storehouse that is far larger than all the rest. "What do you keep in there?" he asks. "Oh, that," responds the Devil, "that holds the smallest but most effective seed of all. That is overflowing with seeds of discouragement." Prayer can be such a wonderful and life-giving relationship. You want to take great care not to allow the seeds of discouragement to grow there. Remember, even an infinitesimal seed of faith grows to the size of a mustard tree, whose roots and shade hold back despair, hopelessness, and fear (see Luke 17:5–6).

> **What specific difficulties discourage you from praying? Why? How can prayer help you to overcome these difficulties?**

Article 46: Ignatian Gospel Meditation

Many different types of Christian **spirituality** offer us valuable guidance in developing our prayer lives. These different schools of thought have developed out of the living tradition of prayer in the life of the Church. Guided by the Holy Spirit, many of these schools of Christian spirituality come from the insights of particular saints. Let's look more closely at one example: Ignatian spirituality.

One of God's greatest gifts to us is our imagination. Through it we can discover possibilities, break down barriers, and solve problems. People have accomplished amazing things because they dared to imagine the world in new and different ways. Christians are able to endure the sacrifices needed to give witness to the Gospel because we can imagine the complete fulfillment of the

Kingdom of God. But have you ever considered using your imagination for prayer?

The power and beauty of the human imagination were not lost on Saint Ignatius Loyola (1491–1556). While recovering from a war injury, he spent months in spiritual reading. Some of the books he read encouraged him to imagine himself being part of the scenes in the Gospels. This use of the imagination for prayer and discernment deeply affected Ignatius, and he took this idea and developed a whole series of spiritual exercises based on it. Imagining yourself as part of a Gospel story can be a very powerful way to hear the voice of God.

Château de Versailles, France / Bridgeman Images

Saint Ignatius gave up the vanity of courtly life after discovering the power of the Gospel and the peace it brought him. His methods for prayer became one of the Church's most well-known schools of Christian spirituality.

The Method

Saint Ignatius developed a method of prayer in which you use your imagination to immerse yourself in a story from the Bible. With this method you visualize in your mind the details of a specific Gospel account. You might think of this method as a meditation that may even draw you into contemplation. As the story comes to life in your imagination, you are brought to a personal and real encounter with Jesus in the present moment. Here is a suggested format to follow for Ignatian Gospel meditation:

1. Prepare yourself for prayer by assuming a comfortable position and allowing yourself to become silent. Select a passage from Sacred Scripture with which to pray. It is usually best to begin with an account from the Gospels, because the details and storyline are especially suited to this method. With some experience you will be able to spot other passages in Sacred Scripture that also work well.

2. Read the passage through once, paying special attention to the characters and the concrete details: What does this place look, feel, smell, and sound like? Who is there? What action unfolds? What words are

spoken? You may wish to reread the passage several times to absorb all the details.

3.   Next, enter the story in your imagination, just as if you were there. Employ your senses to allow the details of the story to come alive. Listen, taste, feel, smell, and see all you can. You can be yourself, or you can imagine yourself as one of the people in the story. Converse and interact with the people in the account. Allow the experience to unfold in your imagination without changing any of the essential details from the Bible passage.

4.   As you experience the story, pay careful attention to all your reactions, all that you are feeling and thinking.

5.   Respond to this experience in prayerful conversation with Jesus.

Did You Know?

Making a Retreat

© Bill Wittman / www.wpwittman.com

Do you go on a class retreat every year? The retreats you are probably familiar with have roots in the work of Saint Ignatius Loyola (1491–1556), founder of the Society of Jesus (or Jesuits). Based on his own conversion experience, he developed the *Spiritual Exercises*—a series of meditations on Christ's life.

The most intense form of Ignatian retreat is the thirty-day retreat. Shorter retreats were later developed to help Catholics fit a retreat into their busy lives. Today some parishes and campus ministries offer a "retreat in daily life," which helps retreatants pray and reflect in their own homes.

Our Holy Father, Pope Francis, is also a Jesuit priest. He once compared the wisdom of Saint Ignatius to the teachings of Saint Paul: "They both let Christ make them his own. I seek Jesus, I serve Jesus because he sought me first, because I was won over by him: and this is the heart of our experience" ("Homily of the Holy Father Francis on the Occasion of the Feast of Saint Ignatius," 2). This is what a retreat is all about.

Any Gospel passage can be used for Ignatian Gospel meditation, but particular passages can speak to us in very powerful ways through this type of prayer. Here are a few you can try:

- Luke 2:1–20 (the birth of Jesus)
- Matthew 4:18–22 (the call of the first disciples)
- Mark 8:27–38 (Peter recognizes that Jesus is the Messiah)
- John 13:1–17 (Jesus washes the disciples' feet)
- Matthew 26:57–75 (Jesus before the Sanhedrin, Peter's denial of Jesus)
- Mark 15:15–41 (the death of Jesus)
- Luke 24:13–32 (the Risen Jesus appears to two disciples)
- John 20:24–31 (Jesus appears to Thomas)

Try It

As an example, let's pray with the passage in John 21:1–14, which describes how the resurrected Jesus appeared to his disciples while they were fishing on the Sea of Tiberius (Sea of Galilee). After you read the passage through a few times, you might begin by imagining the rocking of the boat as the nets are thrown out, the warmth of the sun, and each person in the boat with you. Listen to the quiet conversation as you ponder the meaning of Jesus' death, the empty tomb, and the appearances of your Risen Lord. You work the nets without any success. What are you talking about as you do this? Then a stranger appears on the shore at dawn and tells you to cast your net again. You do so—and the net is so full that you cannot even pull it into the boat. What feelings are you experiencing as this happens? Then John recognizes the figure as Jesus, and Peter enthusiastically jumps into the water so he can be the first to reach the shore. You all come in dragging the full net behind the boat. Jesus himself cooks some fish and feeds it to you, along with some bread, for breakfast. What feelings are deep in

© Brooklyn Museum of Art, New York / The Bridgeman Art Library International

You can use images as an aid to Ignatian meditation. Use this image of the story in John 21:1–14 to help immerse yourself in the story.

your heart? What kind of conversation do you have with Jesus? How will this experience affect your life?

You might be thinking: "This is all just imagination. It isn't real!" Recall that Sacred Scripture is the living Word. When you pray with this method, you will have very real encounters with Jesus and will find that in the experience, God touches you. You can be comforted, healed, and challenged by the living Christ as you meet him through the doorway of your imagination. You find meaning in the story that you might have overlooked before.

As the living Word of God, Sacred Scripture makes a unique contribution to the practice of prayer. *Lectio divina* and Ignatian Gospel meditation are simple ways to start a conversation with God's Word and keep it going. If you aren't in dialogue with God's Word, try these methods when you pray today.

Try Ignatian meditation with a Gospel story that particularly appeals to you. What new insights did you gain during this experience?

Chapter Review

1. What is prayer? Why must we pray?

2. How is a prayer of petition different from a prayer of intercession?

3. Describe some different types of vocal prayer.

4. What is consistent in descriptions of contemplative prayer?

5. Describe some of the misconceptions people have about prayer.

6. How can we overcome being distracted while praying?

7. How can our imagination be helpful in prayer? How did Saint Ignatius Loyola use imagination when praying with Scripture?

Chapter

12 Praying the Triduum

Introduction

In the previous chapter, we looked primarily at the connection between the Paschal Mystery and personal prayer. Now we will turn our attention to the connection between the Paschal Mystery and the liturgy, which is the Church's official, public, communal prayer. In particular, we will look at the Easter Triduum, the three-day celebration that is the heart of the Liturgical Year.

Every Eucharist makes the saving sacrifice of Jesus present to us. And the Liturgical Year commemorates the various aspects of the Paschal Mystery in an annual cycle. But the liturgies of Holy Thursday, Good Friday, and Easter commemorate in a unique way the Passion and Resurrection of Jesus Christ. In our journey to holiness, the Easter Triduum offers us a kind of annual Paschal Mystery retreat. These liturgies are a special gift for us to treasure and celebrate with the Church, the Body of Christ.

Article 47: The Paschal Mystery, Liturgy, and the Triduum

Most people make an effort to celebrate whatever national holidays are important in their country—often gathering with friends, family, and community. For example, perhaps you celebrate Independence Day or Thanksgiving by gathering with loved ones. God created us to be in relationship with one another, and holidays unite us as citizens with a common heritage.

Christians, who are first and foremost citizens of the Kingdom of God, have holidays too—only we call them holy days. Our celebration of **liturgies** on holy days binds us together and strengthens us as the Body of Christ. In our liturgical celebrations, we recall and celebrate God's plan for our salvation, fulfilled through the Paschal Mystery. Before we turn to the specific liturgies of the Easter Triduum, let's first examine how the Lord's Day and our entire liturgical calendar commemorate the Paschal Mystery.

liturgy
The Church's official, public, communal prayer. It is God's work, in which the People of God participate. The Church's most important liturgy is the Eucharist, or the Mass.

Liturgical Year
The Church's annual cycle of feasts and seasons that celebrate the events and mysteries of Christ's birth, life, death, Resurrection, and Ascension, and forms the context for the Church's worship.

The Lord's Day and the Liturgical Year

The most fundamental and foundational holy day is the Lord's Day. We celebrate this day on Sunday, in honor of Christ's Resurrection, which occurred on Sunday morning. We keep the Lord's Day holy by participating in the Eucharist (the Mass) and taking time for rest, prayer, service, and family.

Sunday is the foundation of the **Liturgical Year**, which begins with the First Sunday of Advent. Throughout the Liturgical Year, we remember and celebrate God the Father's saving plan as it is revealed through the life of his Son, Jesus Christ. In Advent we patiently wait for Jesus' birth. During the Christmas season, we celebrate his Incarnation. In Lent we remember his call to a life of holiness and sacrifice, and during the Easter Triduum and Easter season we celebrate his suffering, death, and Resurrection. Forty days after Easter, we recall Christ's Ascension into Heaven. Ten days later, we rejoice in the

Liturgy of the Hours
Also known as the Divine Office, the official public, daily prayer of the Catholic Church. The Divine Office provides standard prayers, Scripture readings, and reflections at regular hours throughout the day.

Sacrament
An efficacious and visible sign of God's grace, instituted by Christ and entrusted to the Church, by which divine life is dispensed to us. The Seven Sacraments are Baptism, the Eucharist, Confirmation, Penance and Reconciliation, Anointing of the Sick, Matrimony, and Holy Orders.

gift of the Holy Spirit at Pentecost. During Ordinary Time we ponder our call to live as disciples while waiting for Christ's final return as Lord of Lords and King of Kings.

The Liturgy and the Paschal Mystery

Liturgy is the Church's public, communal, and official worship. The Eucharist is the central liturgy of the Church and the basis for most other liturgical celebrations. The other six Sacraments are also liturgies, and so are the **Liturgy of the Hours** and Catholic funerals. But a group prayer service is not a liturgy, because it is not an official worship service of the Church.

It is helpful to define some terms. The word *liturgy* is taken from the Greek word *liturgia*, which means "a public work" or "service on behalf of the people." *The liturgy* or *the sacred liturgy* refers to the overall idea of Catholic official worship, but *a liturgy* usually refers to a specific Mass or sacramental celebration. *Liturgical* describes anything related to the liturgy. A *liturgical celebration or ritual* is another name for a Mass, a Baptism, or any other specific liturgy. A *liturgist* is a person who studies, researches, and teaches in the field of liturgy and who may also plan and coordinate liturgical celebrations.

The sacred liturgy is Trinitarian. In the liturgy we bless and worship God the Father as the source of the blessings of creation and salvation. The greatest blessing the Father has bestowed on us is the gift of his Son, Jesus Christ, through whom we have become the adopted children of God. The Holy Spirit makes the Paschal Mystery real and present in the liturgy.

Jesus Christ plays a central role in the Church's liturgy because he not only gave us the sacred liturgy but also makes himself present through the liturgy. This is another way of saying that the liturgy is sacramental—that is, like a Sacrament. A **Sacrament**, such as the Seven Sacraments of the Church, makes Christ's presence real. The Church herself is a sacrament because she makes Christ's saving presence available to all people through the proclamation of the Word and the celebration of the Sacraments. Through the sacred liturgy, the Church is already participating in the divine liturgy, as a foretaste of Heaven. Thus the liturgy is the work of both Christ—the Head—and the Church—the Body of Christ.

The Holy Spirit prepares us to receive Christ in the liturgy and reveals Christ's presence in the community, in Sacred Scripture, and in the physical signs of liturgical celebrations. Through the transforming power of the Holy Spirit, the Paschal Mystery is real and active in the liturgy, bringing us into deeper communion with Christ and with one another. The Holy Spirit gives us the grace

Faith in Action
Celebrate the Triduum with Monks and Nuns

© Bill Wittman / www.wpwittman.com

For an especially prayerful way to participate in the Triduum, visit a monastery of monks or nuns. The monastic life is one of daily prayer and work. Even so, like the rest of the Church, monks and nuns take special care to celebrate the Triduum in the fullest way possible. Visitors find that the monastic observance of the Triduum promotes mindfulness of Christ's Passion, death, and Resurrection, making for an all-encompassing spiritual experience.

What will you find in a monastic observance of the Triduum? Monastic communities celebrate the Triduum with special devotion, centered on the Liturgy of the Hours. You may find more silence than in the usual parish church. You may find a different style of singing, because Gregorian chant (in English or in Latin) is the musical backbone of the Liturgy of the Hours. You may find more simplicity, and even more darkness, because the Hours often begin before dawn. For that reason, you may also find more candlelight. In such an atmosphere of simplicity, you may find it easier to concentrate on Jesus and the great gift of his life, his death, and his Resurrection.

Monastic men and women who regularly pray the Liturgy of the Hours include the Benedictine and Cistercian orders, as well as other communities that follow similar rules of life. You are welcome to visit at any time of the year, but especially during the Triduum.

© Wojtek Kryczka / istockphoto.com

to live as disciples of Christ, participating in his saving work.

It is important that you understand these last points. The liturgy is not just a celebration of past events. It makes the Paschal Mystery available to us right now, just as it was available to the original disciples and Apostles. Of course Christ is close to us all the time, but he is available to us in a unique way through the liturgy and the Sacraments of the Church, especially the Eucharist.

The Significance of the Triduum

Triduum (pronounced TRI-doo-um) literally means "three days." This word can refer to any three days set apart for prayer or some other special service. But it usually describes the Easter **Triduum**, the three holy days that are at the center of the Church's Liturgical Year. The Triduum begins with the Mass of the Lord's Supper on Holy Thursday night, continues with the Celebration of the Lord's Passion on Good Friday afternoon, reaches its climax with the Easter Vigil on Holy Saturday night, and ends with evening prayer on Easter Sunday. (It actually encompasses three twenty-four-hour periods over four days.) The liturgies of the Triduum form one continuous celebration, each liturgy picking up where the previous one leaves off. We follow Jesus' Paschal journey from the Last Supper, through his arrest, torture, and Crucifixion, and finally to the joy of the empty tomb and his Resurrection.

Triduum
The three-day period of the Liturgical Year that begins with the Mass of the Lord's Supper on Holy Thursday and ends with evening prayer on Easter Sunday.

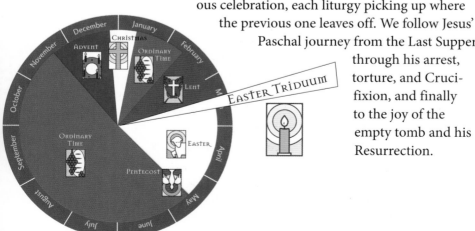

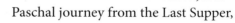

The Gospel readings of the Triduum liturgies roughly parallel these final events in Jesus' mission. The Triduum liturgies are meant not to re-enact these events but to help us to remember them and celebrate them in a sacramental way.

Liturgy	Corresponding Events in Jesus' Life
Holy Thursday	Jesus washes the Apostles' feet and institutes the Eucharist at the Last Supper.
Good Friday	Jesus undergoes his Passion (suffering and death).
Easter Vigil and Easter Day	Jesus rises from the dead, and his followers discover the empty tomb.

The worshipping community has many opportunities to actively participate and to be drawn in to the mystery and drama of the final days of Christ's earthly ministry. All through Lent we seek to deepen our participation with his ministry through prayer, fasting, and acts of charity (almsgiving). On Passion (Palm) Sunday, we enter into Holy Week by recalling Christ's suffering and crucifixion, his sacrifice to save us from sin and death. As Holy Week concludes, the liturgies of the Triduum are filled with special signs and symbolic actions that help us to meditate on the wonder and glory of God's saving plan, culminating in the Paschal Mystery.

It is a shame that many Catholics miss these wonderful liturgies—a gift of the Holy Spirit to renew and strengthen our faith. Try to think of the Easter Triduum as a personal retreat, a time when you can meditate on Christ's suffering, death, and Resurrection and enter more deeply into these great mysteries. You may need to change your ordinary schedule and obligations so you can enter into sacred time and space for these three holy days. Even though you are obligated to attend the Mass on Easter, make whatever sacrifices necessary to attend all the liturgies of the Easter Triduum. This chapter will help you to make the most of this opportunity.

Holy Thursday
The beginning of the Easter Triduum, starting with the evening celebration of the Mass of the Lord's Supper.

Chrism Mass
A special Mass usually celebrated during Holy Week in each diocese. During the Mass the bishop blesses the sacred oils and consecrates the Sacred Chrism used in the diocese throughout the year, and diocesan priests renew their promises to their bishop.

Oil of the Catechumens
Blessed olive oil used to anoint those preparing for Baptism.

Oil of the Sick
Blessed olive oil used in the Sacrament of Anointing of the Sick to anoint the forehead and hands of people who are seriously ill or near death.

Have you attended any of the liturgies of the Easter Triduum? How was the experience different from attending Sunday Mass?

Article 48: Holy Thursday

Holy Thursday, the first day of the Triduum, is filled with anticipation. The Triduum begins in the evening, when we celebrate the Mass of the Lord's Supper. We keep watch with Jesus as the Church remembers the glory and heartbreak of the final night of his earthly ministry. At the beginning of the Mass of the Lord's Supper, we recall how Christ instituted the Eucharist at the Last Supper. In this opening prayer, we ask God to grant us the fullness of love and life through the Eucharistic sacrifice:

> O God, who have called us to participate
> in this most sacred Supper,
> in which your Only Begotten Son,
> when about to hand himself over to death,
> entrusted to the Church a sacrifice new for all eternity,
> the banquet of his love,
> grant, we pray,
> that we may draw from so great a mystery,
> the fullness of charity and of life.
> Through our Lord Jesus Christ, your Son,
> who lives and reigns with you in the unity of the Holy Spirit,
> one God, for ever and ever.
> Amen.
>
> (*Roman Missal*, Mass of the Lord's Supper)

Often, all the clergy of a diocese, along with representatives from every parish, also gather at the diocesan cathedral during the day on Holy Thursday for the **Chrism Mass** with the bishop, although this Mass may also be celebrated earlier in Lent, such as the Thursday before Holy Thursday. At the Chrism Mass, the priests renew their vows to their bishop. The bishop blesses the **Oil of the Catechumens** and the **Oil of the Sick** and consecrates the **Sacred Chrism** that will be used in every parish throughout the next year.

© Alinari / Art Resource, NY

In the Mass of the Lord's Supper, we remember in a special and solemn way the first Eucharist, when Jesus gave his Body and Blood to his disciples.

Liturgical Highlights

The Mass of the Lord's Supper is a Mass, but special rituals make it quite different from Sunday Mass. Knowing their meaning will help you to celebrate the Mass of the Lord's Supper more fully.

The Presentation of the Oils

At the beginning of the liturgy, the Oil of the Catechumens, the Oil of the Sick, and the Sacred Chrism are brought forward in procession by three members of the parish community. This procession represents your parish's connection with the diocese and the universal Church. These oils will be used throughout the year in the Sacraments of Baptism, Confirmation, and Anointing of the Sick. As the oils are brought forward, remember your bishop in prayer; he is entrusted with the challenging task of serving all the people of the diocese. Also pray for the people who will be anointed with these sacred oils. Pray that they will know Christ's saving, healing, and loving presence through these Sacraments.

The Washing of Feet

Following the homily the parish priest washes the feet of some parish members, sometimes with the assistance of other priests. This is done in memory of Jesus' act of washing the disciples' feet and his command to them: "I have given you a model to follow, so that as I have done for you, you should also do" (John 13:15). During this

Sacred Chrism
Perfumed olive oil consecrated by the bishop that is used for anointing in the Sacraments of Baptism, Confirmation, and Holy Orders.

© iamfree007 / Shutterstock.com

At the Holy Thursday liturgy, imagine Christ washing your feet. Let his example inspire you to perform acts of humble service.

ritual, reflect on who has been a servant in your life, and consider whom God has called you to serve. Pray for those people.

The Dismissal of the Elect

If your parish has adults who will be received into the Church at the Easter Vigil, they are dismissed before the intercessions. The Triduum is especially meaningful for them, for it is the last stage in their process of becoming full members of the Body of Christ. Let their faith and commitment to Christ and the Church inspire you to commit more deeply to Christ as well.

The Collection for the Poor

The collection taken up on Holy Thursday is different from typical Sunday collections. It is solely for the needs of the poor; the food and money collected does not go toward parish expenses. Some parishes participate in Operation Rice Bowl, which is organized by Catholic Relief Services. Sometimes parishes encourage people to bring bags of food for the hungry in their community. Encourage your family to participate, and help out with your family's donation. Remember that Christ calls us to sacrifice for the needs of others, and make your donation more than just pocket change. If possible, help to increase the collection total as a sign of your commitment to sacrificial service of those most in need.

The Transfer of the Eucharist

Because the Liturgy of the Eucharist is not celebrated on Good Friday, enough bread is consecrated on Holy Thursday for both the Holy Thursday and Good Friday liturgies. At the end of the Mass of the Lord's Supper, the Body of Christ that will be used on Good Friday is transferred to a separate location, called the reservation chapel, where it remains until the Good Friday liturgy. In some parishes the congregation joins in the procession, following the priest, who is carrying the Body of Christ.

Recall that after the Last Supper, Jesus and his disciples walked to the garden at Gethsemane, where he asked the disciples to stay awake and pray with him. In memory of this, many people stay in the reservation chapel to pray with Jesus, or they come back later that night to do so. This is a wonderful and special time to meditate and pray in the presence of Jesus.

The Paschal Fast

Following the Mass of the Lord's Supper, we begin the Paschal Fast. The Church calls for us to abstain from meat and to eat only one full meal on Good Friday. If we eat other meals that day, they should add up to less than another full meal. But these fasting guidelines are minimal requirements. Some choose to fast all the way to the Easter Vigil on Saturday night, eating very little until that time.

Fasting, along with prayer and almsgiving, is a penitential practice that expresses our conversion—the turning of our lives away from sin and toward God. Fasting prepares us to participate in the liturgical feasts, but it also helps us to control our instincts and act virtuously. Fasting during the Triduum builds our anticipation for the joyous celebration of the Easter Vigil, when we will feast on the Word of God and the Body and Blood of Christ.

Entering into Sacred Time on Holy Thursday

The following suggestions are some ways you can more fully enter into the celebration of the Paschal Mystery, beginning with Holy Thursday:

- If you do nothing else, be sure to attend the Mass of the Lord's Supper. Find out what time it begins, and mark it on your calendar. Encourage your family and friends to go too.

- Decide what you are going to contribute in the collection for the poor. Throughout Lent you might save money you would ordinarily spend on food, clothes, music, or games, and then donate it to the collection. Talk with your family about making this a family effort.

- Before or after the Mass of the Lord's Supper, take time to read and reflect on the readings for the Mass: Exodus 12:1–14, Psalm 116, 1 Corinthians 11:23–26, and John 13:1–15. The Gospel reading is an excellent reading to use for Ignatian Gospel meditation.

- Make a commitment to fast and free yourself of distractions for the next three days. Decide what you will allow yourself to eat, and then stick to your commitment. Commit to not watching television or using the computer or your phone for anything that is not absolutely necessary.

- Spend an hour with the Blessed Sacrament in the reservation chapel on Thursday night. Jesus' presence in the Body and Blood is real and substantial. You can talk with him in prayer, read Sacred Scripture (the Church recommends Psalm 22; the Book of Lamentations; and John, chapters 14–17), pray

Live It!
Remembering the Triduum at Home

Many families have a home altar as a center for family prayer. This can be a simple table displaying a crucifix, Bible, or other religious symbols. If your home does not have one, ask your parents about creating a family altar, or keep a personal altar in your own room.

During the Triduum, you might add pictures, colors, and symbols to your altar to serve as reminders of each liturgical celebration. On Holy Thursday you could put out some bread, oil, water, and a collection bowl for the poor on a white cloth. On Good Friday a crucifix and perhaps some thorns from a bush laid on a red cloth would set the appropriate mood. For Saturday evening and Easter Sunday, on a gold or white cloth you could display a statue of the Risen Jesus along with a large rock that symbolizes the stone rolled away from the empty tomb. What are some other creative and visual ways to bring a prayerful mood for the Triduum into your home?

the Rosary, or just sit quietly and peacefully in his presence.

Which of these suggestions would you like to try as a way to enter more deeply into Holy Thursday?

Article 49: Good Friday

Good Friday arrives as a solemn day, for on this day we especially remember Christ's death, his love for us shown forth in his ultimate sacrifice. When we arrive at Church, it is stark. The altar is bare, the decorations have been removed, the statues are covered, and the fonts have been emptied of holy water. All of these details remind us of how we should approach this holy day—free from distractions so we can meditate on the reality of human sin and cruelty and the enormity of God's love.

At the beginning of the Good Friday liturgy, we recall how Jesus shed his Blood for the sake of our salvation, and we pray for God to make us holy:

> Remember your mercies, O Lord,
> and with your eternal protection sanctify your servants,
> for whom Christ your Son,
> by the shedding of his Blood,
> established the Paschal Mystery.
> Who lives and reigns for ever and ever.
> Amen.
>
> (*Roman Missal*, Friday of the
> Passion of the Lord)

Good Friday is both a day of sadness and a day of hope. It is a day of sadness because our sin made it necessary for Jesus to suffer and die. But it is a day of hope because through his death he has redeemed the world.

Good Friday
The second day of the Easter Triduum on which we commemorate Jesus' Passion and death on the cross.

As the Church remembers Christ's Passion and death, imagine yourself at the foot of the cross with Mary and John. Stand in silent adoration before the God who suffered and died to free us from sin.

Brooklyn Museum of Art, New York, USA / Bridgeman Images

Liturgical Highlights

The Good Friday liturgy is called the Celebration of the Lord's Passion. The liturgy begins in silence, picking up where the Holy Thursday liturgy ended. It is usually held in the afternoon so that the time is close to the time of Christ's death, around 3:00 p.m.

The Liturgy of the Word

The readings in the liturgy focus on Christ's Passion. The Old Testament reading is one of Isaiah's Songs of the Suffering Servant (see Isaiah 52:13– 53:12). In the second reading, from the Letter to the Hebrews, we reflect on the meaning of Christ's suffering and death (see 4:14–16, 5:7–9). The Gospel account of Christ's arrest, mock trial, scourging, and Crucifixion is from the Gospel of John (see 18:1–19:42). It is a long reading, and many parishes include speaking parts for the congregation. As the readings are proclaimed, really listen to them. Let them soak in and touch not just your mind but also your heart.

The Intercessions

On Good Friday, the general intercessions are longer and more formal and are usually sung. We pray for the Church, the Pope, the clergy and laity, those preparing for Baptism, the unity of Christians, the Jewish people, those who do not believe in Christ or God, leaders in the

Pray It!

Prayer for Good Friday

At the liturgy on Good Friday, we come forward individually to venerate the cross and offer praise and thanks for Jesus' sacrifice. You can venerate the cross by kneeling, bowing, or kissing or touching the cross. As you approach the cross, consider praying this brief prayer:

We worship you, Lord,
we venerate your Cross,
we praise your Resurrection.
Through the Cross you brought joy to the world.
   (Catholic Household Blessings and Prayers)

world, and those in special need. Listen carefully to these intercessions so you can sincerely join in praying for these important needs.

The Veneration of the Cross

After the general intercessions, the priest brings up a cross in solemn procession. Three times he lifts it up and sings, "Behold the wood of the Cross, on which hung the salvation of the world," and everyone responds "Come, let us adore." Then the congregation is invited to come forward and **venerate** the cross in some way to show our deep appreciation for Christ's sacrifice. Some people kneel or bow before the cross; others kiss or touch it. Some communities have a local custom to follow, but there is no right or wrong way to express your reverence. Whatever way you choose, let it come from your heart as an expression of your love for and devotion to Christ.

venerate
To show respect and devotion to someone or something.

© Bill Wittman / www.wpwittman.com

Communion

We do not celebrate a full Liturgy of the Eucharist on Good Friday. In a simple ritual, we receive the Body of Christ that was consecrated on Holy Thursday. Then the liturgy ends in silence, a time of waiting that will conclude with the Easter Vigil the next night. As you receive the Body of Christ, be especially aware of his sacrifice, which enables us to live as the redeemed children of God.

As you participate in the veneration of the cross on Good Friday, thank Christ for his sacrificial love. How will you follow his example of loving sacrifice for others?

Entering into Sacred Time on Good Friday

The following suggestions are some ways you can more fully enter into the celebration of the Paschal Mystery, continuing into Good Friday:

- Make a plan to attend the celebration of the Lord's Passion. Find out what time it begins, and mark it on your calendar. Encourage your family and friends to go too.

Stations of the Cross
A devotion for prayer and reflection, popular during Lent, that retraces the events of Jesus' Passion and death in fourteen "stations" represented by artistic depictions. Most Catholic churches have artistic representations of the fourteen Stations of the Cross. Also called the Way of the Cross.

Easter Vigil
The liturgy celebrated on Holy Saturday night. It celebrates the coming of the light of Christ into the world and is also the time when adults and older children are received into the Church through the Sacraments of Christian Initiation.

- Fasting on this day is especially important, as a way to maintain your focus on Christ's sacrifice and to anticipate the celebration of the Resurrection. The Church asks us to eat only one full meal this day (for those between ages fourteen and fifty-nine) and to abstain from eating meat (required of all those over age fourteen). Decide what is possible for you based on your health needs, but make your fast a true sacrifice.

- Some parishes also celebrate the **Stations of the Cross** on Good Friday. In some places, this celebration is conducted very publicly. Sometimes it is even held outdoors, and participants stop at places that symbolize where Christ still suffers in the lives of people today. Find out if the Stations of the Cross will be celebrated in your area, and try to attend this very moving remembrance of Christ's Passion.

- In the general intercessions on Good Friday, we pray for the spiritual and physical needs of the whole world. Take some time to pray for the needs of people who are close to you and who are in your community. Think especially of those people who are sick, hurting, or without work or who don't know Christ.

- Spend some time reflecting on the mystery of Christ's Passion using the Bible. You may wish to read and reflect on the readings for the liturgy: Isaiah 52:13–53:12; Psalm 31; Hebrews 4:14–16, 5:7–9; John 18:1–19:42. Or look for other readings that talk about the meaning of Christ's suffering and death, such as Philippians 2:1–11 or Romans, chapter 5.

Which of these suggestions would you like to try as a way to enter more deeply into Good Friday?

Article 50: Easter Vigil

When we celebrate the Triduum as a kind of retreat, Holy Saturday arrives with a hint of excitement. The sadness of the Passion has passed, and we anticipate the celebration of Christ's victory over sin and death in the Easter Vigil liturgy. Yet Holy Saturday is still a day for reflection, meditation, and even rest. When the Easter Vigil arrives that night, you will want to be fully alert to truly appreciate and enter into the many wonderful signs and symbols that make up this beautiful liturgy that begins our Easter celebration.

© Glenda M. Powers / Shutterstock.com

> Exult, let them exult, the hosts of heaven,
> exult, let Angel ministers of God exult,
> let the trumpet of salvation
> sound aloud our mighty King's triumph!
> (*Roman Missal*, Easter Proclamation)

Liturgical Highlights

Easter is such an important feast day in the Christian calendar that it is not celebrated with just one liturgy. Easter begins with the celebration of the **Easter Vigil**, which many consider the highlight of the Liturgical Year. *Vigil* literally means "to be awake, to be watchful," and it is the name we give to liturgies held the night before an

The empty tomb reminds us that Christ is risen! He is not dead, but alive, and he is present in the world today.

Did You Know?

The Blessing of Easter Baskets

© Nicholas Piccillo / Shutterstock.com

In some parishes, including many Eastern Catholic parishes, parishioners of Slovak or Polish ancestry bring Easter baskets to the Easter Vigil on Saturday evening. After the Vigil, the baskets are blessed by the priest.

These special Easter baskets hold foods traditionally eaten at Easter. In the past, all meats and animal products like butter, cheese, and eggs were forbidden during Lent. So a typical Easter basket holds perhaps a ham, a slab of bacon or a ring of sausage, a round bread made with yeast, cheese, and butter in the shape of a lamb. The bread is a symbol of Jesus, the Bread of Life. The butter honors the Lamb of God and is given a place of honor at the Easter table. Of course, Easter eggs are also included. The basket is covered with a beautiful embroidered cloth that is often handed down through the family for generations.

Easter candle
A large candle symbolizing the light of Christ that is first lit at the Easter Vigil and then is lit for all the liturgies during the Easter Season. It is also called the Paschal candle.

important feast. The Easter Vigil begins sometime after dark on Holy Saturday and must be finished before daybreak on Easter Sunday. Our celebration of Easter continues with the Mass of Easter Sunday. If you have never attended an Easter Vigil, make plans to do so. It is a beautiful, joyful, and powerful celebration of the Resurrection, the culmination of God's saving plan. Let's look at some highlights of this special liturgy.

The Service of Light

The Easter Vigil begins in darkness, outside the church if at all possible. A fire is lit, and the priest welcomes us:

> On this most sacred night,
> in which our Lord Jesus Christ
> passed over from death to life,
> the Church calls upon her sons and daughters,
> scattered throughout the world,
> to come together to watch and pray.
> If we keep the memorial
> of the Lord's paschal solemnity in this way,
> listening to his word and celebrating his mysteries,
> then we shall have the sure hope
> of sharing his triumph over death
> and living with him in God.
>
> (*Roman Missal*, Easter Vigil)

The priest blesses the fire, and lights the large **Easter candle**. Then we process into the church, lighting our individual candles from the Easter candle. When all the candles are lit, the church glows with a beautiful and radiant light. The light of Christ has broken through the darkness of sin and death, illuminating our lives with holy light! As the Easter proclamation (also called the Exsultet) is sung, look around at the people surrounding you and praise God in your heart for his saving love.

The Liturgy of the Word

The Liturgy of the Word in the Easter Vigil is very special. We hear three to seven readings from the Old Testament and two from the New Testament. The readings give us an overview of salvation history, beginning with the Creation of the world and culminating in the discovery of the empty tomb on Easter morning. You have studied God's saving plan in this book. At the Easter Vigil, you can now listen with new appreciation as God's plan of salvation is proclaimed.

The Celebration of Baptism and Confirmation

After the homily the people who are ready to be brought into the Body of Christ receive the first two Sacraments of Christian Initiation: Baptism and Confirmation. Throughout the year leading up to Easter, you will have seen these people in the special rituals that prepared them for this night. We begin by singing the **Litany of the Saints**, a chant that reminds us that we are part of the communion of saints and that asks the saints in Heaven to join their prayers with ours. Then the priest or bishop baptizes those who are joining the Church.

Litany of the Saints
A prayer in the form of a chant or a responsive petition in which the great saints of the Church are asked to pray for us.

Next we hear the profession of faith from the people who have already been baptized and are now being received into full communion with the Catholic Church. They and the newly baptized are then confirmed. As you witness this part of the liturgy, share in the joy of these new Catholics. Let their commitment to our faith renew and strengthen your own commitment.

Liturgy of the Eucharist

We now move into the celebration of the Eucharist. Our Easter fast is over, and we break it by consuming the Body and Blood of Christ, our spiritual food and drink. This is also the first Eucharist for those who have just been baptized or were just received into the Church. We receive Jesus into our bodies, into our hearts, to nourish us and strengthen us. It is a time to be happy and rejoice. Death has been conquered, and eternal life awaits us. Our journey to holiness continues, but in this moment we are given a taste of the communion with God and the saints that await us in Heaven.

© The Crosiers / Gene Plaisted, OSC

During the Easter Vigil, catechumens complete their initiation into the Body of Christ. They, and we, have been baptized into Christ's death so that we may rise with him into new life (see Romans 6:3–4).

Entering into Sacred Time for the Easter Season

The following suggestions are ways you can more fully enter into the celebration of the Paschal Mystery, culminating in the Easter Vigil and Easter Sunday:

- Most parishes have a reception after the Easter Vigil to continue the celebration and to allow you to meet the newly baptized and those received into the Church. Stick around for a few minutes and introduce yourself to these new members of your community.

- Celebrate Easter with your family and friends. If you hunt Easter eggs, remember that eggs, chicks, and bunnies are associated with Easter because they are a sign of spring and of new life. Candy can be a sign of the sweetness of God's gift of salvation. A big Easter dinner is a sign that you are breaking the fasting of Lent and the Triduum.

- Your celebration does not have to end with the Easter Vigil. Consider attending Mass again on Easter Sunday, when a different set of readings will be proclaimed. Or attend evening prayer on Easter Sunday, if your parish celebrates that liturgy.

Primary Sources

Love Is Stronger Than Death

Henri Nouwen (1932–1996) was a Catholic priest, theologian, and psychologist from Holland. He wrote more than three dozen books on spirituality. Today his writings continue to be popular among both Catholics and Protestants around the world. Here he offers us a reflection on the meaning of Jesus' Resurrection:

> The Resurrection of Jesus was a hidden event (from those without faith). Jesus didn't rise from the grave to baffle his opponents, to make a victory statement, or to prove to those who crucified him that he was right after all. Jesus rose as a sign to those who love him and follow him that God's divine love is stronger than death. (*Bread for the Journey*, page 344)

- It is always a good idea to take a few minutes on Easter Day for some praise and thanksgiving prayer. You might want to listen to, or sing, favorite Christian songs or hymns. You might also meditate on passages from Sacred Scripture, especially the Resurrection accounts in the Gospel of John (see chapters 20–21), Paul's reflection on resurrection (see 1 Corinthians 15:1–34), and the reflection on following Jesus found in the Letter to the Hebrews (see chapter 12).

Which of these suggestions would you like to try as a way to enter more deeply into the Easter Vigil and the Easter season?

Chapter Review

1. When does the Church's Liturgical Year begin? Identify some of the major feasts and seasons celebrated during the year.

2. What is the difference between *the liturgy* and *a liturgy*?

3. Why does the priest wash people's feet on Holy Thursday at the Mass of the Lord's Supper?

4. Describe the closing ritual at the end of the Mass of the Lord's Supper.

5. Why is Good Friday both a day of sadness and a day of hope?

6. What does *venerate* mean? Why do we venerate the cross at the celebration of the Lord's Passion? How do people do it?

7. How does the Liturgy of the Word celebrated at the Easter Vigil differ from the Liturgy of the Word celebrated at Sunday Mass throughout the year?

8. What is the relationship between the Easter Vigil and the initiation of new members into the Church?

Glossary

A

adoration The prayerful acknowledgment that God is God and Creator of all that is. *(page 206)*

analogy of faith The coherence of individual doctrines with the whole of Revelation. In other words, as each doctrine is connected with Revelation, each doctrine is also connected with all other doctrines. *(page 66)*

angel Based on a word meaning "messenger," a personal and immortal creature with intelligence and free will who constantly glorifies God and serves as a messenger of God to humans to carry out God's saving plan. *(page 17)*

Annunciation The biblical event in which the Archangel Gabriel visits the Virgin Mary to announce that she is to be the Mother of the Savior. *(page 61)*

Apostles The general term *apostle* means "one who is sent" and can be used in reference to any missionary of the Church during the New Testament period. In reference to the twelve companions chosen by Jesus, also known as "the Twelve," the term refers to those special witnesses of Jesus on whose ministry the early Church was built and whose successors are the bishops. *(page 101)*

Ark of the Covenant A sacred chest that housed the tablets of the Ten Commandments, placed within the sanctuary where God would come and dwell. *(page 47)*

Ascension The "going up" into Heaven of the Risen Christ forty days after his Resurrection. *(page 132)*

B

Beatific Vision Directly encountering and seeing God in the glory of Heaven. *(page 144)*

biblical exegesis The critical interpretation and explanation of Sacred Scripture. *(page 130)*

blasphemy Speech or actions that show disrespect or irreverence for God; also, claiming to have the powers of God or to be God. *(page 102)*

blessing A prayer asking God to care for a particular person, place, or activity. *(page 205)*

C

catechesis, catechists Catechesis is the process by which Christians of all ages are taught the essentials of Christian doctrine and are formed as disciples of Christ. Catechists instruct others in Christian doctrine and for entry into the Church. *(page 176)*

chaplains Specially prepared priests to whom the spiritual care of a special group of people, such as hospital patients, military personnel, or migrants, is entrusted. *(page 94)*

chastity The virtue by which people are able to successfully and healthfully integrate their sexuality into their total person; recognized as one of the fruits of the Holy Spirit. Also one of the vows of religious life. *(page 89)*

chief priests These were Jewish priests of high rank in the Temple. They had administrative authority and presided over important Temple functions and were probably leaders in the Sanhedrin. *(page 101)*

Chrism Mass A special Mass usually celebrated during Holy Week in each diocese. During the Mass the bishop blesses the sacred oils and consecrates the Sacred Chrism used in the diocese throughout the year, and diocesan priests renew their promises to their bishop. *(page 230)*

Christological Having to do with the branch of theology called Christology. Christology is the study of the divinity of Jesus Christ, the Son of God and the Second Divine Person of the Trinity, and his earthly ministry and eternal mission. *(page 64)*

circumcision The act, required by Jewish Law, of removing the foreskin of the penis. Since the time of Abraham, it has been a sign of God's covenant relationship with the Jewish people. *(page 45)*

concupiscence The tendency of all human beings toward sin, as a result of Original Sin. *(page 30)*

confederation An alliance of tribes or nations with no central authority. *(page 49)*

conscience The "inner voice," guided by human reason and Divine Law, that enables us to judge the moral quality of a specific action that has been made, is being made, or will be made. This judgment enables us to distinguish good from evil, in order to accomplish good and avoid evil. To make good judgments, one needs to have a well-formed conscience. *(page 87)*

consecrate To declare or set apart as sacred or to solemnly dedicate to God's service; to make holy. *(page 161)*

contemplation A form of wordless prayer in which one is fully focused on the presence of God; sometimes defined as "resting in God." *(page 212)*

corruptible Something that can be spoiled, contaminated, or made rotten, especially to be made morally perverted. *(page 127)*

D

Doctor of the Church A title officially bestowed by the Church on saints who are highly esteemed for their theological writings, as well as their personal holiness. *(page 114)*

doxology Christian prayer that gives glory and praise to God, often in a special way to the three Divine Persons of the Trinity. *(page 210)*

E

Easter candle A large candle symbolizing the light of Christ that is first lit at the Easter Vigil and then is lit for all the liturgies during the Easter Season. It is also called the Paschal candle. *(page 240)*

Easter Vigil The liturgy celebrated on Holy Saturday night. It celebrates the coming of the light of Christ into the world and is also the time when adults and older children are received into the Church through the Sacraments of Christian Initiation. *(page 239)*

etiology A story that explains something's cause or origin. *(page 30)*

Eucharist, the Also called the Mass or Lord's Supper, and based on a word for "thanksgiving," it is the central Christian liturgical celebration, established by Jesus at the Last Supper. In the Eucharist, the sacrificial death and Resurrection of Jesus are both remembered and renewed. The term sometimes refers specifically to the consecrated bread and wine that have become the Body and Blood of Christ. *(page 79)*

exorcism The act of freeing someone from demonic possession. Exorcisms are also part of the Church's worship and prayer life, calling on the name of Christ to protect us from the power of Satan. *(page 93)*

expiation The act of atoning for sin or wrongdoing. *(page 68)*

F

Fall, the Also called the Fall from Grace, the biblical Revelation about the origins of sin and evil in the world, expressed figuratively in the account of Adam and Eve in Genesis. *(page 27)*

fiat Latin for "let it be done," the words Mary spoke to the angel Gabriel at the Annunciation. *(page 60)*

figurative language A literary form that uses symbolic images, stories, and names to point to a deeper truth. *(page 12)*

foreshadow To represent or prefigure a person before his or her life or an event before it occurs. *(page 64)*

fortitude Also called strength or courage, the virtue that enables one to maintain sound moral judgment and behavior in the face of difficulties and challenges; one of the four Cardinal Virtues. *(page 194)*

G

Gnosticism A group of heretical religious movements that claimed salvation comes from secret knowledge available only to the elite initiated in that religion. *(page 124)*

Good Friday The second day of the Easter Triduum on which we commemorate Jesus' Passion and death on the cross. *(page 235)*

grace The free and undeserved gift that God gives us to empower us to respond to his call and to live as his adopted sons and daughters. Grace restores our loving communion with the Holy Trinity, lost through sin. *(page 163)*

H

Heaven A state of eternal life and union with God in which one experiences full happiness and the satisfaction of the deepest human longings. *(page 153)*

Hell The state of permanent separation from God, reserved for those who die in a state of mortal sin, that is, who freely and consciously choose to reject God to the very end of their lives. *(page 154)*

hermit A person who lives a solitary life in order to commit himself or herself more fully to prayer and in some cases to be completely free for service to others. *(page 170)*

holiness The state of being holy. This means to be set apart for God's service, to live a morally good life, to be a person of prayer, and to reveal God's love to the world through acts of loving service. *(page 161)*

Holy Spirit The Third Person of the Blessed Trinity, the personal love between the Father and the Son, who inspires, guides, and sanctifies the life of believers. *(page 16)*

Holy Thursday The beginning of the Easter Triduum, starting with the evening celebration of the Mass of the Lord's Supper. *(page 230)*

I

Immaculate Conception The dogma that the Virgin Mary, from the moment of her conception, by a singular grace of God, was free of Original Sin and remained free from personal sin throughout her entire life. *(page 61)*

Incarnation From the Latin, meaning "to become flesh," referring to the mystery of Jesus Christ, the Divine Son of God, becoming man. In the Incarnation, Jesus Christ became truly man while remaining truly God. *(page 67)*

intercession A prayer on behalf of another person or group. *(page 207)*

interiority The practice of developing a life of self-reflection and self-examination to attend to our spiritual life and call to holiness. *(page 164)*

K

Kingdom of God The culmination or goal of God's plan of salvation, the Kingdom of God is announced by the Gospel and present in Jesus Christ. The Kingdom is the reign or rule of God over the hearts of people and, as a consequence of that, the development of a new social order based on unconditional love. The fullness of God's Kingdom will not be realized until the end of time. Also called the Reign of God or the Kingdom of Heaven. *(page 76)*

L

laity All members of the Church with the exception of those who are ordained as bishops, priests, or deacons. The laity share in Christ's role as priest, prophet, and king, witnessing to God's love and power in the world. *(page 165)*

leprosy An infectious disease resulting in numbness, paralysis, and physical deformities; also called Hansen's disease. Effective treatment was not developed until the late 1930s. *(page 192)*

Litany of the Saints A prayer in the form of a chant or a responsive petition in which the great saints of the Church are asked to pray for us. *(page 241)*

literary forms (genres) Different kinds of writing determined by their literary technique, content, tone, and purpose. *(page 12)*

literal sense A form of biblical interpretation that considers the explicit meaning of the text. It lays the foundation for all other senses of Sacred Scripture. *(page 39)*

Liturgical Year The Church's annual cycle of feasts and seasons that celebrate the events and mysteries of Christ's birth, life, death, Resurrection, and Ascension, and forms the context for the Church's worship. *(page 225)*

liturgy The Church's official, public, communal prayer. It is God's work, in which the People of God participate. The Church's most important liturgy is the Eucharist, or the Mass. *(page 225)*

Liturgy of the Hours Also known as the Divine Office, the official public, daily prayer of the Catholic Church. The Divine Office provides standard prayers, Scripture readings, and reflections at regular hours throughout the day. *(page 226)*

Lord The word used in the Old Testament to refer to God and in the New Testament for both God the Father and Jesus Christ, to reflect awareness of Jesus' divine identity as the Son of God. *(page 73)*

M

meditation A form of prayer involving a variety of methods and techniques, in which one engages the mind, imagination, and emotions to focus on a particular truth, Scripture passage, or other spiritual matter. *(page 212)*

monarchy A government or a state headed by a single person, such as a king or queen. As a biblical term, it refers to the period of time when the Israelites existed as an independent nation. *(page 50)*

mortal sin An action so contrary to the will of God that it results in complete separation from God and his grace. As a consequence of that separation, the person is condemned to eternal death. For a sin to be a mortal sin, three conditions must be met: the act must involve a grave matter, the person must have full knowledge of the evil of the act, and the person must give his or her full consent in committing the act. *(page 143)*

mysticism An intense experience of the presence and power of God, resulting in a deeper sense of union with God; those who regularly experience such union are called mystics. *(page 212)*

N

New Covenant The covenant or law established by God in Jesus Christ to fulfill and perfect the Old Covenant or Mosaic Law. It is a perfection here on earth of the Divine Law. The law of the New Covenant is called a law of love, grace, and freedom. The New Covenant will never end or diminish, and nothing new will be revealed until Christ comes again in glory. *(page 54)*

O

Oil of the Catechumens Blessed olive oil used to anoint those preparing for Baptism. *(page 230)*

Oil of the Sick Blessed olive oil used in the Sacrament of Anointing of the Sick to anoint the forehead and hands of people who are seriously ill or near death. *(page 230)*

original holiness The original state of human beings in their relationship with God, sharing in the divine life in full communion with him. *(page 23)*

original justice The original state of Adam and Eve before the Fall, a state of complete harmony with themselves, with each other, and with all of creation. *(page 23)*

Original Sin From the Latin *origo*, meaning "beginning" or "birth." The term has two meanings: (1) the sin of the first human beings, who disobeyed God's command by choosing to follow their own will and thus lost their original holiness and became subject to death, (2) the fallen state of human nature that affects every person born into the world, except Jesus and Mary. *(page 27)*

P

paradox A statement that seems contradictory or opposed to common sense and yet is true. *(page 136)*

Parousia The Second Coming of Christ as judge of all the living and the dead, at the end of time, when the Kingdom of God will be fulfilled. *(page 35)*

Particular Judgment The judgment that occurs immediately at the time of our death, when our immortal souls will be judged as worthy or unworthy of Heaven. *(page 147)*

Paschal Lamb In the Old Testament, the sacrificial lamb shared at the seder meal of the Passover on the night the Israelites escaped from Egypt; in the New Testament, the Paschal Lamb is Jesus, the Incarnate Son of God who dies on a cross to take away "the sin of the world" (John 1:29). *(page 79)*

Paschal Mystery The work of salvation accomplished by Jesus Christ mainly through his Passion, death, Resurrection, and Ascension. *(page 42)*

Passion The sufferings of Jesus during the final days of his life: his agony in the garden at Gethsemane, his trial, and his Crucifixion. *(page 78)*

Passover The night the Lord passed over the houses of the Israelites marked by the blood of the lamb, and spared the firstborn sons from death. It also is the feast that celebrates the deliverance of the Chosen People from bondage in Egypt and the Exodus from Egypt to the Promised Land. *(page 79)*

patriarch The father or leader of a tribe, clan, or tradition. Abraham, Isaac, and Jacob were the patriarchs of the Israelite people. *(page 45)*

petition A prayer form in which one asks God for help and forgiveness. *(page 206)*

polytheism The belief in many gods. *(page 43)*

poverty of heart The recognition of our deep need for God and the commitment to put God above everything else in life, particularly above the accumulation of material wealth. *(page 82)*

praise A prayer of acknowledgment that God is God, giving God glory not for what he does, but simply because he is. *(page 209)*

prayer Lifting up of one's mind and heart to God or the requesting of good things from him. The five basic forms of prayer are blessing, praise, petition, thanksgiving, and intercession. In prayer we communicate with God in a relationship of love. *(page 201)*

primeval history The time before the invention of writing and recording of historical data. *(page 11)*

procurator A word used to describe Roman governors, who had administrative and legal authority over a province or region of the Roman Empire. *(page 107)*

Purgatory A state of final purification or cleansing, which one may need to enter following death and before entering Heaven. *(page 156)*

R

redeem, Redeemer, redemption From the Latin *redemptio,* meaning "a buying back"; to redeem something is to pay the price for its freedom. In the Old Testament, it refers to Yahweh's deliverance of Israel and, in the New Testament, to Christ's deliverance of all Christians from the forces of sin. Christ our Redeemer paid the price to free us from the slavery of sin and bring about our redemption. *(page 80)*

Resurrection The bodily rising of Jesus from the dead on the third day after his death on the cross; the heart of the Paschal Mystery and the basis of our hope in the resurrection from the dead. *(page 118)*

resurrection of the dead The raising of the righteous on the last day, to live forever with the Risen Christ. The resurrection of the dead means that not only our immortal souls will live on after death, but also our transformed bodies. *(page 126)*

righteous To be sinless and without guilt; those who are in such standing before God. *(page 132)*

S

Sacrament An efficacious and visible sign of God's grace, instituted by Christ and entrusted to the Church, by which divine life is dispensed to us. The Seven Sacraments are Baptism, the Eucharist, Confirmation, Penance and Reconciliation, Anointing of the Sick, Matrimony, and Holy Orders. *(page 226)*

Sacred Chrism Perfumed olive oil consecrated by the bishop that is used for anointing in the Sacraments of Baptism, Confirmation, and Holy Orders. *(page 230)*

Sacred Scripture The sacred writings of the Old and New Testaments, which contain the truth of God's Revelation and were composed by human authors inspired by the Holy Spirit. *(page 12)*

Sacred Tradition "Tradition" comes from the Latin *tradere,* meaning "to hand on." Sacred Tradition refers to the living process of passing on the Gospel message. It began with the oral communication of the Gospel by the Apostles, was written down in Sacred Scripture, and is interpreted by the Magisterium under the guidance of the Holy Spirit. Both Sacred Tradition and Sacred Scripture have their common source in the revelation of Jesus Christ and must be equally honored. *(page 17)*

sanctifying grace The grace that heals our human nature wounded by sin and restores us to friendship with God by giving us a share in the divine life of the Trinity. It is a supernatural gift of God, infused into our souls by the Holy Spirit, that continues the work of making us holy. *(page 146)*

Sanhedrin An assembly of Jewish religious leaders—chief priests, scribes, and elders—who functioned as the supreme council and tribunal during the time of Jesus. *(page 102)*

Satan The fallen angel or spirit of evil who is the enemy of God and a continuing instigator of temptation and sin in the world. *(page 33)*

Son of Man A messianic title from the Book of Daniel, used to describe a figure who receives authority over other nations from God; the only messianic title in the Gospels used by Jesus to describe himself. *(page 82)*

spirituality In general, the values, actions, attitudes, and behaviors that characterize a person's relationship with God and others. In particular, it refers to different schools of Christian prayer and action. *(page 218)*

spiritual sense A form of biblical interpretation that goes beyond the literal sense to consider what the realities and events of Sacred Scripture signify and mean for salvation. *(page 38)*

soul Our spiritual principle, it is immortal, and it is what makes us most like God. Our soul is created by God at the moment of our conception. It is the seat of human consciousness and freedom. *(page 18)*

Stations of the Cross A devotion for prayer and reflection, popular during Lent, that retraces the events of Jesus' Passion and death in fourteen "stations," represented by artistic depictions. Most Catholic churches have artistic representations of the fourteen Stations of the Cross. Also called the Way of the Cross. *(page 238)*

synoptic Gospels From the Greek for "seeing the whole together," the name given to the Gospels of Matthew, Mark, and Luke, because they are similar in style and content. *(page 78)*

T

temptation An invitation or enticement to commit an unwise or immoral act that often includes a promise of reward to make the immoral act seem more appealing. *(page 36)*

thanksgiving A prayer of gratitude for the gift of life and the gifts of life. Thanksgiving characterizes the prayer of the Church which, in celebrating the Eucharist, offers perfect thanks to the Father through, with, and in Christ, in the unity of the Holy Spirit. *(page 208)*

theological virtues The name for the God-given virtues of faith, hope, and love. These virtues enable us to know God as God and lead us to union with him in mind and heart. *(page 146)*

theophany God's manifestation of himself in a visible form to enrich human understanding of him. An example is God's appearance to Moses in the form of a burning bush. *(page 46)*

Theotokos A Greek title for Mary meaning "God bearer." *(page 60)*

Torah A Hebrew word meaning "law," referring to the first five books of the Old Testament. *(page 46)*

Triduum The three-day period of the Liturgical Year that begins with the Mass of the Lord's Supper on Holy Thursday and ends with evening prayer on Easter Sunday. *(page 228)*

Trinity From the Latin *trinus*, meaning "threefold," referring to the central mystery of the Christian faith that God exists as a communion of three distinct and interrelated Divine Persons: Father, Son, and Holy Spirit. The doctrine of the Trinity is a mystery that is inaccessible to human reason alone and is known through Divine Revelation only. *(page 16)*

V

venerate To show respect and devotion to someone or something. *(page 237)*

venial sin A less serious offense against the will of God that diminishes one's personal character and weakens but does not rupture one's relationship with God. *(page 143)*

virtue A habitual and firm disposition to do good. *(page 194)*

vocal prayer A prayer that is spoken aloud or silently, such as the Lord's Prayer. *(page 211)*

Index

Acknowledgments

The scriptural quotations in this book are from the *New American Bible, revised edition* © 2010, 1991, 1986, and 1970 by the Confraternity of Christian Doctrine, Washington, D.C. All Rights Reserved. No part of this work may be reproduced in any form or by any means, electronic or mechanical, including photocopying, recording, or by any information storage and retrieval system, without permission in writing from the copyright owner.

The excerpts marked *Catechism of the Catholic Church* or *CCC* are from the English translation of the *Catechism of the Catholic Church* for use in the United States of America, second edition. Copyright © 1994 by the United States Catholic Conference, Inc.—Libreria Editrice Vaticana (LEV). English translation of the *Catechism of the Catholic Church: Modifications from the Editio Typica* copyright © 1997 by the United States Catholic Conference, Inc.—LEV.

The excerpt on page 13 is from "Homily of Pope Francis, Mass, Imposition of the Pallium and Bestowal of the Fisherman's Ring for the Beginning of the Petrine Ministry of the Bishop of Rome," March 19, 2013, at *www.vatican.va/holy_father/francesco/ homilies/2013/documents/papa-francesco_20130319_omelia-inizio-pontificato_en.html.* Copyright © LEV.

The quotation on page 14 is from "Address of His Holiness Pope Benedict XVI to Members of the Pontifical Academy of Sciences on the Occasion of the Plenary Assembly," November 8, 2012, at *www.vatican.va/holy_father/benedict_xvi/speeches/ 2012/november/documents/hf_ben-xvi_spe_20121108_academy-sciences _en.html.* Copyright © 2012 LEV.

The excerpts from the Nicene Creed on pages 17, 67, 106, and 132 and the prayers on pages 22, 210, 230, 235, 237, 239, and 240 are from the English translation of *The Roman Missal* © 2010, International Commission on English in the Liturgy (ICEL) (Washington, DC: United States Conference of Catholic Bishops [USCCB], 2011), pages 527, 1291, 522, 299, 315, 330, 353, and 344, respectively. All rights reserved. Used with permission of the ICEL. Published with the approval of the Committee on Divine Worship, USCCB.

The excerpt on page 31 is from *Pastoral Constitution on the Church in the Modern World* (*Gaudium et Spes*, 1965), number 16, at *www.vatican.va/ archive/hist_councils/ii _vatican_council/documents/vat-ii_cons_19651207_ gaudium-et-spes_en.html.* Copyright © LEV.

The excerpt on page 39 is from Saint Leo the Great, "Sermon 73," number IV, found at *www.newadvent.org/fathers/360373.htm.*

The quotation on page 42 is from *Declaration on the Relation of the Church to Non-Christian Religions* (*Nostra Aetate*, 1965), number 4, in *Vatican Council II: Constitutions, Decrees, Declarations*, Austin Flannery, general editor (Northport, NY: Costello Publishing Company, 1996), page 573. Copyright © 1996 by Reverend Austin Flannery.

The second quotation on page 42 is from a note by Pope Francis to the chief rabbi of Rome, reprinted from *nationalcouncilofsynagogues.org/sites/default/files/docs /Pope%20Francis%20note%20and%20Rabbi%20DiSegni%20reply.pdf.*

The excerpt on page 53 is from *Saved by Hope (Spe Salvi)*, number 1, at *www .vatican.va/holy_father/benedict_xvi/encyclicals/documents/ hf_ben-xvi_enc_ 20071130_spe-salvi_en.html.* Copyright © 2007 LEV.

The excerpt on page 169 is from "President Obama Awards Medal of Honor to Father Emil Kapaun," at *www.whitehouse.gov/blog/2013/04/11/president-obama-awards-medal-honor-father-emil-kapaun-0*.

The excerpt on page 191 is from "Address of Pope Francis, Way of the Cross at the Colosseum," at *www.vatican.va/holy_father/francesco/speeches/2013march/documents/papa-francesco_20130329_via-crucis-colosseo_en.html*. Copyright © LEV.

The excerpt on page 202 is from *Gratefulness, the Heart of Prayer: An Approach to Life in Fullness*, by Br. David Steindl-Rast (New York: Paulist Press, 1984), page 41. Copyright © 1984 by David Steindl-Rast.

The quotation on page 204 is from *Bone Rules, or Skeleton of English Grammar*, by John B. Tabb (New York: Benziger Brothers, 1901), n.p. Copyright © 1897 Benziger Brothers.

The quotation on page 220 is from "Homily of the Holy Father Francis on the Occasion of the Feast of Saint Ignatius," number 2, at *www.vatican.va/holy_father/francesco/homilies/2013/documents/papa-francesco_20130731_omelia-sant-ignazio_en.html*. Copyright © LEV.

The prayer on page 236 is from the English translation of an Antiphon for the Veneration of the Cross from *The Roman Missal* © 1973 ICEL, and is reprinted here from *Catholic Household Blessings and Prayers,* by the Bishops' Committee on the Liturgy (Washington, DC: United States Conference of Catholic Bishops [USCCB], 1989), page 146. Copyright © 1989 by the USCCB. All rights reserved. Used with permission of the ICEL.

The excerpt on page 242 is from *Bread for the Journey: A Daybook of Wisdom and Faith*, by Henri J. M. Nouwen (New York: HarperCollins, 1997), page 344. Copyright © 1997 by Henri J. M. Nouwen.

To view copyright terms and conditions for Internet materials cited here, log on to the home pages for the referenced websites.

During this book's preparation, all citations, facts, figures, names, addresses, telephone numbers, Internet URLs, and other pieces of information cited within were verified for accuracy. The authors and Saint Mary's Press staff have made every attempt to reference current and valid sources, but we cannot guarantee the content of any source, and we are not responsible for any changes that may have occurred since our verification. If you find an error in, or have a question or concern about, any of the information or sources listed within, please contact Saint Mary's Press.

Endnotes Cited in Quotations from the *Catechism of the Catholic Church,* Second Edition

Chapter 7
1. *Romans* 6:4; cf. 4:25.

Chapter 9
1. Cf. *2 Timothy* 4.
2. Cf. John Paul II, *Redemptor hominis* 18–21.
3. *Lumen Gentium* 34; cf. *Lumen Gentium* 10; *1 Peter* 2:5.